GENESIS IN JAPAN

THE BIBLE BEYOND CHRISTIANITY

Thomas Dabbs

Texas Review Press
Huntsville, Texas

Copyright © 2013 by Thomas Dabbs
All rights reserved
Printed in the United States of America

FIRST EDITION, 2013
Requests for permission to reproduce material from this work should be sent to:

> Permissions
> Texas Review Press
> English Department
> Sam Houston State University
> Huntsville, TX 77341-2146

All unmarked scripture quotations are taken from The Bible: Authorized King James Version. ed. Carroll and Pricket. Oxford: Oxford UP, 1998.

Although actual student comments are used in this work, the names of these students in all cases have been changed to protect their identities. The names used for students are common surnames in Japan (in English speaking cultures they are as common as the surnames Smith, Jones, etc.). Any similarly between the surnames used in this book and the surnames of one of the many students I have taught over the years is purely coincidental. No surnames reflect the actual identity of a particular student.

Cover art and design by Jenny Gorecki

Cover image: Nanban Carrack
Cropped from a Japanese Nanban folding screen by Kano Naizen.
Azuchi-Momoyama period (approx. 1573 to 1603).
Kobe City Museum

Library of Congress Cataloging-in-Publication Data

Dabbs, Thomas, 1957-
 Genesis in Japan : the Bible beyond Christianity / Thomas Dabbs.
    pages cm
  ISBN 978-1-933896-99-1 (pbk. : alk. paper) 1. Bible--Meditations. 2. Spiritual life--Christianity. 3. Christianity--Japan. I. Title.
  BS491.5.D33 2013
  220.60952--dc23
                              2013001406

To Nell and Eugene Dabbs, in loving memory

CONTENTS

Section One: The Faces of the Deep

In the Beginning..3
A World Without Sin..9
Normal and Not-So-Normal...............................15
The God Who Is Not There and
    the Gods Who Are..18
The Fault Line..22
The Face of Things; the Face
    of Nothing..24
Unintelligent Designs..31
Highly Inspired Designs......................................35
The Man Who Didn't Fall;
    The Teacher Who *Did*...................................39
But What about the Dinosaurs?.........................45
The Great Shazam...51
The Un-shazam..58

Section Two: Desert Storm

Free Association I:
    Gaskets and Rods..67
Free Association II:
    Snakes and Alligators..................................82
Free Association III:
    Line Dancing with the Gods......................103
Free Association IV:
    The Problem with Pronouns......................117
Free Association V:
    The White Lines of the
    Freeway...127

Section Three: Creating Gods in Creation

The Curse of the Colonel..................................137
In Search of the River God:
    Part I..142
In Search of the River God:
    Part II...150
In Search of the River God:
    Part III..154
The Bible of Sky and the
    Bible of Earth...158
The Education of God......................................163
The Double-Edged Sword...............................171

Section Four: On the Offensive

Gods and Christians..179
The New Testament
    vs. Christianity...185
A World Without Stained Glass......................197
The Jesus There..203
Scary Christian Things I:
    Eating Jesus...220
Scary ChristianThings II:
    Going to Hell..231
Scary Christian Things III:
    Members and Persecution........................236
Epilogue: Shinjuku..246

GENESIS IN JAPAN

THE BIBLE BEYOND CHRISTIANITY

Section One: The Faces of the Deep

Nothing that is not there and the nothing that is.
—Wallace Stevens, from "The Snow Man"

In the Beginning

"Living backwards!" Alice repeated in great astonishment. "I never heard of such a thing!" —from *Alice in Wonderland*

This book rises from a journal of reflections that I have kept while teaching the Bible to Japanese university students in Tokyo. Diverse responses to the Bible have rebounded, subtly but forcefully, back to me from my students—extraordinary responses, in that they are simple, pure, ordinary, and entirely disorienting. Teaching and learning the Bible in Japan has led me to another view of the Bible, one that stands in stark contrast with the Bible in the Bible-heavy culture that was my beginning at a small crossroads in central South Carolina.

This book is not just about teaching the Bible. It is also about how this experience has shaken my view of the Bible and the Bible's relationship with the Christian world. My students come from a culture that is not Christian. They are not un-Christian, or non-Christian. They are not against Christianity: They are detached from it, though they are sincere about wanting to learn about the Bible. They come to the Bible from a place *beyond* Christianity. Their distance from the Bible makes their responses to it seem radical, but they do not mean to be radical. Their understanding of the Bible, tossed into a volatile mix with my own thinking, has jarred me into seeing the Christian world as having a marginally insane relationship with the Bible.

This view is not panoramic. There is no high definition. It is only partially visible when you look at the Bible first and Christianity second. In the Christian world this is the reverse order of things. We learn something about Christianity before getting to the Bible. Christianity leads us to the Bible and also eclipses our view of the Bible. In his letter to the Corinthians,

Paul talks about seeing life through a glass darkly. Japan holds up such a glass when it comes to seeing the Bible, one without the glare of latter day Christian thought disrupting the view, one that is deceptive in that you think you are looking through at something else when you are in fact seeing a darkish silhouette reflection of self. At first you do not recognize what you see.

While teaching, the biblical images that return from your students also reveal that you are on a circular, not a straight, journey through the Bible—as if you are unable to exit the D.C. Beltway, or the rapid, crowded juggernaut of a train line that circles central Tokyo, the Yamanote line. As soon as you leave any station you are circling back to that same station. Heading back just as you are trying to leave. I left home years ago and thought I was heading straight to a place far away from the Bible and the religion that permeates my home front. It turns out that I have always been circling through the Bible-soaked religion of my childhood. This is a fresh but uneasy look at the Bible and its uneasy relationship with Christianity, a raw look from the land of raw fish. Anyone from a Christian culture, religious or not, interested in Japan or not, should be forewarned. We cannot go gentle into The Good Book, not from the perspective of teaching and learning the Bible in Japan.

I grew up close to the Bible: at least I thought so. All of us did. We went to church. We were taught Bible stories. We learned, sometimes memorized, verses from the Bible. Throughout America and in other Christian cultures, even those who have not spent much time with the Bible still have had passing contact with the Bible and Bible-based religion through popular culture or secondhand sources. Those of us from the Christian world, devout Christians or not, cannot view the Bible with the objective detachment that my students have. Whatever angle we are seeing it from, we have an attitude about the Bible, a strong attitude, and this attitude is set in place before we reach for a Bible. The Bible in English permeates our language so deeply that we refer to it while talking and writing even when we do not know we are. We cite quotations that we think come from the Bible even when

they do not. It is impossible for us to see the Bible, the Bible itself, through the haze of the many things thought and said about the Bible in the Christian world.

The story about the fellow who knows nothing about the Bible, who picks it up, starts reading, and suddenly finds God, is a fairy tale. In the Christian world it would be hard to find a person who has had no exposure to the Bible, who knows nothing of things said about what the Bible is supposed to be, before getting to the Bible. It would be easier to find an unbiased juror for an O.J. Simpson trial.

My new view of the Bible comes from a place that is, in terms of the Bible, more pure or Eden-like. The Bible and Christian ideas about the Bible have little influence in Japan—almost no influence. What the Bible says would never enter into political debate. Political candidates in Japan are not asked if they believe in Jesus. Japanese students enter my class without knowing much about the Bible's greatest hits. They are well educated, but they have not heard much about Noah and the flood or Joseph and his coat of many colors. They may have seen *Raiders of the Lost Ark*, but they do not know what the Ark of the Covenant is, except what they draw from the movie: that it is an ancient tub-like container with an unstable element that will blast the flesh off of anyone who opens it, particularly Nazis. They are unschooled in the ideas that hover over the Bible in the Christian world. The idea of being saved, the notion of falling from grace—both of these abstractions fly over their heads. "Saved from what? Falling from *where*?"

Beyond the country crossroads where I grew up, throughout Europe and the Western Hemisphere, throughout large sections of Africa, throughout Australia and the Pacific, in Christian cultures across the world, we can refer to the Fall from Eden, to David and Goliath, to Daniel in the Lion's Den, to Judas betraying Jesus, because we know the person we are talking to will recognize the reference, whether he has read it in the Bible or not. There are assorted images and stories from the Bible that are as familiar to us as a Rolling Stones song or a Clint Eastwood movie (both of which have references to the Bible). We might come across a pamphlet where kids are warned not to bite the apple, during an abstinence campaign against underage sex. We might turn on the T.V. just when a local weatherman advises us jokingly to get ready to build an ark when an extended rainstorm is on the way. We may have seen a recent commercial for a famous delivery service where the diligent courier walks on the water to deliver his package. We get the reference. We get the humor.

We might remember the Last Supper scene with the surprise appearance of Leonardo Da Vinci in Mel Brook's *History of the World: Part I*. We might recall the guys nailed on crosses singing, "always look on the bright side of life" in Monty Python's *Life of Brian*. We laugh at these scenes—or are offended—but we respond. We automatically associate the title of this section, "in the beginning," with the Bible. We grin if we get the connection made between the McIntosh apples of New England with the forbidden fruit of Eden and combine these with the computer byte that helps to produce knowledge and the biblical bite that produced too much knowledge in Eden. Where would the Apple brand be without the Bible?

These biblical references and images register little seismic activity at all on the Japanese cultural terrain. An apple is simply a fruit and, yes, an Apple is a computer, too. But here is where the association stops, long before reaching Adam and Eve in the Garden of Eden. The book and film *The Da Vinci Code* and its sequel were widely seen in Japan because of all of the fuss over its premise in the States. Several Japanese acquaintances of mine saw the movie and wanted to know what all of the fuss was about. They simply did not get it.

In Christian cultures, to repent means something—a big something. We might talk about resurrecting an old idea. On any given night, we could find ourselves watching a feature film about the Old Testament, one that stars Charlton Heston as a Nordic Moses. We respond to the scene in which the waters are parted: We may be in awe of this wondrous miracle or we may scoff at the special effects and at people who believe in wondrous miracles. There is the controversy of the human Jesus in Martin Scorcese's *The Last Temptation of Christ* and the controversial graphic torture of Jesus in Mel Gibson's *The Passion of The Christ*. These feature films, in order to be controversial, require prior knowledge of the parameters of religious taboo. They draw audiences who are predisposed to respond strongly to the story of Jesus. Whether we see the story as a miracle or a tall tale, we have already read or heard about Moses parting the waters. We are familiar with the problem of Jesus being both God and man, and we already know about the rough go of it Jesus had in the end. So many of us have feelings, strong feelings, about these stories, whether we believe them or not.

The average Japanese person would be familiar with the name, Jesus, and might be familiar with a few biblical references and images, maybe the ones mentioned above. A young person might run across a Bible reference in one of the many *manga*, or comic books, that are popular in Japan. Sometimes the illustrators borrow images and names from the Bible to enhance a hero story. There is even a Bible in comic book form in Japan. According to several of my students, it is not the most popular comic on the shelf. References to the Bible do not have the penetration that they do in Christian culture. You would not likely hear two Japanese people, when talking to each another, echoing deeper religious thought with references to someone being crucified or someone who walks on water or someone having to repent for a sin or resurrecting an old idea.

You would not likely hear someone talk about the cross he has to bear or of a colleague being made a scapegoat. Making personal sacrifices and setting up an individual to take the fall for a larger group is common in Japan, but the language for these concepts is not drawn from the Bible. You would not hear a Japanese person talk about being thrown to the lions or tell another person to go to hell or curse about how crowded the goddamn subways are. They live outside the world of the book that teaches us how to talk this way, the book that teaches us how to curse.

There is no Last Supper in Japan. Knowledge about the Sacrifice of Isaac or the sounding of the final trumpets would be a rare find, and there is only a trace of the tale of a man swallowed by a big fish. The fish story draws some attention in Japan, given the never waning interest Japanese folks have in fish. But the source of the story in the book of Jonah would rarely be recognized. You would have better luck with the Rolling Stones and Clint Eastwood.

Of course we are much more connected with the Bible in the Christianized world, but often we are connected in unconnected ways that we do not see or understand. Some of us might be so comfortable with biblical images and stories and ideas that we might be talked into teaching a basic class on the Bible to students who know little about the Bible. This was my case. I had regular and strong doses of the Bible from early childhood on, at least I thought I did, so, sure, I'll take on that class on the Bible.

You might think, as I did, that teaching a beginner's class on the Bible to people who do not know much about the Bible is light work and, for whatever reason, good work. But as it turned out, the responses and questions that my students have had about the Bible have been hard to handle. The work I did was not good, at least at first, because I really did not know the Bible. As a result, my students put me to shame, even caused hardship, including the hardship you feel when you repeatedly stumble in front of an audience.

I was arrogant about what I thought I knew about the Bible, and this arrogance was a religious arrogance born of the culture I was born to, an arrogance that I could not see in myself. This blindness might be the source of religious arrogance—the inability to look through the glass darkly and see. My case is the same for a number of people who were brought up in the world of this book that is at once so familiar and yet so unknown. While I am apologizing—we apologize a lot in Japan—I will also apologize for the fact that the strange view of the Bible that I see in Japan is sparked from detail, harsh detail—that place where the devil is. If you want to find your way through the looking glass with me to this raw and incomplete Bible of the other side, I am afraid I am like that fellow circling the lower regions with Dante, the pagan poet who could not take the Christian poet the distance. I can only take you so far.

A World Without Sin

Since sin is a moral evil, it is necessary in the first place to determine what is meant by evil, and in particular by moral evil.
  —from *The Catholic Encyclopedia*

You are teaching the Garden of Eden story in your beginner's Bible class. A student asks, innocently, "Why would any fruit be forbidden?" You laugh, but no one else is laughing. Your student wants to know what this God character has against fruit. Your student has support from the class. You are in a place where asking direct questions about the Bible is not remotely irreverent. The question does not have a comic edge. It is just a straight and simple question. And this question is packaged with similar questions. Other students might ask abruptly, "What kind of fruit? How big was the tree?"

Now you are re-reading the text in front of class, fumbling for an answer because you are not quite sure how to explain why the fruit was forbidden because you do not know why the fruit was forbidden. A flashback circles you back to when you still believed in Santa Claus. You are in a Sunday school class, in my case in a Presbyterian church in small-town South Carolina. You ask the teacher, "How did Adam and Eve's two sons have children?"

Your teacher glares, "we don't ask that kind of question." You better shut up or else no juice and cookies after class. No teacher in this gone world of childhood—a world where Santa is alive and well, a world where not asking the wrong question can be redeemed for juice and cookies—no teacher has to explain the answer to a religious question that children are not supposed to ask in the first place. But in Japan you look over puzzled stares, faces innocent of Sunday school rules. They have heard little to nothing about the tree of the knowledge of good and evil. It strikes you in a moment of clarity how marvelous the story is—and how we from the world of people who think we know the story so well may not know the story well enough to marvel at it.

The raw material from this story prompted the exquisite sensual imagery in Renaissance paintings, in Milton's grand epic, that were not part of our Sunday school education—the two naked people, the green world with fruit and flowing streams, and the voyeuristic voice, the God of earth and soil who walks within his creation. Your students have not received the unwritten memo that there are certain questions about this question begging narrative that you are not supposed to ask. You are not protected from hard questions by the invisible force that protected your old Sunday school teacher. You have just been initiated to the new view, marvelous but under-explained.

You try to mutter something that sounds like an answer, and you also sense that some from your flock are starting to sense that their Bible teacher does not seem to know the Bible. You recover by saying that the story is not just about the tree or about fruit, but about the fact that when the God of the Bible makes a rule, you have to follow it, you have to do what you are told, for your own good. The voice of the story itself insists that there are questions that should not be asked.

Your students stare at you blankly. You have just been taught something that you did not know you knew: The *point* of the story is not to ask questions. Enjoy childhood, and listen to the story and understand that it means that we should do what we were told by God. Curiosity is what got us tossed out of paradise in the beginning. You look over your students of a culture where this God of Eden has no purchase. You clear your throat and say, "In this story you have to follow the rule or else you have done something very bad in the Bible. You have sinned against God."

Your students remain blank—a couple of them look cross as they search for *sin* in their electronic dictionaries. Maybe they are wondering if they will be flunked for asking questions. They have no idea what sin is, even what the word, *sin*, means. Of course there is the idea of right and wrong in

Japan, even a Japanese word that Christian ministers use for sin or flaw, but there is no tradition of *original sin*, of being born into sin. You are in a modern culture with a strong economy, where public health officials smile on fruit eating, where young people are encouraged, forced, to learn things, where they are given homework assignments to get knowledge or else fail examinations and disgrace their family.

You wonder how to explain sin to your students. You are from sin central, a place where the word, *sin*, is used casually. But you do not know enough about sin to explain what sin is to the sinless. After class you return to your office to look for a hard, clear definition of sin.

Sin is an act committed against God's rules and laws, and there is also sin of omission, when one fails to carry out the will of God. But the first sin was provoked by the desire to be godlike, an urge for personal betterment that was curiously damned from the start, given that the two sinners were made in the image of God. But the first sin was big. This is made clear in Genesis. What is not clear is where sin came from, but it certainly got our earthly father and mother harshly evicted from paradise. No one in this class would identify with Adam as their first father. He wasn't Japanese. Wrong passport.

Sin is a moral evil according to the person who wrote the entry to the Catholic Encyclopedia. Japanese students can of course fathom morality and evil but not in relation to the idea of sin in the Bible. The words *moral* and *evil*, in relation to each other and the Bible, are in a place thousands of miles from where I stand in Tokyo. When I put these words together, they even fly over my head, no matter where I am standing. The words *sin* and *moral* and *evil* do not appear with each other in the King James Bible. I cannot even find the word *moral* in the King James Version, after a digital search. Is moral evil, whatever that is, really what the story of Adam and Eve is about? And what to make of being damned for eating one piece of fruit. "*Sore dake?*" "Only that?," one of my students quips in Japanese.

Sin changes when you consider the whole Bible. Centuries beyond Adam and Eve, Jesus reportedly gets testy about the God of Moses' hard-line Old Testament law that it is a sin to work on the Sabbath. Jesus' attitude toward the authorities indicates that, along with my testy students, he might be someone who would ask, "Why would any fruit be forbidden?" Explaining sin is difficult, and it is one of the many elements in the Bible that you think you understand but do not understand. Japanese students follow rules, even stupid rules. In fact Japan may be the global leader in stupid rule making. But restrictions on fruit are out of line, even in this rule making culture.

You have to manage the next level of student questions, those about modern Christian practices that are asked because Japanese students, following our lead, link the Bible to Christianity, not to Judaism, which produced roughly 75% of the books inside—this is another enormous issue—but to Christianity. They link the Bible to Christianity even though they do not know much about the Bible or Christianity.

A student wonders, "Do modern Christians still have sin?" She pronounces sin carefully, with a long "i," this strange, foreign word.

"Yes," you answer.

But teaching sin makes you wonder if you ever really knew what sin was, or is. You even begin to think, along with the God of Eden, that it is not a good idea to expose the knowledge of sin to the sinless.

You may feel familiar with the story of Noah and the big flood, but in Japan you must explain every detail of the story in the text of the Bible. You re-read this section in Genesis carefully before class. You get through it in class without having to answer a hard question, like, "How did Noah's grandchildren have children?" But one of your sinless students looks up from her Bible and asks,

"Do Christian people think this story is true?"

"Yes, sometimes."

"Really?"

They view you as someone from the world of Bible belief, so letting them in on the fact that people in your world believe every word of the Flood story is like outing a family secret. No, it is not *like* outing a family secret: It really *is* outing a family secret. After the outing, you feel you have betrayed a confidence. You begin to look suspect yourself.

"Many people, even devout Christians, just see the Flood as an interesting story," you add, trying to distance yourself from the people you have informed on.

But your students do not know what a devout Christian is. You realize that you do not either and that we do not agree on what a devout Christian is in the world where many think of the Bible as a devotional guidebook. So many examples flash to mind of issues that Christians disagree on. Is suicide wrong? Is capital punishment just? Is abortion a moral evil? What is a moral evil? Is it okay to be gay? The punishment for working on the Sabbath in the Old Testament is death. Isn't that too severe? You sum up by saying something to your Bible students that would sound insane in your hometown:

"Reading the Bible is not the best way to learn about Christianity."

Then you check the hallway to see if a stray Christian has overheard you and is off to report you to the God of juice and cookies.

It is a downhill rather than an uphill struggle, teaching the Bible to the uninitiated, the biblically innocent. Beyond linking the Bible to Christianity, there are no pre-installed Christian views of the Bible in the minds of my students. This slope becomes steeper when you try to explain what we think, those of us brought up as Christians, to those who do not approach bible study under the stern binary gaze of the One God, the God of love and damnation, or under the auspices of one of the many branches of modern religion that have appropriated this God as their own.

Let's look closer at this map of my misguided journey my pilgrimage, not away from home but back from whence I came—just off the circular Yamanote line of central Tokyo and back to the Bible, this time going ass around elbow due West to the far East which, from America, is actually the far West. This is a pilgrimage that I have taken with my Japanese students who have been my burning bush, my collective voice in the wilderness, telling me unintentionally how strange the connections are between modern Christianity and the Bible in my religious homeland. It is a tricky map with a course as roundabout and whimsical as Abraham's wanderings through the desert. In order not to get lost, we should consider the layout of the terrain.

Normal and Not-So-Normal

The Bible is not normal. —Overheard in the hallway outside a Japanese university classroom

I do not scream out my Bible lessons from a megaphone in a crowded Asian marketplace. I do not teach in a robe before a golden Buddhist deity with eighteen arms. Nothing in my teaching resembles the old *Kung Fu* television series. I teach the Bible to normal students in a normal classroom at a normal university. I am not a Japanese culture expert, but I have lived in Japan for over fifteen years and counting. I am not a preacher, or a born-again Christian, or an expert on the Bible. I am the Shakespeare guy. I teach in central Tokyo at Aoyama Gakuin University—Blue Mountain U., in English, drawing from the meanings of *ao* (blue) and *yama* (mountain).

Like many Western universities, Aoyama Gakuin was founded as a Christian school. In 1874, during the Meiji Restoration, Shibuya, Tokyo was "discovered" by Methodist Episcopal Missionaries from the United States who were doing what the faithful from Christian institutions have often done: They set up small schools to spread Christianity and then fall back as the small schools become much larger schools full of teachers and students who do not care much about spreading Christianity. If you build it, they will come—but 100 years later, they won't come for the same reasons.

The Shibuya area, once an outpost, is now one of the Japanese homes to the global fashion industry. Within a minute's walk of our front gates are abundant and opulent brand-name bases that lend an air of fashion to the university. But the university began with a humble and austere mission. The original, small Aoyama Christian school became a college in the 1940s and then expanded rapidly into a modern comprehensive university with large schools in various disciplines—the humanities, law, business, and engineering. The term *Gakuin* means that the facility also runs schools continuously from kindergarten level through to post-graduate degree programs.

The university has retained ceremonial hand-me-downs from the Christian founders, however remote their mission is to the faculty and students now. The vast majority of our faculty and students are not Christian—we are in Japan after all—but in good Japanese fashion, university authorities have put in place memorials, rituals, and slogans to show respect for the Methodist founders.

There is an enormous, elevated statue of John Wesley at the front gate with the inscription, familiar to many Christians, from Matthew: "Salt of the Earth, Light of the World." I do not think our students ponder the meaning of these words. In my not-so-precise polling, students agree that the statue of Wesley, with his stern look and outstretched hand, is scary. The chimes for our classes come from the Methodist church hymnal. They sound a melody that is hauntingly familiar to me, but not my students. We have a Christian chapel with its regrettably underused pipe organ. The darkly stained wooden pews are familiar to me, depressingly familiar, but not to my students, who view this area as a formal meeting room, which it often is.

I teach in the Department of English within the School of Humanities. We offer a class on the Bible, another hand-me-down from the old days. A few years ago, this class came open due to a faculty retirement, and I was asked to teach it because my mostly Japanese colleagues shied away from taking on the class, because they did not feel qualified to teach the Bible because they are smart. They understood the difference between thinking you might know a subject and really knowing a subject.

But I had some pressure. Our then scheduling czar, a Japanese woman with an Ivy League education, had three questions for me, and she did not wait for an answer: (1) You teach Shakespeare, so the English in the King James Bible is no problem for you, right? (2) You are from the American South. You are familiar with Christianity, right? (3) Certainly you would be willing to help out?

"Yes ma'am." Christian or not, Japan is a culture of sacrifice—and when in Rome . . . . This said, there was part of me that wanted to give this class a go. That part was the overconfident, arrogant—at least arrogant about my knowledge of the Bible—grandson of a Methodist minister.

The Bible class I teach has 20 to 50 students. These students on the balance have excellent English skills, and the class is taught in English. Nearly all of my students were born in Japan and are of Japanese heritage. Many of them have had international experience and on the whole are bright and outgoing. In this environment the teacher can become familiar with the attitudes of a given group of Bible students.

Often when an educator talks about teaching, the underlying message is "look at how good I am." I am a good teacher when teaching Shakespeare. But during my first, even second year of teaching the Bible, I was a bad Bible teacher. Now I get more things right, after a few years, but when I started—the memory is painful. But sometimes pain is good, so I will focus here on where things went wrong. Old Testament authors teach us through their descriptions of the stiffnecked Israelites that failure is more memorable than success, more provocative, more interesting.

There are faiths in Japan. Certainly one of those faiths (confirmed on many occasions by my Japanese colleagues during university faculty meetings) is manifested in the relentless and tiresome and frustrating devotion to detail. Japan is a precise culture, abnormally precise. You can find this precision in education. Though the Japanese educational system has been criticized from within and from without for its strict commitment to method, it produces impressive results, particularly in Math and Science. Japanese students are inclined do their homework and do it systematically. They read closely and they listen carefully, at least the top students do. The devil is not in their detail. Detail is God, their ultimate authority. Therein lies the challenge.

The God Who Is Not There and the Gods Who Are

Detail is God. —A grumbling Japanese colleague, overheard during a four-hour faculty meeting.

    Japan still has rustic charm, but, in Tokyo, Japan presents itself as a hyper modern country with cutting-edge technology, a large economy developed by a legion of workaholic men and women in dark-blue suits, lopped quickly and incongruously on top of a long history of samurai warriors, geisha, and sushi. The past has been largely left in the past. The sushi survived, though I do not think the fish would agree.

    Japan is not a land of godless heathens brandishing huge swords in highly choreographed *Kill Bill* style fights. Most people know this, but one cannot underestimate the influence of Hollywood on human consciousness. We should look specifically at religion in Japan. Most Japanese will describe themselves as Buddhists, but only as mild Buddhists, whatever it means to be a mild Buddhist, and they will usually give a passing nod to the Shinto religion, which still has significance in Japanese life. Buddhists follow the teachings of Buddha, who is not a god, as the Christian world understands God.

    In the life of a normal Japanese person, Shinto is a series of rituals more than anything else. The idea of the emperor as a human deity is officially, and pretty much unofficially, a thing of the past. There are gods out there somewhere in Japan, but you will not run into many Japanese who talk of having a unique relationship with a single, all-powerful divine being. Along with forbidden fruit and sin, a Bible-like God, an immense, merciful, but dangerously mercurial supreme being, is not present in Japanese culture. My students draw a blank on original sin. They also lapse into confusion over the God of the Bible, who, to them, comes off as strange, foreign, and scary, along with the statue of John Wesley at my university.

But Japan does have religion. Though Japanese statistics show a very low level of religious belief, Japanese people routinely practice religious observances and often "turn to God," to use Ian Reader's expression from *Religion in Contemporary Japan*. They turn to God, sometimes one of the many *kami* or gods of Shinto tradition. These moments of turning happen at weddings, at funerals, during the Japanese New Year and each August, during *o-bon*, or the Festival of the Dead. (The festival is a picnic with a traditional dance, a pleasant outing despite its name.) There is also a need to perform rituals at critical times, say, before university entrance exams, when in Tokyo many test-taking hopefuls make a quick visit to the shrine of the Japanese God of Education (but not to the statue of John Wesley).

It is difficult to gauge levels of religious belief. Most of us are unsure about exactly what religious level we are on. "On a scale from 1-10 how religious are you?" Next question: "Are you lying to us or to yourself?"

In my Shakespeare classes, when we run across the ghost scene at the beginning of *Hamlet*, I ask students if they believe in ghosts or in life after death. Usually about half of them will say no, they don't. At that point I ask the non-believers if they would take a walk with me at night through nearby Aoyama Cemetery. Several of the non-believing students will shake their heads—an emphatic, "No!" It's too scary.

I agree. The cemetery is a large, scary place, and it does have ghosts. If any of these students ever call my bluff, they will have to go without me because I will be damned before I go there at night. But my point is that my students' belief in life after death, or, in this case, their non belief, does not hold up when put to the test. A simple question about ghosts, asked to bring some humor to the humorless task of teaching tragedy, exposes how inaccurate surveys of religious belief can be.

And this is not only in Japan. It is well known that Americans insist on having high levels of religious belief. But how strong is this belief? Flannery O'Connor's famous story, "A Good Man is Hard to Find," set in Georgia, features a self-righteous Christian in the character of the Grandmother. At the end of the story, she is quick to deny Christ when an escaped convict named The Misfit points a gun at her. This story makes one wonder how much a loaded gun would queer the pitch of religious polls in a Christian culture should respondents be put to a similar test. Most estimates on the number of Christians in Japan currently hover between 1% and 2% of its population, but some argue that this percentage is low. Again, it is difficult to be precise, but you can assume that any Japanese fellow you are talking to in Tokyo does not see himself as a Christian or know much about Christianity.

Sometimes stereotypes are not true. Recently a Japanese professor from our School of Business Management ran me down on campus to tell me that he had found Jesus in Oklahoma. He had heard I was teaching the Bible, and he wanted to talk about Jesus with me. My first thought was that a Business Management school in Japan is a strange place to find a born-again Christian. I explained to him that I had to get going because I was late for a meeting. Meetings trump Jesus in Japan.

The lack of Christians in Japan is The Good News for a Bible teacher. It is difficult to teach the Bible here, but you do not have to concern yourself (normally) with Christian students disagreeing with you or with each other during class. There are no conflicts in class between the Jesus of Oklahoma and one of the many other views of Jesus. For those who believe that a lack of Christian faith leads a culture to moral oblivion and chaos, Japan stands as a strong example that a modern civilized society can get along well without Christianity and its morality stories to keep civil order. Excepting the rush hour human traffic in busy terminals and some other public nuisances—*kamikaze* cyclists, motorbikes, and scooters careening through public areas (sans samurai swords)—Japanese citizens are on the whole painfully polite and obsessively orderly. Japan maintains a low crime rate, particularly when compared with the U.S.

You can find bad behavior in Japan (as you will find even

in Oklahoma). But if you can accept the word of someone who has lived in Japan for an extended period, the Japanese have a strong sense of personal responsibility and duty and are driven by a rigid understanding of right and wrong. Japan is what you could call a religious culture, and it is also a moral culture. It is a normal culture, a democracy with a strong capitalist economy. But it is also an abnormally precise culture. It is not a Christian culture, which may seem abnormal to us, but not to the vast majority of Japanese.

The Fault Line

Ooo—Oak-lahoma, where the wind comes sweepin' down the plain.

So here lies the template for my biblical revelations in Japan—the foundation for the life through the looking glass of seeing the Bible first, before the many latter-day versions of Christianity, before any religion that holds the Bible as sacred. My students typically feel no more closeness to the God of the Bible than we in the Christian world feel for Zeus. And this lack of recognition, reverence, and respect comes from students who are good and polite, who bow incessantly to me and to each other. They approach the Bible by reading the sections they are assigned word for word, trying to translate the exact meaning of abstract concepts, in order to determine the *precise* idea that is being expressed.

On the surface, it is a dream world for religious fundamentalists, who tout the truth-value of every word in the Bible. But it is a stark, real world for a teacher, who has to explain not only such large concepts as original sin but each and every word or idea coherently and then be ready to comment on what all of these concepts, words, and ideas have to do with modern Christianity.

A student stops me in the hallway at the beginning of the school year. She is carrying her recently purchased classroom text, her King James Bible. She has the large book open and is pointing to the word "firmament," which first appears in Genesis 1:6. She asks me, in Japanese, *"Dou yuu imi desu ka?"* Would you please explain why you made us buy this enormous book that I can't understand?

That's a joke. She asked, simply, "What is the meaning?" But because she is Japanese, her real question is, "Precisely, would you please tell me exactly and precisely, what the exact and precise meaning of this word is? The exact meaning." I scratch my head and say that I will get back with her later because I am late for a meeting.

In the King James Bible the firmament is the sky, the solid or "firm" sky. It is a big dome that covers their flat earth in a world that is shaped something like a huge, a very huge, indoor stadium—the original mega church. This is a dome that the writer or writers of these verses did not describe in much detail or accurately because they had never been that high. They did not know that there was no firmament. Before our next class, I landed this explanation on my student, sans the mega church. Her eyes blinked. Maybe she was thinking that she had signed up for the wrong class. What I saw in her eyes was fear. My eyes blinked, too, as I saw much more trouble coming. How do you teach this writing? How does a Bible teacher explain these ancient attempts to describe the nothing that is not there and the nothing that is?

Many of us from Christian cultures feel familiar with the Bible. I did, and it was precisely my lack of precision that made me feel more familiar with the Bible than I should have. Japanese students are not very familiar with the Bible, but they come to Bible study with a stronger skill set for reading the Bible than I have. On the surface it seems easy enough to expose students who are not from a Christian culture to the Bible. It is simple enough to stress that the modern Christian world, the modern religious world, is a diverse place with diverse readings of the Bible. But in Japan, in a land where the gods live in coexistence with themselves but not so much with the God of Christianity or the Jesus of Oklahoma, in a land where being precise overrides any abstract notion of the Bible as God's authoritative Word, it is difficult to find any area of the Bible that does not become a problem on a number of levels, particularly when you try to square the Bible with modern Christian beliefs and practices. This knowledge gap is embarrassing for those of us who are expected to know the answers but who do not. If you want to find a good example of one of the biblical problems I am talking about, open the King James Version to any page and point.

The Face of Things; The Face of Nothing

Lead me, Lord, lead me in thy righteousness; make thy way plain before my face. —Adapted by Samuel Sebastian Wesley, from the *Methodist Church Hymnal*

The musical accompaniment for the above quotation is used for the chimes to begin and end classes at my university, the hauntingly familiar chimes that are from a hymn inspired by Psalm 5. The melody is supposed to reinforce piety among the faithful, and in the case of my university, it fails to do this. The source of the melody is unknown. Students do not hear the chimes and look to God. The religious infrastructure for this response does not exist on our campus.

I remember the hymn from the occasional visits to my maternal grandfather's Methodist church as a child. When I hear it a part of me still fears that God or, worse, my long deceased Methodist minister grandfather might round the corner at any second and catch me doing something wrong. At first I could not remember the exact source of the melody, so I thrashed through the Internet to chase it down one day with the determination of a religious zealot trying to convert the damned.

My students expect a Bible teacher to lead them down the paths of plain understanding of the Bible, so spirited onward by my Protestant past, I hammer down biblical connections that pop up like whack-a-moles. This hardly seems fair. It is plain that there are far more references to the Bible out there than any one person could learn and explain clearly. The people who wrote, who write the hymns and the poetry, the people who crafted, who craft the paintings and art, the people who interpreted, who interpret the Bible were and are driven to make the meanings of the Bible plain before their face and before the faces of others. They have mostly done this not by explaining the Bible but by adapting select biblical passages to the spirit of their experience and desires.

There are no Methodist hymns in the Bible. A Bible verse may bring meaning to the hymn but the hymn does not explain the Bible verse. Nothing in my background, Shakespeare and Southern Protestant roots included, makes it easy or natural for me to make the Bible plain before the faces of my Japanese students. Also troubling is the fact that I teach a class on the Bible under the false, even deceptive idea that there is one book called the Bible. There is no one Bible, even though people feel so, many with all of their hearts. There are of course many different Bibles, many versions in English that read differently from each other, and there are also Bibles in many other languages, including the ancient languages of the Bible that were not English. We cannot get bogged down in this quagmire here. When I use the term, the Bible, unless otherwise noted, I mean the King James Version. Teaching a class called the Bible using only one of the many Bibles, albeit the most famous version in English, is like offering a class on the history of the hamburger and only covering the Big Mac. But I have to live with this.

Why do I use the King James Version? The quick answer to this is in the wording of the first verses of Genesis, the 23rd Psalm, the Christmas story from Luke 2, and other places where the King James Version is superior to other English versions. In the King James Version, the familiar opening verses resound profoundly. I think most readers from Christian backgrounds will quickly scan this passage. I did at the time I was preparing my first class on the Bible. I added the italics:

> In the beginning God created the heaven and the earth.
> And the earth was *without form, and void*;
> and darkness was upon *the face of the deep*.
> And the Spirit of God moved upon *the face of the waters*.
> And God said, Let there be light: and there was light.

Imagine explaining the meanings here to someone who has

never heard these verses while growing up, someone who is trying to determine the precise meaning of each word, someone who has never felt familiar with this God or these words.

Japanese students often ask questions without actually asking a question, by changing their facial expression. This is the case everywhere, but from my experience the habit is pronounced in Japan. So you have to read faces closely. After we read the verses above from Genesis in the first Bible class I ever taught, I was getting unsettling facial reads.

The classic perplexed face in Japan is an upward glance accompanied by a sideways twist of the chin, sometimes with the index finger touching the bottom lip, sometimes with a quick intake of breath through the teeth, a look and style that has been mastered by Japanese students and is in its own quaint manner a no less subtle way to signal *Halt!* than a police dragnet.

There was a problem with detail. The main problem was with the word "void" and the phrase, "face of the deep." I assumed that void meant nothingness, but then it struck me, during class—a bad time to be struck—that nothing, located as it is in darkness, cannot have a face, or at least a face that can be perceived.

While reading the next line, which states, "the Spirit of God moved upon the face of the waters," it also struck me that the nothing in darkness cannot have a perceivable face of the waters, either. Before we had gotten through three verses of the Bible, I was dumbstruck before the class. How do I explain this description of the nothing that is not there with the dark nothingness that is? How do I make plain the face of the deep in a way that would un-trouble the faces of my students?

I mumbled the weak response that, "it appears as if nothingness and water are closely associated in this passage." Professors sound the most professorial when they don't know what they are talking about, and this was an unsatisfactory answer in a culture of students concerned about what, exactly, precisely, might be moving along the face of their next test. Words and images and passages from the Bible seem clear and plain to those of us who feel familiar with them, but the students I teach are not culturally pre-disposed to allow the sense of the familiar to eclipse the need for precise understanding.

We had practiced the King James Version vocabulary, going over older versions of current words ("forth" as an honorific form of forward), special words, ("wroth" as an old word for angry) and special idioms that come up (and the evening and the morning were the first day). And of course I covered and explained the words "thus" and "thee" and "saith" and "'tis." But I was not yet prepared to explain the firmament, the most significant something made from nothing in the Genesis story. That word got by me in the beginning.

No matter how much you prepare, some terms cannot be explained to the satisfaction of these students. To take a non-biblical example, when you use the term "son of a gun" in Japan, you find yourself having to explain what "son of a gun" means. "Son of a bitch" is easier to explain, but how often is this phrase used literally? Can you imagine, 2,000 years from now, students who speak a language that does not currently exist, students in a class studying a novel in English from the ancient 21st century? They come to this sentence: "And then the big sum bitch barreled through the door of the bar and said, 'Whar's my wife?'" Can you image a future professor trying to explain, using a translation of this sentence, the precise meaning of the words in this sentence?

But you do not even have to imagine the problems with word meanings in the distant future when you are in Japan. Many of us are fond of the phrase "get outta here," when we mean, "wow, what you just said is hard to believe." If you say, "get outta here," in this context, to a Japanese fellow, even an excellent English speaker, he will look toward the door, wondering why you just told him to leave. I know this from experience. And let's not go into the look you get when, after a nice stroll in the park, you turn to your Japanese friend and say, "The ice cream is on me."

In the Bible we are all struggling with words and phrases that had slippery meanings to begin with, meanings that may have been lost more than once in translation. Some might feel that I should use a modern English version of the Bible. But so-called modern English versions are not a bit more clear or plain, not to me or to my students.

The New International Version of the Bible, translated in modern English, renders the problem words above, "Now the earth was formless and empty, darkness was over the surface of the deep." I do not think "the surface of the deep" is any less cryptic than "the face of the deep" or any easier to understand. Again, how can formlessness and emptiness, coupled with darkness, have a perceivable surface? The original meaning of this passage, if we could channel the spirit of the ancient writer, might be just as difficult for that writer to explain to my students and me.

"Did you fellows closely associate water and nothingness?" I would ask the spirit when he appears. At which point the spirit, who in my mind looks vaguely like Charlton Heston in *The Ten Commandments*, would respond, "Who are you? I didn't write the story for you." He would say this in English like the English-speaking aliens in *Star Trek*.

It takes time to gather precise meanings from the Bible, or to gather that you cannot reach a precise meaning, and I entered this void before we finished the first three verses of Genesis. In Japan, my lack of precision is embarrassing, and it is also time consuming. A Bible teacher trying to scrunch even a short section of the Bible into a single class, from one of the many Bibles he could have chosen, has to minimize and push forward. Jesus fed the many with a few fish. I must try to achieve the reverse miracle of taking a book that has fed the multitudes and reduce it to a few fish.

Only twenty minutes at best can go to the Creation in Genesis 1. With this sparse amount of time it is difficult to do justice to the sublime theme of the writers reckoning with the beginnings of their race, the beginning of their world. And how can we fly through the ambiguous wording? *And all was void, and the ice cream is on me.*

Anyone who studies the Bible, the whole of the Bible, is in for a challenge, one that requires large amounts of time and thought and one that is played downed by the popular notion in Christian cultures that serious Bible study is something the average Joe can pull off daily. My students think that the Bible is quick work for us in the Christian world, that we read the Bible with the same ease that we read the Sports or Fashion section of the news. I think many of us think this way too.

Often religious groups believe that the study of the Bible can be worked seamlessly into day-to-day routine—short spurts of mild reflection. Let's get out of bed, shower and brush our teeth, sit for a moment with our morning coffee, then pause for a while to read a rough translation of an ancient vision of the eruptive creation and catastrophic destruction of the world. Then feed the dog and get dressed for work. Maybe if we start a group of people to distribute Bibles to hotel rooms across the world, Joe businessman, after a hard day's work on the road, will elect to read the hard and boring book of Leviticus rather than watching a pay-per-view movie. This type of thinking, the type of thinking that insists that anyone can handle the Bible given a little time set aside for reading, that anyone who picks up a Bible and begins to read will be struck by the clarity, the plainness of the Bible's meanings, was what led me to believe that I could jog through the Creation story in twenty minutes in a Japanese classroom.

It was clear that we would not have enough time to cover even selected passages in a way that would lead us to feel that we had made each verse plain before our faces. From the first few verses of Genesis, here are some examples of time-consuming student questions over the years, students who read carefully:

> Why is it dark, before it is light?
> Why does darkness have to be separated from light?
> What waters were divided?

Here are some examples of answers:

> I don't know; let's move on.
> I'm not sure; let's move on.
> I think water and nothingness are closely related, but
>   let me get back to you.
> I'm late for a meeting.

The Bible is long, wide, deep, and disturbing. Maybe Bible study group leaders in the Christian world can get through the Bible by controlling renegade questions about specific words and images; maybe they can overstep the challenges by stating that it is time to trust God. Maybe you can just neglect to invite the renegade question asker to future Bible group discussions—no juice and cookies for him.

To my students, teaching the Bible in this manner might make me seem too much like the scary God they meet early in the Bible.

Unintelligent Designs

Banish me from Eden when you will; but first let me eat of the fruit of the tree of knowledge! —Robert G. Ingersoll, from "Oration on the Gods"

The text of the Bible is hard at the get go, and the Bible makes us all feel ignorant. Because the Bible is hard, because so many people, including me, do not understand key words and verses, it is vulnerable to people bringing in shoddy ideas to make the Bible look like it makes sense by insisting that the Bible is something it is not. One year when we were covering the Creation, my student—let's call him Mr. Takahashi—asked me about the debate surrounding the theory of evolution and the recent push on American school boards from certain Christian groups to adopt intelligent design as an alternative to teaching evolution. You never know what fragments of American culture will bleed in through special news reports on T.V. or the Internet.

I asked him if we could discuss this idea in the next class. I will give over a trade secret. When a student asks a question that I have no clue how to answer, I put the student off and then head back to my office after class and look up the information, then pretend that I knew the answer the whole time. The keywords "intelligent" and "design" bring up some scary websites. Once you reach the sane side of the web, or hard-copy universe, you will find that the idea of intelligent design originally had nothing to do with the Bible or with science. Even so, some groups use the idea to bolster their notion that the Creation story presents the exact truth, to argue that this pre-scientific idea should be treated as a branch of science in schools.

Intelligent design, simply put, is the idea that creation was the result of an intelligent cause. The idea has roots in pre-scientific philosophy ranging from the medieval period, a time that came about a long time after Genesis was written. And the medieval period is a time that most of us would like to believe we are not still in. On the surface, it is easy thinking, the type of thinking John McCain, as a presidential candidate, used when he was asked about his religious faith. McCain answered that he feels the hand of God at work when he walks along the Grand Canyon, either at sunset or sunrise, I can't remember.

The Grand Canyon is beautiful and awe inspiring. But there is an obvious flip side to the grand image of the Grand Canyon. Using the idea of intelligent design we have to conclude that the same intelligent designer who brought us the Grand Canyon also came up with lice, stomach viruses, and large reptiles that eat people. I wish someone had asked this followed up: "Senator McCain, do you also see the hand of God at work when you consider, say, the image of a German eco-tourist being ripped to bloody shreds by a den of Komodo dragons in the island jungles of Indonesia?"

During the next class, instead of covering the Bible, I had to start by explaining to Mr. Takahashi and to the rest of my students that *intelligent design*, in its pure form, does not align itself with a particular god and that the designer does not have to be pro-human being. I added that Genesis tells us that God puts people, at least *His* people, first. I thought, *Why do you need a medieval idea that allows you to argue that the intelligent designer created the earth for the Komodo dragons and that we were added as part of their food supply? And how did your thinking end up in my Bible class?* So much for intelligent design, or so I thought.

"Do you believe the Bible is true?" back to Mr. Takahashi, who erupts like a small volcano because he originally brought up intelligent design and Creationism because he wanted to argue that the earth could not have been created in the way it is described in Genesis. I wanted to avoid discussing my personal beliefs because I am self-trained to be on the defensive. I am from a culture where people want to know your position on religious issues when you would rather be left alone. You would rather be left alone because you wish that these types of Christians would first figure out exactly, precisely, what their beliefs are before they ask you if you believe the things they do. And some of these people, depending on what faction they are from, will persist on wanting to know your position even after you lie to them about being late for a meeting. Where I was born, meetings do not trump Jesus.

But I did not need to be on the defensive. Original sinless Takahashi was not asking a religious question. He was asking a fair question, from a side that does not see the Bible as a sacred text and from a side that is well trained in basic science, a fair question that was intelligently designed to determine if the teacher was a lunatic or not.

"Well, no," I answered. "I don't believe that the creation of earth took exactly six days. And while we're discussing what I don't believe, I don't believe that the earth and heaven are surrounded by water, either. Genesis 1:7 says, 'And God made the firmament, and divided the waters which were under the firmament from the waters which were above the firmament.'"

Takahashi nodded politely. *What a strange thing to say*, I think he was thinking. He was fishing for my position on Christianity and instead heard me proclaim that I didn't believe that outer space was actually water.

"Some Christians believe Genesis tells the exact truth, but a number of Christians don't. I don't know the exact numbers." Then I quipped—quipping in English is not a good thing to do in Japan—"Some people need to figure out if they believe in outer space before they try to shoot down Darwin." I should not have said this because evolution can also be a touchy subject in Japan, where a certain number of Japanese, I am not sure exactly how many, would like to believe that they descend from a unique Japanese race.

My comment confused Takahashi, who thought for a moment. Then he asked, "Don't you have to believe that the Bible is true to be a Christian?"

"Well, there are many types of Christians," I answered. I have found that this evasive non-answer usually works. You can move on if you say it firmly and with the same tone of voice that my old Sunday school teacher used.

This answer even stopped the determined teacher baiter, Mr. Takahashi. But he had let the genie out. Just then about half of the students in the class had on their perplexed faces, so we were stuck. We lost valuable minutes of Bible study just as we lose many more minutes any given year to various modern Christian groups, members of which are not in my class. My students have trained me to be in a state of constant readiness to explain wild connections that people from my own culture make with the Bible.

"Professor, my American friend said something last night that I don't understand. What does *holy shit* mean? Does that come from the Bible?"

Highly Inspired Designs

But nothing is perfect in God's perfect plan —Neil Young

It is not only the anti-outer space, Intelligent Design people who latch on to Genesis and the rest of the Bible, but others who see the creation story, and other Bible stories, not as literally true but as inspirational. The Bible may not be exactly true, they say, but we can draw wonderful spiritual feelings and ideas from these stories.

This type of thinking is mixed with my thinking because I come from this group, vaguely called moderate mainline Christians. In the context of this book, I will group these people with a larger group, the Cookout Christians. These are nice, religious folks who, on my trips home, treat me kindly. They have forgiven my long rap sheet of assailing their religious, middle-class values and have resumed inviting me to cookouts. More on these people, my people, later, but they are the ones who, in the end, I can trust to give me a decent Christian burial. I do not find their spiritual inspiration stupid or delusional, but I do think some of us might be fuzzy about what inspiration is when we look to the Bible for it.

Many of my cookout brethren like to think of the Bible as a source for inspiration. Inspiration, to them, is a synonym for gaining pleasant, warm feelings about life. Life can be scary, and we should put as much warmth into the mix as we can to ward off the ever-encroaching feelings of despair that are always lurking about. The idea that the Bible is a fine source for warm inspiration was reinforced when I traveled to the States recently and wandered through a soon-to-be grave in a new graveyard, a big chain bookstore, before heading off, honestly, to a cookout. There was a section called "Inspirational," which caught my eye. There I found a number of spiritual self-help books and a number of bibles. Now the Bible teacher, I wondered about the intelligent designer of the bookstore, the person or people who created this section, who created a market sector with the word, Inspirational. Was there darkness before light or the converse? Were the inspirational books in this section written before there was an inspirational section? Or was the section created first, and then came the writers of the books arranged in this section? And why were ancient Bibles dumped in this soon-to-be archaeological area?

I indicated before that some references to Bible stories have made their way into Japanese *manga* or comic books. Kids and even adults find comic books inspiring across the world, and there is a type of religious devotion to manga in Japan. There are fantasy elements in the Bible that often make it read like manga, so why not add illustrations and put the Bible in the comic book section as they do in Japan? Samson killing one thousand men with a donkey's jawbone right there with Spiderman swinging through the midtown skyline. Given the Bible's cultural power and its uniqueness, though, I think that bibles and books about the Bible should be taken from the Inspirational section and put into a section of the bookstore called "The Bible." But it would be difficult to market the Bible as the Bible, and bookstore intelligent designers know this. You have to attach the Bible to a category it is not in to sell it.

I find the Bible inspiring, but I do not think I am channeling the bookstore designers. Once I was hit by the absurd image of Ham feeding the Komodo dragons on Noah's ark after rereading the Noah story. But of course the average Cookout Christian shopping the Inspirational section of an American bookstore is looking for a different type of inspiration, something apart from Noah's son having to feed big lizards that will eat you and each other.

What type of inspiration would this shopper look for in the opening chapters of Genesis? Inspiration is not always a good thing. The 9/11 terrorists were inspired, as was Timothy McVeigh. Genesis is a book that starts with two fantastical creation stories that are followed by stories of mass destruction, that are followed many other books with even more stories of mass destruction. Is this the inspiration a religious, middle-class book buyer wants? My middle-class Japanese students find much of the Bible scary instead of warm. I do too.

In the Bible, the reader is told that God loves us, that Jesus loves us, and these words can inspire us in a happy way. But you have to be careful where you go to the Bible searching for warmth. Open it to the wrong page and you find God killing people—even his own people—and many people killed in his name. The book of Revelation, as Northrop Frye points out, has been described as "a book that either finds a man mad or else leaves him so." This idea expands beyond Revelation and into much of the Bible.

The Bible is too violent and strange to fit in with other polite inspirational coffee table books. It is largely maladapted for the modern middle-class Christian. I do not think it could be published and distributed as an inspirational book if it had just been written yesterday. It is too hard, too *hard,* and it would not sell.

Intelligent Design and Inspiration: These lurches at the Bible never bothered me much until I had to explain them to students. To each his own. But now these attempts to absorb the Bible into other unrelated ways of thinking seem blatantly disrespectful of the Bible and the culture—my culture—in which the Bible has so much influence. The Bible in the grip of these and other strange ideas make my home culture look like the twilight zone to my students.

And I am sure that my students cannot understand why I get so worked-up over the Bible in the first place, why I keep insisting that the are many types of Christians in that restrained, righteous tone of voice. As a foreigner teaching in Japan—as an American—my thoughts on just about any issue could be received as an authoritative American perspective to my students. I sometimes become the subject of an impromptu cross-cultural study, and that's fine. Many Japanese feel like they live under American policies. They do not have the opportunity to meet many Americans, so their interest in my views as an American is understandable. But I do not like the idea that my opinions on religion, what many of my American cousins might see as jaded opinions, could be taken to represent The American Perspective.

I cannot speak for all Americans. I cannot begin to get a grip on religion in America. America does not have a firm grip on religion in America. I could refer my students to Harold Bloom of Yale, who writes faster than I can read, for gripping portraits of the American religion, but that would be different subject, another class. It is difficult enough for me to cover the Bible, a series of books that came into being hundreds of years before anyone set up weird websites to abuse the Bible with half cooked and unrelated medieval ideas, hundreds of years before bookstores and their inspirational sections were conceived, hundreds of years before anyone assigned the word America to a enormous section of dry land, and hundreds of years before I moved across the surface of the deep to teach the Bible in Japan.

The Man Who Did Not Fall; The Teacher Who *Did*

The history of the Fall is recorded in Gen. 2 and 3. That history is to be literally interpreted. It records facts which underlie the whole system of revealed truth. —The Christian WebBible Encyclopedia

Literally there is no fall. The Bible is difficult, and it is enormous. I came across explanations that do not explain anything and that somehow seeped in to my class to stir up more confusion. The Bible does not forward a philosophy that the earth was created for the Komodo dragon. The Bible does not always inspire us to be good in the way we see good.

These ideas started to send my thinking in circles about the differences between the Bible that I was teaching and the other views of the Bible from my homeland. I started to have feelings of righteousness, which is not good. I have had to edit these feelings from my teaching and from the early drafts of this book. Back in our history, righteousness was a good thing, something that we asked God to lead us with. But I tend to view righteousness with suspicion, and this is good, I think. Righteousness is not the feeling you have when you are right and someone else is wrong. Righteous feelings come when I know someone else is wrong, and I sense that I am wrong, too.

Instead of admitting that I am wrong, I insist that I am right. I do not want to see myself as being just as bad as all the other wrong people. The words *righteous* and *wrongheaded* are now synonyms, and teaching the Bible has helped me understand my own righteousness better though this understanding proffers no warm feelings. Lead me, Lord, lead me in Your righteousness—make it plain to me that when I feel righteous, I am wrong.

I, too, had my own pre-packaged ideas about the Bible, ideas drawn from my religious background, ideas that I thought were good general overviews but that did not stand up against the text of the Bible. In the early days of teaching the Bible, I brought forth the idea of the Fall of Man after we had finally made it out of the first two of fifty, 50!, chapters of Genesis.

We were covering Chapter 3. The serpent talks Eve into giving the fruit a try. She does and offers the fruit to Adam, who also takes a bite, and then they both realize they are naked. What an unforgettable miniature of human angst—that is, the realization that doing just about anything that feels good will be met with punishment.

It does not need an overblown overview like the Fall of Man to explain it. But I was sold on the Fall of Man idea, and I realized, too late, that this idea comes from Christian interpretations of the Bible that had somehow wormed their way into my thinking. The Fall of Man is a later Christian view of Genesis that is not in the actual words of Genesis 3, King James Version.

I did not learn this from my own reading. I learned it after a class, from a polite mature student who shyly approached me, pointing to the words in his Bible, to point out that he could not find any line in Genesis 3 where the "fall" happened. It was late, and I was hungry, so I wanted to glare at him and say, "Mr. Yoneda, just trust God, and get outta here."

I righteously defended my view. I explained to him that the idea of the Fall of Man is metaphorical. Adam's fall represents the fall of everyone. Yoneda persisted, showing me his text and saying, "but Adam does not fall." I stared with him at the lines of Genesis 3. He was not righteous, but he was right; I was righteous but wrong. The verb, to fall, in any form, is not part of the King James Version's description of Adam and Eve being driven out of the Garden of Eden.

I am no better than the Intelligent Design and Inspirational people, I thought, using big ideas to describe what is not in the Bible. I failed to read the section I was teaching closely enough, and this positioned me uncomfortably close to the people who replace outer space with water. No one actually falls. I did not read each word of Chapter 3 carefully.

But I cannot take the full blame for teaching the Fall of Man in relation to the Bible. The idea has a firm institutional history. It is the product of hard thinking intellectuals, not members of the Intelligent Design crowd or those who want to put man-eating giant lizards that are not indigenous to the Middle East on Noah's ark. Bible stories and themes that have been rendered part of what we need to know are received and absorbed by us in ways that, well, ways that I cannot remember. I know how to read, but I cannot remember much about how I was taught to read.

I was given a number of biblical ideas going to church as a kid. Setting aside a few select verses that we read here and there, church Bible teaching was mostly oral or visual. I picked up some more ideas through popular culture, which is mostly oral and visual and unexplained. I learned in classes that I took, maybe a history class or a humanities class, ideas about the Bible by reading things written about the Bible instead of the Bible itself. I cannot help but think that there is a quiet consensus in Christian cultures that knowing the Bible is not actually reading all of the words of the Bible closely; knowing the Bible is absorbing uncritically what others tell us the Bible is.

The devil is in the detail, or detail is God—however you want to look at it. I introduced an idea about the Bible that is not in the text. I got busted by my Japanese student, a volunteer member of the Detail Police Force of Japan. If I had been teaching in a Christian culture, in a place where most of my students would be in Fall of Man Land with me, I think the mistake would have gone unnoticed. We are all acolytes of the oral and visual Bible, with a few actual verses thrown in for good measure. But these students read word by word, often negotiating, word for word, the dark matter of meaning between the cryptic English text and their native tongue. And in come more vexing questions for those of us who think we know the Bible. In Genesis 4:17, where did Cain's wife come from? Why was Ham cursed by his father (9:25)? A student asks, "Why Ham? It was his father who got drunk and fell asleep naked."

Because I had heard of the Ten Commandments, I thought I knew the Ten Commandments. In order to save the reader from tedious detail, and to save more embarrassment, I will just say that I did not know exactly, precisely, what the Ten Commandments were, and I did not know that the King James Bible does not make it clear what they are either. Can you recite what we, not the authors of the Bible, call the all-important Ten Commandments in the right order? Both versions? They are not the same, and different church traditions number them differently. I do not think many of us can recited any whole version of the passage that we call the Ten Commandments, even the righteous who want to display them in courthouses.

Do we understand the precise differences in the two versions of the creation story in Genesis 1 and 2? Do we know the names of the twelve disciples? Do we know how many books are in the New Testament and the names of these books? Was it really an apple that Eve, then Adam, bit into? Look closely at Genesis 1 of the King James Version, before you answer.

Or try to pick the best answer for this test question I created in the beginning:

> According to the King James Version, God created the heavens and the earth
> (a) after the great flood.
> (b) in seven days.
> (c) in forty days.
> (d) in six days.

I gotcha if you jumped for answer (b) instead of answer (d)—at least that is what I thought when I made the question.

I wanted to see if my students knew that God rested on the seventh day and that the creation was completed in six days. But in another embarrassing teaching moment, it struck me while I was grading the test, a bad time to be struck, that I had to throw out the question. None of the answers is correct. I made a spelling error in forming the question because I thought I knew the King James line by heart.

In the King James Version, the actual word is *heaven*, not *heavens*. The word *heavens* is used in Genesis 1 in a number of modern English versions of the Bible but not the King James

Version. The word *heaven* is a concrete image, one that works well with the concrete image of the firmament. The word *heavens* is an abstract image that fits better with our now more abstract scientific understanding that we are not living under that big dam above that holds back the space water.

In the King James Version, Genesis 1, God did not create heavens, plural. Those students who chose answer (b) got a break. But I did not get a break. And I cannot find anyone else to blame for this mistake. All I can say is that we have all made spelling errors and have come short of the glory of our middle-school English teachers.

You might argue—I would argue—that passing a picky objective quiz on the Bible is not so important. But you might argue, as I would, that Bible students should know that the creation took six days instead of seven. Resting on the Sabbath is a big mandate throughout the Bible. Small details reflect large Godly meanings. So close reading is the key to studying the Bible.

I have recently re-read the richly poetic 23rd Psalm, word for word. "The valley of the shadow of death." These words are abstract, but I think my students and I can draw clear meaning, even inspiration from them. I get too close to the valley of the shadow of death every time a flight I am on starts its turbulent approach for landing—a good time for prayer.

But close reading cannot always ferry you across the Jordan into the Promised Land. Sometimes you read every word of a section and still cannot find even a vague meaning or find anything to say about what you cannot find. There are ideas in the Bible more difficult than the hard firmament, than the watery void. The first two chapters of the richly poetic *Song of Solomon* gives the reader no clue as to what these chapters mean, even after a close reading, even now that I have been self-trained not to let any word go by unnoticed. In the first three verses of Chapter 1, from the King James Version, the speaker says:

> The song of songs, which is Solomon's. Let him kiss me with the kisses of his mouth: for thy love is better than wine. Because of the savour of thy good ointments thy

name is as ointment poured forth, therefore do the virgins love thee. (1-3)

Is Solomon the writer here, and, if so, is he reflecting on how he is viewed by lovers and—let's clear our throats—virgins, in the plural form? But let's move on. Like so many Bible teachers before me, I have now been seduced by the benefits of passing over these songs in silence.

Each time I do not know the answer, and each time I think I know the answer but do not, I believe my students think I am a fake, a fake who is on the verge of becoming self-righteous, who is frequently late for meetings and who thinks that he knows more than he knows, a fake who is a product of a culture that has given the Bible the status of holy writ, of ultimate truth, but a culture that feels more familiar with the Bible than it really is, a culture in which religious folk insist that everyone should read the Bible, but a culture in which those same people often do not know what the Bible is or what it says.

But What about the Dinosaurs?

In a single stroke with a medium-grained nail file you could eradicate human history. —John McPhee, from *Basin and Range*

That the writers of the ancient texts of the Bible did not know the shape of things in their solar system is understandable. What gets to my students is that their religious beliefs might still be held as true, and that those who still cling to this old cosmos come from the West, from the same sponsor that brought in space travel, the Internet, the human genome project, and CERN.

This non-scientific belief in the modern religious symbol called The Bible, in their minds, stands in opposition to the menacing truths of science. This gap between science and religion of course also presents a dissonant split in Western thinking. Science has a long history of cutting the gods down to size, showing the Christian world, the religious world, even the enduring mythologies of the Japanese world, where lightning really comes from, showing us how the earth was not created in six days because the galaxy does not have days, showing us the earth's atmosphere then outer space, instead of a firmament holding back the deep watery void. In the minds of my students, in my mind, science presents no challenge to the continuing importance and pertinence of the Bible as book, even as a wider institution of study. For starters, as long as people do not insist that we live on a flat earth that the sun rotates around, there is no reason why the two could not find a way to co-exist peacefully.

A teacher does not have to be concerned about the relationship between modern religious belief and science when teaching other ancient texts. If I were teaching *The Odyssey* in

Japan, I would not have to stop and explain to students that, yes, some people in Idaho still believe in the Cyclops and the Sirens. This is not so with the Bible. All too often science becomes mixed in with my Bible class. And I am not a scientist.

"But what about the dinosaurs?"

Ms. Sano blurts out while I was trying to cover the Creation during another year of class. My answer was that my understanding of dinosaurs comes from Michael Creighton's *Jurassic Park*, and little else. Dinosaurs do not appear in the ancient creation story in the Bible, which makes it seem as if the writer of the story did not know about the dinosaurs, not unless a T-Rex qualifies as a "beast of the earth."

Wolves and lions and other beasts are mentioned in the Bible, but the writers left out velociraptors. Some Creationists think that the behemoth mentioned in the book of Job is evidence of dinosaurs, which would put dinosaurs on earth less than three thousand years ago. But, science aside, other ancient writers, including those who wrote the other books of the Bible, missed remarking on what would be some uncanny, fearful, and, indeed, remarkable creatures food stalking beneath the great firmament.

The dinosaur question is a fair question from a Japanese Bible student who has some understanding of global Christianity and how it is practiced. Ms. Sano, like Mr. Takahashi, had heard that the creation story was believed to be true in the Christian world. Mr. Takahashi, in another group of students, was the one who approached the creationist issue via intelligent design in a polite attempt to smoke me out on my specific beliefs. Both of these young people, I am certain, came to class with respect for the Christian world or Western civilization or whatever you call what they see when looking outward to the enormous and lasting cross-continental influence that European history and religion has had on our spherical earth.

Ms. Sano, though, took the direct, hard-science route of the dinosaurs to attack the problem of why the same cultures that discovered dinosaurs have people who believe an ancient description of a dinosaur-less world. She did not care what I believed. She was prepared to defend science if, say, I dared to proclaim in class that Genesis is true. (I responded to her that there are many types of Christians.) She had not heard about the recent 27 million dollar Creation Museum in Petersburg, Kentucky, where dinosaurs are introduced as part of the museum's creationist mission to show the behemoth dinosaurs alongside the Garden of Eden. The museum's website promises to "bring the pages of the Bible to life." They advertise that "our dinosaurs cater to groups."

Dinosaurs. Should we make our exodus from the Bible that is not there and head to the Bible that is, would there be anything left? The intrusion of science on mythological thinking, on modern belief in mythological thinking, is a problem. Science tells us that the big picture is much larger and much smaller than us, and many people find this notion troubling. But science could also present a solution, or so I thought. Science has yet to explain why bad ideas too often come in disguise as the divine muse, but in one such moment of false revelation I got it in my head that I could use popular science as a teaching aid, a way to gain entrée into the ancient mythological mind of the Bible.

A teacher can exacerbate a teaching problem by making up a way to explain the problem that is more difficult to understand than the problem itself. At the beginning of the Bible, a number of my students were confused by the disconnection between their modern world of dinosaur discoveries and the ancient world of the flat earth and firmament but no dinosaurs—that is unless you buy in to the notion that you can just put dinosaurs in the Bible, as they do in a certain part of Kentucky.

The next year I reorganized the class by creating a module for the creation story—a module is what a teacher uses when he is not certain what it is he is teaching. I created a module for teaching that I thought would brilliantly diagram the Creation, my own little ark that I hoped would rescue us from the deluge of belief systems and the interpretations of these belief systems and the interpretations of the interpretations.

I came up with the idea of the reverse planetarium. On a summer afternoon, it is hard to imagine a more pleasing place than a planetarium, a place that is edifying and truly fun, not to mention quiet, relaxing, and cool, with comfortable, cushioned seats—a good place to enjoy a cold bottle of water. The house lights go down and a simple domed ceiling transforms into darkness and space. You see the stars as you would on the clearest night. How quickly the imagination takes over in a planetarium, how easy it is to feel that you are gazing at real stars and planets, real meteor showers and comets.

The strength of the imagination is what the poet Samuel Taylor Coleridge called, when speaking about drama, "the willing suspension of disbelief." We understand imagination and scientific reasoning as two different things, but the planetarium reminds us that there would be little science without the imagination.

With the aid of modern science, with measurements and calculations, with lighting and graphics, the planetarium draws us into a vision of planets and space that is imagined but unreal. We make it real by imagination, but through the imagination that science has taught us. We forget that we are looking at a domed ceiling with a host of variously tinted lights aimed at it. The planetarium is an unreal place where we can imagine the reality of our universe. *My students are wondering what a planetarium has to do with the Bible at this point.*

But I continue. It is easy to see how an ancient, pre-scientific visionary might look up to the real sky on a clear night and imagine that the sky itself is a type of planetarium, a firm domed ceiling with the animated moon and stars. This view of heaven and earth was real and close to our ancient visionary, though his perception of the dome was based on perception alone and not the findings of science.

The ancient world assumed that the world is a flat plain with mountains because the world looks flat. The flatness of planet earth is not hard to imagine. The sky, the firmament, must be a dome that fits over this horizontal plain, this earth, this "dry land," surrounded by water. If dry land is surrounded by water, then water is the void that is under dry land and also above the firmament. The ancient visionary reckons that somewhere in the domed sky, in the firmament, is Heaven.

This vaulted or arched firmament, a ceiling replicated

by so many cathedrals, is a term that has been made obsolete by science. We no longer see the sky as a domed ceiling with a sun and moon and much smaller stars that rotate over us. In a planetarium, though, if we discount science and scientific discovery and instead remember the domed ceiling, we can imagine a view of the sky that is similar to that of the ancient writer, teacher, thinker, and priest, the one who made up his own module for showing us the shape of his world through the Creation story in Genesis 1. In order to design a planetarium, the makers must rotate the sun, moon, and stars with much the same view of the ancient visionary. *Ms. Yoshikuni yawns.*

If I could take you to a place outside on a clear night, preferably in a desert located somewhere between Egypt and Iraq, not Tokyo, we could look to the sky and imagine this natural planetarium, this dome, this firmament with its lamp-like stars and understand how the ancient saw this ceiling, not so far away but still unreachable.

A modern imagines the scientific reality of space from the known unreality of the domed ceiling. But the ancient reversed the planetarium by perceiving the apparent and natural reality of the domed ceiling, the firmament, and imagining the unknown, a world, a heaven over dry land, now with light, that had taken shape "in the midst of the waters."

When putting my teaching creation to work explaining the Creation, I saw the perplexed faces moving along the face of this deep. I tacked and tried to reduce my module to a simpler formula: In a planetarium we moderns imagine what is real from what is not real. The ancient imagined what is not real from what is real or at least what seemed to be real.

I had confused myself, so I tried a more reduced version: We imagine the known; the ancients imagined the unknown. This is, roughly speaking, what I concluded in class. The students looked stunned, with the exception of Mr. Matsuda, who had nodded off to sleep. I added that of course the biblical view of creation was based on a perceived cosmology that (almost) all agree is not really the case. Nicolaus Copernicus, who lived some three hundred years before Darwin, let his contemporaries in on the then troublesome fact, highly troublesome to the Christian church that Copernicus belonged to, that the earth revolves around the Sun, not the converse.

Before Copernicus, long before Darwin, but after our biblical ancients, nautical navigators were figuring out that our globe was a place where, if you went in the same direction long enough, you would end up where you started. And Mr. Matsuda is still sleeping. Ms. Yoshino, judging from her face, is wondering what Copernicus has to do with the Bible. Mr. Aoki is brave enough to raise his hand and ask if the class is expected to know about Copernicus on a test about the Bible. He was being a smart aleck, I think, but I ignored him because I was too busy thinking about Copernicus.

I forge ahead, saying that oddly in the Christian world there are modern Creationists who, along with their ancient Hebrew brethren, believe that the earth is a flat place under a heavenly firmament, an area where water, being the chief primal element, was parted to allow our existence. I did not mention the patrons of the Creation Museum, but I guess those folks believe the airline company that flies them from Salt Lick, Montana, to Petersburg, Kentucky, for creationist vacation lies to them with their curved navigational charts. Google Earth lies, too. But not all Creationists agree on how we were created. Indeed, Creationists, too, have their own polarized denominations. Some do not believe that dinosaurs ever existed. These folks must believe that all of those views of the earth from space were provided to us by the same global demonic conspiracy that salted our dry land with fake dinosaur bones.

Where was I? Right, the failure of my creation. Even the most reduced version of the planetarium in reverse idea, triggered a volley of perplexed faces among those students who were still awake, and several of those faces took on a look of abject despair. So much for using science to explain non-scientific thinking. My module, my creation, my planetarium in reverse was a failure. After class, I angrily dumped my class notes in the garbage. I destroyed my planetarium world, then I thought, *Didn't something like this happen early on in the Bible?*

The Great Shazam

I wish people would stop putting my name under sayings that I never said. —Mark Twain, maybe

Mark Twain did not care much for religion, but he did share with God the fact that he has had a number of sayings attributed to him that he did not write or say. God and Mark Twain. We are familiar with their names. We tend to accept what others say about them without checking sources because the famous have authority and quoting the famous makes a speaker seem authoritative, so we tend to overlook the fact that the sources of quotations should be confirmed before we repeat them.

I felt this authority at once as a Bible teacher. My students know that I am teaching the most famous and authoritative book produced in the Western world. The Bible's authority gave me authority, an authority that I did not deserve, teaching ideas that I was somewhat familiar with but that often were not confirmed by the source. I was a charlatan, an impostor, when the source, time after time, tore down what I thought I knew about the Bible.

Again, there is an arrogance in repeating quotations without checking the source—an arrogance that comes with thinking you are familiar with something you are not. The arrogance that is not there but that is there. This arrogance made me worse than the dinosaur lovers of Kentucky. I am supposed to come from the right side of the intellectual tracks. I am supposed to know the source.

I needed to repent. I needed redemption. Early on, I knew that I owed it to my students and to the gods of Japan to sit down and read every single word of the Bible, to read it closely and carefully, to gain, at least in my own mind, real expertise on the actual words of the Bible. I did this. I sat down and read every single word of the King James Bible—every word, even the parts I thought I knew. Actually I read sizeable portions of the Bible standing up rather than sitting because I did much of this reading on overcrowded Tokyo trains.

Reading the Bible while standing in a train is painful. The Bible is and is not all of the things I have mentioned and more. It is physically heavy, particularly a real study Bible, not one of those fragile thin-paged non-books with typesetting that was never meant to be read by human beings. Japanese commuters on the subway sometimes seemed shocked by the shear size of the Bible I was carrying—the Oxford World's Classics edition of the King James Version.

A Japanese office lady stares blankly at my big book, then blinks and goes back to her mobile phone. Another Japanese fellow, from his enviable seat below, looks up and does a double take at the cover, a close up of the head of Michelangelo's Jeremiah. Michelangelo thought that Jeremiah should look like God when God is vexed and angry.

However time efficient, reading the Bible on the Tokyo train system made me nervous. An older lady, an American from the look of things, gives me a warm, approving smile. I return the smile nervously, taking a short break from reading about Jezebel being eaten by dogs. Another fellow, a Brit from the looks of his soccer jersey, scowls at me. I ignore him as I read about Elijah challenging, beating, and then destroying the priests of Baal.

During this period I experienced back pain and went to see my doctor. He asked, "Have you been over-exerting yourself physically?" Yes, by God. I had been carrying around a heavy book for three hours of my life every day, trudging distances with it, heaving it countless times up stairs and hills, holding it precariously while being jostled around standing on crowded, careening trains. Adding the Bible to the already heavy load was more than my back muscles could handle. My Bible is not a cross, but I did have to bear it through the Tokyo underworld transit system and then up the hill or *yama* that is part of my university's name.

I changed from a satchel to a backpack, which helped with the back problem, but not the emotional problems. Reading the Bible before going to sleep is a bad idea. Reading in the subway is better than falling asleep with images of people being eaten by dogs. There are large sections of the Bible, the entire bipolar book of Jeremiah, that are not good for your mental health, no matter when or where you read these passages.

> Therefore deliver up their children to the famine, and pour out their blood by the force of the sword; and let their wives be bereaved of their children, and be widows; and let their men be put to death; let their young men be slain by the sword in battle. Let a cry be heard from their houses, when thou shalt bring a troop suddenly upon them: for they have digged a pit to take me, and hid snares for my feet. (Jeremiah 18: 21-22)

In any Christian Bible study group, members should follow the study of such verses by segueing into a group therapy session to recover from what they have just read. Drinking two or three beers also works well to numb the image of children being slaughtered by swords and also the enduring image of the warrior king in the book of Judges who has a tent peg nailed through his head.

There are scarier things than the Bible. Nearby Aoyama Cemetery is scarier than the Bible. There are movies that are scarier than the Bible, but when you watch them you are not besieged with painful reminders of your own shortcomings as someone who is supposed to know the Bible but who does not. You are not confronted with your own arrogance as the Bible itself weighs and measures you and finds you unworthy as a teacher. The scariest thing about reading the Bible is the empty feeling, the hollowness of heart that occurs when you see just how much of this big book is incomprehensible.

The more or less comprehensible areas are often angry and threatening and designed to fill your heart with fear. The Passover is fearful. You wonder why first-born human children and animals have to suffer so much in this world.

Less hyperbolic and more fearful is the ugly scene in which Moses, always mindful of God's judgment and, once enlisted, quick to carry out God's will, commands the slaughter of the captured Midianite women and male children after the Midianites had been soundly defeated in Numbers 31.

Joshua, in dead sync with God's will, orders the death of every man, woman, and child in Jericho after the siege (aside from one prostitute and her family—she had served the Israelites as a spy). This is in Joshua 6. You feel that there are shades of real history here, that these and a number of other brutal, bloody slaughters carried out in the name of God are not just tall tales. Such massacres did occur. These ugly scenes eclipse the general theme of God's goodness and mercy, which the writers of these books continually insist upon.

Joshua wipes out a number of tribes in Joshua 10:40, "utterly" destroying "all that breathed, as the LORD God of Israel commanded." Speaking on behalf of God, the priest Samuel tells Saul to "smite" the city of Amalek and "slay both man and woman, infant and suckling" in 1 Samuel 15:3, and speaking for God, Ezekiel repeats the commandment to, "slay utterly old and young, both maids, and little children, and women" in Ezekiel 9:6. It is not clear why murdering women and children is sanctioned, even encouraged, by God, even if those women and children do not belong to the Chosen. Are we supposed to like the Israelites and their God after these genocidal rampages?

It is also fearful that normal dramatic devices used to elicit normal responses are out of kilter in the Bible. In Shakespeare, Richard III and Macbeth both want to be king, so they do horrible things in order to capture and maintain the crown. They both order the murder of children. Both lose our sympathy, and both are punished. Whatever other bad things these kings have done, the slaughter of innocents is unforgivable.

Shakespearean stories, which are complex enough, seem to have simple morals when placed beside the stories in the Bible. How are we supposed to identify with Moses as a good man, as a hero we support, after he orders his troops to slaughter children? I finished my close reading of the entire Bible, and the experience was long and painful.

I was arrogant. I attempted to redeem myself by reading every word of the Bible, much of it standing up. Where did this arrogance come from? If someone had asked me to teach a class on dinosaurs, I would have refused because I am not a dinosaur expert. I am not a scientist. I made a D in high school Chemistry, and that was a gift from a teacher who felt sorry for me. No arrogance there. Why was it that I thought I could teach a book that I had not carefully read myself? And why was it that anyone in my department thought that I was the person for the job?

Now I am certain that my own arrogance came from a much larger wellspring than just my own arrogance. It came from a very long, wide, and deep false consciousness. Being from the American South was a major credential for teaching the class. This is like assuming that anyone who grows up in Stratford, England, whether an accountant or an auto mechanic, is mystically able to teach Shakespeare without really reading and studying Shakespeare. It is also like assuming that, being from the American South, I would also be able to up and teach a class on the Paleolithic fossils of the Carolinas.

I wanted to find someone else to blame for these biblical miscalculations. I did not want to see myself as a liar and a fool, the kind of fool who lies convincingly to himself. I did not want to start sounding like an angry adolescent, calling other people liars in order to hide from the lies that I had told myself. This is the path to the worst kind of self-righteousness.

But the word *lie* is a strong and brutal word, and the term *liar* really does not come close to describing a host of us who bend the truth, even to ourselves, from time to time. A bad guy pushes over an 82-year-old grandmother and then runs down the street and points at another man, accusing him of the crime. This is a lie, a horrible lie, and just the type of lie expressly forbidden when God warns his people against bearing false witness. And for a good reason. Bearing false witness is the worst of all lies because it undermines justice and civilization. There is a difference between this hard, low lying and the instinct for deception, the real need for self-deception as a shelter from uncomfortable, horrible truths. The German eco-tourist, when he finds himself surrounded by Komodo dragons is thinking, no doubt, *This isn't happening to me.*

In my own defense I began to concoct the idea that there is a unique brand of deception, including self-deception, in how we in the Christian world view the Bible. It is a strong deception, a type of indoctrination that we have experienced on levels invisible to us. But the word *indoctrination* misses the mark as badly as the words *lie* and *liar*. The term indoctrination is too strident, heavy-handed, inaccurate, and even paranoid. The problem was that I could not find a better word to replace the ideas of lying and indoctrination, so I invented one, or modified the meaning of an old word used by Gomer Pyle: *Shazam*. In the old T.V. series, Pyle says "shazam" whenever he has a revelation.

But, in the Christian world, revelations are so commonplace, even mass-produced, that the shazam effect reverses itself. Shazams that come off the religious assembly line—a big one being the notion that the Bible is one book instead of many texts cut and pasted together—close us off from the truth. Religious shazams present things as true that simply are not true. There is no mention of an apple in the Garden of Eden.

God is easy to give quotations to. While teaching the Bible in Japan, it has become clear that many Christians have either been shazamed or have shazamed themselves into thinking about the Bible in varied contexts in which the Bible does not fit. People in the Christian world, me included, have been shazamed or have shazamed themselves into thinking they know a book they do not know at all. I am just a microscopic part of this large world of the Bible, submerged in the watery void of its ardent and deceptive unknowing.

Long before we get to the actual texts of the Bible, our world, the world of my upbringing and maybe of your upbringing, too, puts the Bible in contexts where it does not belong because of our religious need to shelter ourselves from uncomfortable truths about our own religious foundations. But should we let this instinct to bend the truth lead us to bear false witness? Of the many Bibles out there, no serious version makes for quick and easy reading, but reading the actual text does have its moments of truth.

The Bible I have learned through now years of reading and studying and teaching is not about intelligent design or self-help inspiration. There are no dinosaurs. There is no Fall of Man. The Bible cannot be fit securely into general teaching modules. The American woman in the subway sees me reading the Bible and thinks I am a good man doing a good thing. The British soccer fan sees me as a prick. Both of these assessments are made from shazamed ideas about the Bible, and both assessments are wrong. The Japanese people in the subway quietly see me as a nervous foreign guy reading a big, scary book.

Bingo.

The Un-shazam

You Have Questions. The Bible Has Answers.
—Catchphrase for BibleStudy.org

Moving deeper into Genesis, the story of Lot from Genesis 19 shows how the shazam holds us. Many of us know how the story begins. Angels appear to Lot to warn him of the imminent destruction of Sodom and Gomorrah, the twin sin cities that made it onto God's hit list because of "grievous" sins committed against God (18:20). We are not told precisely what those sins are, a fact that prompts our imagination.

We *are* told that Lot and his family, his wife and two daughters, are the only good people in town, and Lot and his family are warned by angels to get out of town in a hurry. And they are warned to "look not behind" (19:17). Lot, his wife, and two daughters, flee just as God "rained upon Sodom and Gomorrah brimstone and fire" from Heaven (19:24). They get away safely, but Lot's wife looks back, and for that she is turned into a "pillar of salt" (19:26). Here, traditionally, or at least in my case, is where the oral telling of the story ended in Sunday school.

It was an abrupt ending, we thought, back when Santa was alive and well, when the story was told to us by our Sunday school teacher. We also thought this was a mean punishment on God's part. "What is the moral?" little Johnny Witherspoon asked. This question was allowed. Our teacher paused, then said. "Well, first, you should be good. Second, if God tells you not to look back, then don't look back."

To this day, I suppose Johnny Witherspoon and some of my other Sunday school classmates hesitate to turn around when there is a loud sound behind them. For me the moral of this story was further complicated by the fact that, in Southern dialect, the word "pillar" sounds almost like the word "pillow," so for some time after, I also wondered why God would turn Lot's wife into a pillow of salt. I was also confused about the stone pillow that Jacob used and later turned into a pillar. These thoughts returned just before I went to sleep at night.

When teaching children the Bible, it is appropriate to end the story of Lot just when his wife is turned into a pillow (and begin after Lot offers his daughters to the horny townsmen). But I think that teaching children these stories in any framework is inappropriate. For adult Bible students, the whole story, as I would find out from my own students, is important when trying to trace and understand the family, tribal, and racial lines in the Old Testament.

Three problems were created for Lot during and after his exodus from Sodom. First, he was afraid to live in *any* city after a sudden volley of piping hot rocks from the firmament rained on his hometown. Second, his sons-in-law were not smart enough to get out of town with him, and, third, God turned his wife into salt. Lot ended up in no-man's-land with his daughters and with no way to continue his family line. The rest of the story from the King James Version goes like this:

> And Lot went up out of Zoar, and dwelt in the mountain, and his two daughters with him; for he feared to dwell in Zoar: and he dwelt in a cave, he and his two daughters.

Lot felt that a cave, even though it does not offer the comforts of home, is the only safe place to dwell in a world where the sky rains fire. But a cave, however safe, can be a lonely place:

> And the firstborn said unto the younger, Our father *is* old, and *there is* not a man in the earth to come in unto us after the manner of all the earth: Come, let us make our father drink wine, and we will lie with him, that we may preserve seed of our father.

At this point, the teacher explains to his Japanese students what the verbs *to come* and *to lie* mean in this context. His students struggle in vain to confirm meanings in their electronic dictionaries. Then they continue, reading together.

> And they made their father drink wine that night: and the firstborn went in, and lay with her father; and he perceived not when she lay down, nor when she arose.

Lot was a big drinker. Who wouldn't want to drink after the sky rains fire, after God kills your wife.

Still, who could drink so much wine that he couldn't remember having sex with his own daughter? But not remembering the encounter is the point. And never underestimate the virility of a Bible hero.

> And it came to pass on the morrow, that the firstborn said unto the younger, Behold, I lay yesternight with my father: let us make him drink wine this night also; and go thou in, *and* lie with him, that we may preserve seed of our father. And they made their father drink wine that night also: and the younger arose, and lay with him; and he perceived not when she lay down, nor when she arose.

Here the teacher points out how patriarchs from early civilizations learned to deal with hangovers by drinking their way through them:

> Thus were both the daughters of Lot with child by their father. And the firstborn bare a son, and called his name Moab: the same *is* the father of the Moabites unto this day. And the younger, she also bare a son, and called his name Ben-ammi: the same *is* the father of the children of Ammon unto this day. (Genesis 19:31-38)

These passages are difficult to separate from the earlier part of the story of Lot. If a teacher wants Mr. Matsuda to wake up and listen, there is no better way than reading and explaining the story of Lot. It puts students on red alert.

The class watches my face closely, perhaps wondering if the mating habits of my culture are the same.

Each year when we cover Lot and his daughters, my face turns into a beacon, the faces of my students go from being perplexed to being startled. Mr. Matsuda is awake and transmitting. No one bothers to ask if modern Christians believe this story is true. And no one asks if this type of family gathering is common in modern Christian culture—although they may wonder.

Maybe I should avoid this story like everyone else does, except a number of famous painters from the Renaissance and beyond, but it would look suspicious to end this lesson at the same place that my Sunday school teacher left it off in her oral rendering, at Genesis 19:26, where Lot's wife is punished in a way that has disturbed the sleep of children for many generations.

The writer intended readers to continue, and by this time we want to learn more about what happened to Lot. The rest of the story sparks more interest from my students than the destruction of Sodom and Gomorrah. It is interesting to wonder why Lot went into the mountains. Why did he not go and join Abraham, who lived nearby? Maybe he felt the cave was safer, but the Bible does not tell us why. And there is the other question we cannot answer that bears repeating: How can a man get so drunk that he would have sex with both of his daughters and not remember?

And what did God think about these sex acts? We know what he thought about the way people behaved in Sodom and Gomorrah. Besides explaining where the often troubling Moabites and Ammonites came from, what did the writer think the story meant, and what was the writer trying to say in this tale?

Each time I teach the Bible, this classroom moment is one of the rare times when I feel that we are beyond Christian culture and deep into thinking about meanings in this ancient pre-Christian, not-Christian writing. Maybe people from my Christian world are not as familiar with the incest portion of this story because we have never been taught this part because, let's face it, how do you tell eight-year-olds on Sunday morning the story of a drunk father unwittingly having sex with his own daughters?

The full Lot story is a good example of how to undo the Great Shazam. What we generally think we know about Sodom and Gomorrah only takes us through half of Genesis 19 because we have to stop due to certain boundaries we have placed on Bible discussion for moral reasons. We do not know much about the other half because we were never taught the other half. What self-respecting citizen would teach this story to children in Sunday school?

But what a story. Like the Adam and Eve story, it does not need theology because it means, it means deeply, on its own. Any person, ancient or modern, who wants to link himself to a racially unique group is necessarily linked to incest, in the beginning. This is an inspiring thought that, if thought through, would give despairing pause to any group of people who view themselves as racially unique, whether white Southern Sunday schoolers in the American South or Japanese college students. Here is the Bible with the director's cuts, the uncensored stories of how those drunk and disorderly desert tribesmen managed the traumas of uncertain life, of their brutal history of quick and catastrophic death.

The Lot story and its reception in Japan is an unsavory springboard. In the next section I will wander like a desert tribesman through my own origins, through the nexus of free associations that clouds the inbred theology in my homeland, and look at a different type of incest, this time in a sober religious culture that lies frequently with the Bible, a religious culture that has spawned any number of tribal denominations with the seminal act of mating select Bible verses with social and political agendas far beyond the reach of the Bible.

For those who wish to ponder over being lost with the Bible in a savage and brutal desert wilderness of church slogans and bumper stickers, for those who would will risk excommunication from the people who truly think the story of Lot and his daughters is an answer to their questions, for thrill seekers who would chase storms of brimstone and fire on modern asphalt highways, who would risk being turned to salt by guilty association with an author who is not-so-slowly being driven crazy by the Bible, then read on with the promise that the following pages will not have one good answer to any of your questions.

Section Two: Desert Storm

. . . though I were perfect, yet would I not know my soul: I would despise my life. —Job 9:21

Free Association I: Gaskets and Rods

I really don't know clouds at all. —Joni Mitchell

The first Iraq War, or Gulf War, began with a massive air strike that was labeled "Operation Desert Storm." Now the terms *Gulf War* and *Desert Storm* are used synonymously, but Desert Storm is far and above the best title for the war. Sitting in my tiny apartment in Tokyo, the term had just stormed into my head. I was having a free association moment, one in which I was relating something from time past with my life in the present, perhaps associating the massive oil spills in the Gulf of Mexico with the oil rich countries around the Persian Gulf. These distractions had to do with teaching the Bible in Japan.

The new Bible that I was learning as a Bible teacher was mixing badly with the old Bible of the South I grew up in. It was like mixing sushi with mashed potatoes and gravy. Why Operation Desert Storm? Not the military initiative, exactly, not the homed in cruise missiles lighting up the night over Baghdad or General Schwarzkopf's Abrams tanks charging over the dunes, but the words *desert* and *storm*. Words, when put together, that I had never thought about, never made a mental picture of, swirling expansive words that signified something that I had never really *seen*. I looked out of my window at the view, three feet away, of the wall beside my neighbor's house.

The reader is invited to free associate with the Bible, to look out of your own window. But be careful. Thinking about the Bible can bring strange and scary images to mind. You may have a better view than I do. Maybe your neighbor's wall isn't so close by, maybe you can look out over a freshly cut lawn or into the woods. But freshly cut lawns and woods are not any closer to the desert of the Bible than my neighbor's Japanese wall is.

You might even have a real sense the desert if you live in West Texas or Arizona. Still your desert view is not the desert of Lawrence of Arabia, a desert that has spitting camels, flowing mounds of hallucinogenic sand, parched and dying men who can't find water, half-burnt dead men who are dead because they were caught drinking from someone else's well, and wandering caravans of robed people who will kill you for drinking from their well, and who will kill you for a long list of other reasons, including no good reason at all.

Or at least they will kill you in the movies. Most of us do not know much about those people, that desert and its storms, in real life. There is a church named after Sinai in the verdant, tree clustered mountains of North Carolina, but what does this church in the Blue Ridge have to do with the biblical desert? We live thousands of miles, and years, years, and years away from the rocky, bald, sun-torched mountains of the mythical lands of Moses. We do not know much about the vast history of that desert land beyond a montage of latter-day images imprinted on our minds, images that have been delivered on the wing of the desert's two gargantuan, multinational exports: God and Oil.

There is more God and Oil in that desert to this day, but it ran short of Christians long ago. Modern Christianity is not really part of that world. I am not part of that world. Yet sometimes I still find myself free associating elements of my own life with narratives and themes in the Bible even though I know little about the turf. For those of us who were brought up Christian, the Bible has been made to seem so close and pertinent that we often fail to see how far away it is.

The Bible is a foreign book to my students. But the Bible is also foreign to those of us who were brought up with it in the Christian world.

I free-associate Egypt, a place that plays an enormous role in the Bible, with pyramids, but I cannot find pyramids in the Bible. This absence makes you wonder if the men who wrote about Egypt in the Bible had ever been to Egypt. You wonder how much they knew about foreign Egypt. I am a foreigner teaching a book that is foreign to my Japanese students, even foreign to us from the Christian world. I am also teaching stories given to us by writers who were writing about places foreign to them.

A bible written from my own experience, from a chapter of growing up in the American South, would have abundant pine trees and oak trees and swamps and golf courses, indigenous snakes, alligators, maybe an escaped convict, certainly barbeque, but no camels. I have no idea what it would be like to wander in the desert of Lawrence of Arabia without paved roads or an air-conditioned car.

There are large and abundant deserts in the Bible. Deserts circumscribe the Bible much like the image of the high seas circumscribes *Moby Dick*. There is the desert in Exodus 20:18, the backside of which gives way to the temperamental mountain of God, where "the people saw the thunder and lightning and heard the trumpet and saw the mountain in smoke," and where "they trembled with fear. They stayed at a distance." There are the deserts of Sinai, Zin, and Gaza—settings for exile, suffering and death. That is, unless you are Abraham, who, unlike our Abram tanks, had an easygoing relationship with the desert, if not desert people who were not part of his tribe. Jesus goes to "a desert place apart" to tell a large group of desperate followers that he is the Son of God, and he feeds thousands of them with a few fish and some bread. This is a less despairing image of the desert. But Jesus reportedly flees by ship to get to this desert to avoid the same fate as the recently beheaded John the Baptist. The desert is still the fearful stormy desert that you head to only when you need to get out of town. We know nothing of this life surrounded by sand.

There are many wildernesses in the Bible. The word *wilderness* brings to mind a wooded place, similar to the site of the great Wilderness, where two large armies wandered and then clashed during the American Civil War. A wilderness is difficult to imagine without greenery. A wilderness should at least have prairie grass, maybe an open range from an old cowboy movie—a little rough, but a good place for backpacking. But wilderness is a word that the King James Version associates with the desert, not the western plains or tree-rich Virginia or even the Arizona desert, not a wilderness we know but the Lawrence of Arabia desert of the Bible.

This foreign wilderness of time long passed is a fearful place. It is the vast uncharted region for abject suffering, for having hot run-ins with a fearful God of sand and mountain. There is the wilderness of Beersheba, where the bondservant Hagar and her son Ishmael were sent into perilous exile by a distressed Abraham, the father of Ishmael. There is the wilderness of Paran, where the mother and son almost died. There is the wilderness of the Red Sea, or the Reed Sea, which was a fearful place for the Israelites fleeing from Egypt. But it was even more fearful for the soldiers of the Egyptian army in pursuit who were drowned by parted water that suddenly un-parted, a scene that reminds my students of the waters that were parted during the Creation and that un-parted on all of God's desert creation thereafter.

There is the wilderness of Sin, where the starving Israelites whined about their hunger until the manna started to fall. And there is the wilderness of Shur, where the Israelites whined about their thirst until God led them to water. There is the unnamed wilderness where they whined so much about what any of us would understand as severe hardship that an angry, and to my students an intolerant, God finally sent in a horde of desert snakes to bite them for complaining too much. In most of the Christian world, the character of God is less brutal than this desert God of Moses, but my students do not know this.

There is the wilderness before Moab, the location of menacing, uncircumcised hostiles. "Uncircumcised" is a pejorative term in the Old Testament, almost a synonym for a "no count" in vernacular English. (My mostly uncircumcised male students do not cotton to the notion that the uncircumcised are lower beings who should be slaughtered in mass quantities.) The wildernesses continue, including the wilderness that runs out from the "coasts" of the Amorites, where the Israelites, given to complaint, were insecurely located between two large tribes, totaling three large tribes in the wilderness, all of whom were ready to kill each other, circumcised and uncircumcised alike, before anyone drank from anyone else's well. There is the wilderness on "this side of Jordan," one of the many places where Joshua, who never complained, set out to destroy the enemy, those who were inconveniently located in Joshua's promised land before Joshua arrived.

The wilderness beside Jordan, we are told, is also where Satan, who in the New Testament is not God's advocate, tempts Jesus. At that point Satan did not look like a serpent or a dragon, or at least no writer explains this difference in detail, and this new character, with his familiar name, confuses my students. What they do understand clearly from these stories is that it is good to have God on your side in the wilderness, even if he is angry and hurtful, and it is better to have Satan far behind. But you do not want God too close by, because if you complain, even for good reasons, and even if you do not complain, that same God will punish you. He will let Satan, his advocate, kill your children.

These old and foreign desert narratives are cruel and unjust to my students, and one wonders how we in the Christian world would view them if they were not placed in the Bible. How would we view an ancient, foreign, Mesopotamian God of the killing deserts? Add storms, with too much water from the watery void, add brimstone and fire from the sky dome, and as the horror show expanded, our sympathy would quickly shrink for this unruly God.

My polite, mature student is in a kimono today, just in from arranging flowers and having tea with her *ikebana* club. She sits in the front row and looks at me with the same expression a polite southern grandmother would give you if you farted, by accident but loudly, at her dinner table. A good Buddhist from a good Buddhist family, my student expected a different, more affirming course of study. Maybe someone led her to believe she would be studying a religious text where, among other happy things, an ancient predecessor to Julie Andrews sings "The Hills are Alive" from atop Sinai before God's chosen people sign a peace accord and walk hand in hand in the land of milk and honey with their new uncircumcised but beloved neighbors.

Instead, the polite mature student is verbally assailed

with storms and more storms, glossed by death and despair, and from her look I'm certain she thinks the Bible is my fault. The first storm that swirls into my class is the great rain and flood that blew up when God decides to destroy almost all of his people. That is the largest storm. Another memorable storm is the tempest that inspired Jonah's dodgy shipmates to toss him overboard before he becomes human sushi for a big fish. The storm that Jesus calms is also stamped on my memory but not my students'. Jesus's reprimand, "O ye of little faith," is as familiar to me as the phrase "to thy own self be true," which comes from *Hamlet*, not the Bible, but which, along with a number of other sententious quotations, seems to have been imprinted on my DNA as coming from the Bible.

"O ye of little faith," Jesus says as he calms the storm before the skeptical apostles in their boat on the stormy sea. Jesus says this several times in the Gospels, and this phrase has become one of the most repeated phrases in the history of preaching, echoed as it is by righteous folk who all share in common the fact that they are not Jesus. My students side with the apostles in this story in tsunami-stricken Japan. O ye who have never witnessed the primal surge of the watery void. Speak of fearless faith when the deep surges in.

More foreign storms, the brimstone and fire that rained on Sodom and Gomorrah—a desert storm *that* was—one that is doubly terrifying because you cannot look back. These storms, caused or overseen by an ancient, foreign God in an ancient, foreign place oddly resound as indigenous events in the conscious and sub-conscious thoughts of Christian culture, but they fail to ignite the same lightning flashes of thought and memory in the minds of my students. Often these stormy narratives just irritate certain students who came to Bible study with higher expectations for Christianity.

In the King James Version, the word *storm* is used as a noun or an adjective, not as a verb. In the New International Version, the word *storm* has developed into its modern use also as a verb: to storm. *To storm* can be and is used as a metaphor for battle in this version. A desert storm, in our time, can mean a storm in the desert, or it can mean a military attack in the desert. Perhaps the stormy deserts of the Bible found their way into the minds of those who name modern military initiatives. In this case the ancient desert storms we do not know were free-associated into an analogy with us. We are ancient Hebrew warriors? The Bible just might be our fault.

How to teach the stormy Bible to students who do not wildly free-associate the foreign Bible with the echoes of their own thoughts and memories? The biblical free associations emerging from my own memory may be associated with a biblical vision or dream that heroes in the Bible have, one that haunts my efforts to abbreviate the stormy confusion of my bible classes. A short list of people who have visions includes Abraham, Jacob, Joseph, Pharaoh, Samuel, Solomon, Job, all of the prophets, Nebuchadnezzar, Paul, and the seemingly crazed writer of the book of Revelation. I cannot find where Moses had dreams. God speaks directly to Moses, who himself admits that he is a little thick in the head. In one instance, a student wanted to know why God does not tell people plainly what he wants, as he did with Moses. I do not know why, but I would like to know the answer to that question.

Unless you are Moses or Abraham, both of whom God was direct if not straightforward with, God communicates to you through a vision/dream that must be interpreted to make sense. You have to be a hero or visionary yourself, or you have to bring in a strongman, say, Joseph or Daniel, to explain what your dream/vision means. It is clear to my students that I am not a hero or a visionary. I am just their teacher, not a hero, and the foreign book we are studying is fond of producing questions that only heroes can answer.

Neither Joseph nor Daniel can be invited to my class as guest lecturers to explain how the foreign Bible still works its way into the mind of modern Christianity. I stare at my neighbor's wall, which I have appropriated as my own wall. There is no writing, but some of the sooty spots on the concrete bricks could pass as Rorschach Ink Blots. I look at my wall, at my non-view and try to see how ancient deserts and storms meld with modern times. I wonder what would be the best way to import this eternally foreign book to people who find the desert God in it foreign, brutal, and unfair. Even though I know it is a mistake, I feel the urge to free associate my situation with the Bible, to describe myself as a pensive wanderer in a type of biblical desert, a stormy wilderness of thought.

What we do with the Bible is make analogies in an effort to map and control its wild wildernesses, those of us who are the religious descendents of those who carried the books of the Bible from the ancient desert lands into newer foreign lands, into new worlds without so much sand. There were wanderings in the stormy desert wildernesses in the Bible that we equate by analogy to our own struggles in imagined wildernesses that we are familiar with in our green lands far away from the sandy Bible. But there is a limited relevance in relating images of another biblical place you know nothing about with your own thinking when you do not understand the other place, when you do not understand your own thinking.

It is impossible to parse the Bible from the memory of what the Bible signifies when you grow up with the Bible, a memory that soaks into your DNA. When asked to come up with a name for a military initiative in Iraq, the words *desert storm* might pop into your head from seemingly nowhere. If you were high up in the military, you might float the term to the higher command, and you might hear from the stern visages at the table that, yes, you are spot on. Desert Storm sounds appropriate for a military campaign in the Middle East.

I grew up in a religious culture that can churn fabulous and strange ideas from the Bible. But my students are not the people from my home front. They do not vet the Bible for modern experience or get haphazardly struck by biblical imagery when they are trying to name a military offensive. They cannot tap that seminal biblical branch that streams into the great rivers of our consciousness. They do not warm their imaginations from the same generator, the same power source, our Christianized nervous systems use to spark our brains into biblical analogies, often stretched or flawed.

But I talk of nothing. A college professor grumbles to himself after class in private in his office, for a few moments, courtesy of the Bible, after he becomes confused before an audience, after he stumbles before his class and after he realizes, as he returns home and sits in his tiny apartment staring at a wall, that he will continue to stumble. Everyone has bad days on the job: A lawyer receives an angry letter from his ex-wife's new boyfriend, who is a judge, about a late alimony payment; a hotel manager receives a call from a housekeeper, who angrily announces that someone is pissing on the wall by the elevator on the 14th floor; a toilet clogs and overflows just when it's time to pick up little Jimmy from soccer practice; an engineer writes the wrong specs for a small gasket and an engine blows.

Everyone has bad moments on the job. My neighbor's wall—the wall that lacks writing—stands as my own little testament to my smallness in my own world, because why would this wall, sitting here in the depths of Tokyo and being stared at by me, sans a train of wives and concubines, merit writing? I'm not a Babylonian or Persian king. And why am I making weak connections between large desert storms and kings and me in my tiny life as one 35 millionth part of the population of greater Tokyo. *Retrench and start over*, I thought. *Settle down, follow Paul's advice and drink a little wine, and for God's sake don't bore people with your teaching crisis.*

But if the engineer's small gasket were on a space shuttle—*ka boom*. Small thoughts can trigger large explosive ideas. My mind shifted from desert storms to gaskets and rods, not in space shuttles but in broken-down cars in various wildernesses. I drifted with my neighbor's wall to memories of growing up in the American South, in a region where the men of my father's generation, of my generation, too, felt acquainted with gaskets and rods. We also felt we knew the Bible, the old Bible that unifies us with ancient desert regions and peoples we do not know, not with my new Bible that, when read with a discerning eye, shatters us apart.

There, when a car breaks down, when a driver stops because his car is billowing smoke from the engine or the tailpipe, the sight of a lifted hood in a parking lot or gas station draws local, self-appointed car experts. Someone in the crowd will scratch his head and speculate: "Not the radiator? I dunno, maybe it's a blown head gasket or maybe she threw a rod." Most of the spectators do not know what a head gasket or a rod looks like, or what a head gasket or a rod is, or how these parts function. I doubt that the head-scratching guy has a clear image of a car engine. People who know car engines do not have to speculate.

Blown head gaskets and thrown rods were among the unknown familiar things that the people of this memory, of this familiar but gone world, talked about over raised hoods, even if they were not sure what these things were. This is what blown gaskets and thrown rods and the Bible had in common in those parts. What they still have in common. They remind us of the not known but familiar and binding force of catastrophe, even small catastrophes, the communal urges that attend the congregation of those who meet with malfunction and failure.

It is easy to see how the "engines, invented by cunning men," the engines of war in the book of Chronicles, could bring about catastrophe. But there is also catastrophe in the failure of engines, failure brought about by small malfunctions in those engines that are mechanical, and those engines that are powered by connections, large and small, that we make, those engines that power the great shazam. It is the bigness of the images of the old Bible that is not there that draws us in. Getting beside the big images of the Bible makes many from the Christian world feel big, too.

But in Japan, in the land of detail, small things are big. Hamlet tells us that there is "special providence in the fall of a sparrow." Something as small as a broken down car has special meaning. If it is your car that is breaking down, you might see this small example of engine failure as a sign from God. A broken down car is a small problem for the next guy, but a matter of divine importance for you, and for those who lend their time to help you, even if they are lost over the solution to your problem.

Mechanical engines fail when you do not pay enough attention to the small details of maintenance. Maybe my Japanese colleague is right. Detail is God. And the binding group attention to the elusive details of reparation is divine. But the engines of thought that power the foreign Bible through our world seem to break down exactly when you do pay attention to detail. It is the catastrophe that occurs when we look closely at how we have engineered our connection with a collection of ancient books written in entirely foreign places and languages, books filled with catastrophes, the catastrophes brought to us by a God who, when dealt with in detail, billows smoke and breaks down. But there may be reparation in looking at the details, in the precise and exact engineering and maintenance of a thinking that might bring us closer to this biblical God. The great quake is yet to come. As is the next quake and the next.

There was not any writing on my neighbor's wall—just two words in my head: *desert* and *storm*. I was relieved. In the Bible, that guy sees the writing on the wall just before someone from Persia kills him. Still, I was staring at concrete trying to figure out why my internal combustion engine of a brain was smoky, was locked up at the same time that I was trying to gain a precise understanding of the engines of the Bible and the secondary series of engines that belong to the entirely separate enterprise of how we think about the Bible.

I was being assailed by random swirling biblical images that were following me from of the university out into the windy streets of Shibuya, beyond class, through town, on the train, and back to my tiny apartment. Can a human being blow a head gasket, throw a rod? Desert Storm—I think the term itself refutes anyone who argues that the Bible has lost its place in modern consciousness, a grand consciousness that includes many weak and tiny biblical analogies.

It is a literary maxim that rings true: arrogance leads to catastrophe. And it was a machine-like arrogance that possessed me as an organic, mechanized, sub-particle of the Christianized world. I realized that it is my culture, not Japanese culture, that was and that is making a small teaching debacle in Japan take the shape of something larger, even catastrophic. It is a catastrophe for anyone from my culture to begin to look at the foreign Bible too closely, for anyone who begins to hold the Bible as close as a pillow to his thoughts, the catastrophe that could be sparked by the details of a new Bible, the anti-Bible, the Bible that is there.

This journey through smallness and detail is like a Bible story itself, one about wandering, stiff-necked, people in the wilderness getting lost, losing track of God and themselves, and breaking down and blowing up across and throughout the stormy desert. But let's for once skip the bad biblical analogy. My thought journey was not anything like the journey of the Israelites. It is my home culture that made my teaching efforts harder than they needed to be. My culture, even more than the culture in which I was teaching, was pushing me to make the Bible plain before the faces of my students and before my own face, and the Bible is not plain.

I never thought that the big mountain God of Moses was behind my broken down revelations in my tiny apartment in Tokyo. But these thoughts were bigger than I, of the small pronoun, I. These would be significant small thoughts, if I could show something of the strange organic but mechanized way we from the Christian world, including people from my old home front, connect with the old foreign harmonized Bible that is not there by analogy.

I could expose the bad connections we make with the foreign Bible while at the same time show how we connect the Bible of our minds in powerful and significant ways to modern life, show how the Bible really does not connect at all, then show how it connects completely and absolutely as it is mechanically forced through currents of our consciousness, how it powers the wheels of modern engines of thought, how those wheels often spin off their own axles, charged by our own haphazard neurological, cranial sparks over time and terrain. The Bible fuels a big, powerful, broken down machine that still runs, still draws communal gatherings with its scary, smoke billowing failure to function.

We all associate the Bible's foreign deserts and storms of yore with the stormy wildernesses of modern life, those of us among the shazamed. The associative power of the Bible we think we know overpowers us in ways that we do not comprehend. This book, what the poet William Blake called "the great code," is the source of the fearful but fetching smoke that flows from so many mountains of modern Christian thought.

My Japanese students cannot feel the choking and sputtering Bible of the Christianized subconscious; they cannot feel its eruptive power. We from the Christianized world, particularly the devout among us, are a people who live our entire lives next to an active volcano trying to reckon exactly how the volcano shapes our view of the world. The Bible is our volcano, our mountain of God. As a Bible teacher in a foreign volcanic land, I often wonder: How we can know the power of our volcano without knowing life without the volcano?

Someone takes a can of spray paint and writes the word ISRAEL on a concrete wall somewhere in Tennessee. ISRAEL—the word in big, black, block letters. Passers by would pause—then free associate. What does this mean? ISRAEL. Is it a pro-Israel statement? Pro Palestine? Anti-Semitic? Patriotic? Religious? Racist? Demented? If the word were on a billboard, a bumper sticker, or on a T-Shirt, then you would assume it is a statement in support of Israel.

But, no, there it is, painted on a wall, presumably by a vandal with a can of black spray paint. There would have to be an official meeting. How to interpret the writing on the wall? Gut reaction: clean up the wall, and save us from interpretation. But to do that you would have to erase ISRAEL. Would that be disrespectful? Even the fact that I have mentioned the word *Israel* over six times in the past few sentences might have some readers concerned, though it is a place most of us have never been to and know little about.

Would anyone be so concerned if the single word on the wall were CANADA?

The word *Israel* does not bring to mind images from a country of roughly 7 million people in the Middle East, a country roughly the size of Maryland, a country roughly one fifth the size in population of greater Tokyo. The word *Israel*, if you were to use it in a word association exercise, would not provoke respondents to blurt out the word *fig* or even *fruit*, which is Israel's chief agricultural export. Fruit eating is good from their point of view. Historically the chief overall export from and around that place we now call Israel, its countryside and surrounding areas, is the Bible. It was the Bible Belt long before the Southern Bible Belt was a twinkle in God's eye.

These foreign words, *Bible* and *Israel*, are so powerful that putting them together might make some readers a little nervous. Both words are not what they are, but are part of the temperamental mountain standing close by on the dry land of the mind of the shazamed. Both words are so familiar, so together, but both in essence are so little known yet so strongly powered by our failed engines of thought. Our volcano—to know the fearful God of this mountain, would we have to forget that we thought we knew him at all?

But my free associations, those crafted from my own home culture, have to stand trial by a jury of the bible-less un-shazamed. Take the obscure example of God's judgment of the idol-worshipping Jeroboam, the king of the breakaway northern tribes:

> Therefore, behold, I will bring evil upon the house of Jeroboam, and will cut off Jeroboam him that pisseth against the wall, and him that is shut up and left in Israel, and will take away the remnant of the house of Jeroboam, as a man taketh away dung, till it be all gone. (I Kings 14:10)

In Japan I have no straight analogy or direct association I can draw into the modern world from this passage, one that makes its own analogies and, in the King James Version, a passage that is hard to discern the meaning of. But in the Christian world next to the volcano, I can do much with this verse by virtue of the fact that it is obscure and from the Bible.

In our world, Israel has resonance. So do angry judges and walls and people pissing on walls, and houses turning to dung, after the toilet gets clogged. These images can relate us to the Bible in oblique but profound ways. You can take almost anything you come across in the Bible, bang on it a bit, and fit it to your own experience. The very foreign-ness of the familiar Bible makes these free associations possible.

But the thought machine we create is vulnerable to breakdowns. These associations, even when we do not sense the association, expand into new meanings or they can hide obvious and essential meanings from us. These associations can give us brilliant insights, and they can be idiotic. Many hold that these associations give true spiritual meaning to life. But the late Christopher Hitchens has reminded us turgidly that they can also kill. These associations can be meaningless, particularly those meanings that seem the most meaningful. But in the end, there is meaning.

  I cannot find blown head gaskets in the foreign Bible but, yes, rods are thrown in the Bible. I ask my neighbor's wall, *Do any of these foreign thoughts mean anything?* The Japanese wall says nothing, which I take to mean yes, and no.

Free Association II: Snakes and Alligators

for there is nothing either good or bad, but thinking makes it so
—Hamlet

    Staring at my neighbor's wall, I began thinking about bubbles, an image that I freely associated with the Bible when I heard the finish buzzer beeping on my washing machine. In my religious homeland, the foreign but familiar Bible is like the soap in my washing machine: There you can throw in the Bible and watch it make bubbles as it reacts with the watery void of thought in modern Christian culture, beyond the foreign deserts of the Bible.
    Bible bubbles are not delightful, as bubbles should be. They confuse and irritate. The Dinosaur in Eden museum, a bubbled-up complex, is one enormous example of making bubbles from the Bible by mixing two components, the Bible and not-Bible science thrown into a holy beaker to form one highly unstable compound. The museum will be bankrupted, padlocked, and abandoned after a couple decades, then broken into one night by a couple of dope smoking teenagers who wander dumbfounded around the dinosaurs of paradise: *Dude, what the hell was this place?*
    There are also the bubbles of church tradition, those that are the froth the Bible produces on the dinosaur-less side of the theological world. These bubbles are difficult to sort out because they seem part of the Bible but are not. The Fall of Man concept is a more seductive idea than the dinosaurs of Eden. It is less delusional, and its far-reaching hold on our thinking is testimony to how necessary it has been for Christianity to garner the vast, foreign Bible into clear and compact components of non-biblical metaphysics in order

to keep the biblical wilderness under control. The concept of the Holy Trinity is another large, controlling, metaphysical bubble blown over the Bible that has little to do with the Bible.

There are other baffling bubbles blown that are difficult to burst even after they are identified. These are highly sensitive, smallish but abundant bubbles blown from mainline areas of Christianity, thought bubbles that transform the stormy Bible into something comfortable and middle class, inspirational bubbles that are regenerated from the Bible to make the Bible seem finely structured and harmonized with itself and with us.

These are the bubbles blown in the religious world I grew up in, closer to me and even more difficult to detect and parse. These are the bubbles of moderate, mainline Christianity, bubbles blown over, around, and through the homes and lawns of middle-class Christians, bubbles that allow the Bible a place in the Inspirational section of bookstores. It is my closeness to these Christians that fuels the confusion and irritation when teaching the biblically bubble-less in Japan.

I am borrowing the term "mainline Christianity" from the researchers at The Pew Forum on Religion and Public Life, who conducted a survey on what they have termed the "Religious Landscape" of the United States. The survey covers a range of interesting data. For instance, it indicates that only 1.7% of the U.S. population views itself as Jewish and only 0.6% of the U.S. population views itself Muslim. Given the vexing concerns in the U.S. surrounding both religious groups, these two small percentages are surprising.

But here I am interested in how this study moves over the face of the Christian void of the U.S. It is a starting point for sizing up and explaining my own wilderness when my students want to know more about how the ancient, foreign Bible functions in modern Christianity, particularly in America. According to the Pew study, American Christians fall into three primary but distinct religious groups, all three of which view themselves as Christian: Evangelical Protestants (26.3%), Catholic (23.9%), and Mainline Protestant (18.1%). These three self-described Christian groups comprise over two-thirds of Americans surveyed. Only 16.1% of people surveyed view themselves as "unaffiliated," and the Pew study has no category for intellectually challenged wall gazers who are religiously trying to figure out how to teach the Bible to people who are not Christian.

If you ask specific questions about religious beliefs and practices, you find that each of the three major Christian groups is highly diversified within their respective categories. Certainly not all Evangelical Protestants believe that there were dinosaurs in Eden (although it might be difficult to find one who does not believe that Eden was a real place). Not all Catholics agree on the issue of divorce.

There are overlapping opinions. The Pew study shows that there are high percentages of pro-lifers in both the Evangelical and Catholic faiths, and more than a few in mainline traditions. Beyond the study, you can assume that there are a number of evangelical Catholics and mainline Christians who resemble evangelical Protestants in their zeal to save souls, although evangelicals are, by name, the friskiest in their efforts to spread the Good News.

Certain sub beliefs and sub-rosa beliefs shared within and between larger groups bind people religiously. These often hidden or soft categories are devilishly difficult to map in the American religious landscape because few individuals feel a need to express or even to hold strong religious views on every single issue important to religious leaders. Also people change their minds, and, as a follow-up Pew study indicates, they frequently change their affiliations.

In terms of how I present modern Christianity to students while trying to hold to the more pressing concern of teaching the Bible, Christians must be defined outside of the diverse and hyper-delineated theologies presented by Christian leaders within and among the ostensibly solid categories of the Pew study. I route my explanations of modern Christian belief through what I have divided, roughly and unscientifically, into a second set of three Christian groupings or categories.

The first group is the Cookout Christians, the moderate Christians I was brought up with, an overlooked group that I will focus on in this section. There are a large number of mainline Protestants who belong in the category of

Cookout Christianity. There are also a large number of moderate Catholics and a smaller but significant percentage of Evangelicals who would fall into this category. These are regular Christians who enjoy back yard cookouts with family and friends, maybe with a couple of cold beers and some irreverent jokes. In the right context, they are happy to share their religious beliefs, but they are not obsessively concerned with saving souls. Many of them admit that other religions and ways of life can lead people down the right path also.

It is impossible to subject this un-scientific category to the rigors of science, but I estimate that Cookout Christians comprise well over half of the practicing Christians in the U.S. I suspect that these types are largely middle to upper middle class. Were they to see themselves as a distinct group and become active as moderates, they would be a formidable lot. However, one of the defining principles of bubbled-up Cookout Christianity is to avoid activism whenever possible, a trait that I have grown to like, at least as it concerns religious practice.

These largely middle class, reasonable, responsible, and fun loving Christians attend and support their churches but do not let the preacher or the Pope interfere too much with their desire to be normal and happy. These are people who may quietly dissent on this or that theological principle on the basis on science, reason, and good sense.

A Protestant church member who does not believe that it is a mortal sin to work on Sunday and a tithing Catholic who practices birth control are both good candidates for Cookout Christianity. Those who would like to live reasonable and spiritual lives in middle-class comfort are Cookout Christians. Still, these moderate souls hold to a belief that there is an afterlife, they strive and hope for salvation through God. Their beliefs are fine, but when the Bible is involved, the clouds gather for the stormy thoughts that bring on confusion and irritation.

The second group includes loosely affiliated people cloistered within strict but ephemeral sub-groups of euphoric Christian worship. These people might classify themselves as evangelical Christians but, in my unscientific polling, self-described evangelical Christians often want nothing to do with other, self-described evangelical Christians. This second group is the Highway Jesus Christians, a group that is largely evangelical but certainly not all evangelicals would fall within.

The leaders and members of this group have earned the title, Highway Jesus Christians, because of their energetic mobility, their feel good acumen in the areas of raising money and building celebrity, their obsession with signs, and the ability of their leaders to leave town, often in disgrace, just as quickly as they came in. They use various and arbitrary biblical passages to splinter off in a dazzling variety of directions. Using Genesis as their beacon, a group of them might find the resources to run off and build a dinosaur and Bible museum. Notable fallen angels from this non-group grouping are Jimmy Swaggart, Jim Bakker, and Ted Haggard. And the list, of course, is much longer.

The third group of Christians is the Hooverites, who are drawn from the amorphous wellspring of so-called fundamentalist Christians. Hooverites seize hard upon the idea, drawn from the Bible, that a privileged few (the Hooverites themselves) are soon to be hoovered, or vacuumed, or sucked, into God's Heaven whilst the rest us are hurled into a burning lake or some other torment for eternity. They live close to the cosmic world forwarded in the Bible, although, inspired by their predecessors in the medieval church, they have added to the Bible annexes of fear, particularly as concerns the workings of a notorious and nefarious devil.

These believers had their comeuppance via the Protestant reformation in Europe during the 16th century, but they have been a vociferous mainstay of Christian thinking since the beginning of Christianity. Cookout Christians, in my experience, quietly wish that the Hooverites would be sucked out of town with the next wave of Highway Jesus Christians, whom they share some extreme theological views with but that Hooverites tend to grimace rather than smile when they express these views.

This grimace signals a fundamental difference between the Hooverites and the Highway Jesus Christians. To the Hooverite, religion is not happy go lucky; religion is a grim business. And Hooverites do not leave town. They never leave town, because they are damned determined to root in for years, generations, to scowl at people, family members included, who are not as divinely informed as they are. The Hooverites like signs, too, but are drawn to those signs that relate to the last days and the imminent and catastrophic and horrific end of the world. In modern times, they are largely Protestant and often self-described biblical Christians. The Bible is inerrant in their view. But their belief in biblical inerrancy is not what defines them as a group because other, less mean types of Christians also view the Bible as inerrant.

What defines them is their primary need for power, not divine riches and eternal celebrity, as in the case of the Highway Jesus Christians. They are religious hardliners who do not fit in well with others. Responding to a deeply seated but oblique low-church legacy, they have a powerful need to judge others, so they form their own congregations that are invested with the divine power to designate others for everlasting agony. Examples of famous church leaders with strong Hooverite tendencies are Oral Roberts, Jerry Falwell, and Pat Robertson.

There are hybrid forms of these three groupings. Sometimes Cookout Christians are stimulated by Highway Jesus feel-good preaching or are drawn into contemplating the Apocalypse with the Hooverites. Given the diverse practices within Christianity, it is impossible to detail the exact borders of religious groups, so it is fortunate that trying to define modern religious groups is not my job as a Bible teacher. Though it is part of my job, here, to describe what has been revealed to me about the desert of modern Christianity from my wall gazing and stormy thoughts about the Bible.

I will first go into my grumpy relationship with bubbly Cookout Christianity. Then I will enter, for a desperate moment, the stormy wilderness of Highway Jesus Christianity and then shoot a yellow glance towards the horrific cosmic universe of the Hooverites. I have to confront Highway Jesus Christians and Hooverites because, like me, they are suspicious of the smallish frothy bubbles of Cookout Christianity, and I should show how and why we differ.

Before I began teaching the Bible in Japan, I thought that I had moved far away from organized Christianity, even mild Cookout Christianity, and far away from the mainline Christian views of the close but distant Bible that I had grown up with. This is what I thought I thought. Now I realize that I am not, and never have been, aloof from mainline Christianity. When I was a boy, I walked away from the Christianity I grew up with and ran at a full sprint away from odd forms of Christianity that revolved around my mainline Christian world. I may have sought out academia because I wanted to replace religious reckoning with thinking that was then, on the surface, more reliable.

I learned how to seek and destroy the bubbles of what we strident humanists call false consciousness as we assail mainline Christian values. But, when you set yourself up as the bubble burster while teaching the Bible, you often miss the point because you are too busy bursting bubbles to see the point. This blindness to the obvious is an often-stated problem with academic training. Missing biblical meanings because of knee-jerk intellectual reactions is one bad habit that has been revealed to me by teaching the Bible. Recently I was teaching the famous edict expressed in the Bible to love your neighbor as you do yourself, a core Jesus directive drawn, like Paul's directive against homosexuality, from Leviticus. When we were covering the idea of neighborly love expressed by Jesus, one of my students blurted out: "That's crazy."

Crazy? I was in the habit of scoffing at people who do not like their neighbors but who put on a display of neighborly love as a bubbly, feel-good standard. And I was prepared to explain to my class that this standard is not really followed in the Christian world. But I had not thought about the pure craziness of the ideal of neighborly love. Crazy love. My student was not scoffing at modern Christians, just reacting to what she saw as an outlandish idea presented in an ancient, foreign, desert text.

I wanted the false, feel-good standard of neighborly love set in the familiar parameters of the Christianity I knew, so that I could stand in judgment of people who really do not love their neighbors but who stand in judgment of people who do not love their neighbors. But there was no point in bursting the love-your-neighbor bubble of Cookout Christians or any modern Christians in my Japanese classroom because none of these people are in the Bible.

My Japanese students are tightly packed in with neighbors they do not love, just as I am tightly packed against my neighbor's wall. He is a pleasant enough fellow to meet on the street, but we do not share love for one another. A Cookout Christian or any Christian who claims to hold to the idea of neighborly love but who does not love his neighbor is self-deceived. But, in the view of my Japanese student and, now, me, he is just behaving like a sane person.

And who is more self-deceived that the teacher who wants to burst bubbles in places where no bubbles exist? When I began my journey as a Bible teacher, I did not see the Eden story as the literal truth, but I still saw the story as representing the flawed or sinful nature of human kind. I learned this view somewhere; I am not sure where. Our failure in Eden was encoded in my DNA like a quotable quote. But it dawned on me through my wall gazing that this idea of our flawed nature was imparted to me through the mysterious bubbles of Cookout Christianity and that this was my Christianity, whether I walked with it or not.

Cookout Christians, those from my tribe, see the Eden story not so much as a true story about the damnation of the first two humans and, by proxy, all of us, but a story about how we humans have been flawed and sinful from the start. There is another idea, drawn from a literal Hooverite view of the Eden story, that we are all damned to hell for eternity by default. Cookout Christians like to keep some distance from this unpleasant type of thinking. So do I.

It is better to use the Eden story, as my Sunday school teacher asserted, as a message that we should try to do what God tells us to even though we know that we are flawed. This begins as a stern message from God that happily segues into a comfortable understanding of God's kindness and forgiveness because we know how the story ends: God sends Jesus later to save us from our own nature.

This is a comfortable and civilized reception of one

of the most famous Bible stories. But when you think about the Eden story in the Bible while staring at a Japanese wall and recalling student responses to the story, you realize that it does not show our flawed or sinful nature being exposed and then erased by a stern, but ultimately kind, redeeming, and perfect God. Via the embers of the Cookout Christianity still glowing in my subconscious, though, I continued to hold on to what I have been steered to see as its essential meaning: We are flawed.

During some confusing and irritating moments, I have gathered from my students when covering the Garden of Eden that (1) They do not understand how you get from breaking a rule made for the sake of rule-making to the fact that all mankind is flawed. This is too broad a leap for them because they feel no more related to Adam and Eve than we do to the Romulans in Star Trek; (2) They think that God over-reacts to the rule breaking. And they hold God responsible for the failure in Eden because God created it all. God should be held responsible for the things God created, including the reptiles; (3) They miss the tragic theme of the story and often find Adam and Eve and the talking snake funny.

I have a more recent snake story that was told to me by an old friend who used to be a real estate developer, a Creator, before he found Jesus and took a different course in life. Years ago my ex-developer friend managed a picture-perfect subdivision next to a lake. As the story goes, one Friday evening he received an angry call from a new homeowner in the development. She was upset because she had just spotted, from her sun porch, a large black snake in her back yard. During the call, she threatened to sue the developer, my friend. In her mind, the snake was a breach of contract because the snake violated her ideal image of what she had purchased: her perfect house and her perfect back yard next to the perfect lake, her lush garden.

The story of the lady and the snake carries new meaning for me. This is the Garden of Eden turned upside down. This lady would not have been drawn into a fatal conversation with the serpent. Instead she would have called God and threatened to sue him for letting a snake in her garden to begin with.

There is another story my friend told me about another developer, a successful then young entrepreneur in ritzy Hilton Head, South Carolina, who had his bubble burst one afternoon. As the story goes, he returns home from work to his large house next to a beautiful marsh. His wife mixes him a scotch and water and asks him to take their little dog out for a walk in their expansive back yard. He walks toward the marsh and views the idyllic watery extension of his estate. He admires the rosy image of the sun descending in the firmament above his own garden as he sips his scotch, and—let's say for the sake of story telling—he thinks about how perfect and great life and creation are.

While he stands bathing in the glowing embers of his success, the family dog wanders toward the edge of the water to sniff around as dogs do. The developer has another sip of scotch. He hears a swishing sound from the water and looks down to find that there is no little dog at the end of the extension leash. He eyes a large alligator, retreating slowing into the grassy marsh. Just like that. Now he's standing there, in a fit of despair, wondering how to explain to his wife and to their two small children what had just happened, certain that he would be sent to hell courtesy of his family for the outcome. He should have called the Creator and threatened to sue him, but he was in his own sub-division. He would have to sue himself.

Another bubble burst by reptiles beyond control. We did not make the reptiles, but we look for someone to blame for what reptiles do. Even God, who created them, is not able to control them, although, unlike the real estate developers, it is reasonable to hold God accountable for their existence. Reptiles—snakes and alligators and Komodo dragons—make the Creator seem not in control. Reptiles do what reptiles do. We might think they are bad or evil, but it is only our thinking that makes them so.

Looking to my wall, I was struck by the despairing thought that I had been approaching the Garden of Eden story in the wrong way. I was focused on the flaws of the created. In the story, the humans do human things. Curiosity gets the better of the innocent, childlike couple in the garden.

They taste the forbidden fruit, they realize that they are naked, exposed, and then they try to hide and blame others for what they did.

We are flawed, sinful? Is this all we can get from the story? What about the larger point that my students get at the onset? God's Garden is not perfect. There we are with the tree of knowledge, under-explained, the serpent, who is smart, and the people, who are dim wits. And there is God, who wanders the perimeters of his creation, but who does not have full control over what he created.

Why is it that Christianity, not just odd dinosaur Christianity but Cookout Christianity, too, goes back to what my students see as the God of the comedy of errors in the Garden of Eden in order to find bubbly perfection? Why was I blind to the flaws of the creator when it is so clear that the the creator is to blame for the reptiles? And what is so bad about flawed creations? If we were perfect, we would not know our souls. Maybe to be flawed is divine.

In my flawed teaching, I missed key elements of the Garden of Eden story because I was still under the auspices of Christian thinking. I had to work through my own rejection of this thinking during childhood to see through it. My irritation echoed God's irritation with his one busy-body serpent and two gullible gardeners of his own making. God seems to want the project to fail. He wants to be irritated—maybe he just wants to know his own soul. It took the perplexed faces of my students to separate the Garden of Eden story from the Cookout Christian tradition, one that has bubbled it over as a story about the inherent flaws that precedent our quests for comfort and perfection in the afterlife and even in the here and now. But this quest for perfection even overreaches the abilities of the God of Eden.

I may be on the verge of finding a cure for my irritation with mainline Christianity, a redeeming cure that comes, oddly, through the repeated practice of reading and teaching the Bible to the uninitiated. Teaching the Bible in Japan has taught me the futility of scoffing at the flaws of bubbly religious ideas that have little to do with the text or the students I am teaching. And there are times when there is no need to interject, in my classes and elsewhere, anti-bubble ideas of my own. But I also have my own bubbled-up religious ideas still loitering about, and I have grown so cautious about busting the bubbles that are not there that I avoid bursting the bubbles that are. Certain bubbles must be identified and burst beforehand else they lead to more flaws.

Though easy targets for hyper-righteous souls on both the extreme right and left, Cookout Christians are not as bubbled-up or self-deceived as outspoken fundamentalists and left-leaning intellectuals and stand-up comics and people like me make them out to be. In my experience, they are strong and trustworthy people—citizens. They would like things to be as ideal, as un-flawed, as possible. They are well aware that there are reptiles lurking on their borders and that there are things amiss about the Bible. They are not perfect, and, by and large, they have had a glimpse of their souls and do not despise their lives.

Gertrude Stein says about religion in America: "Religion. They like religion. Why do they like religion? They like religion because if they like religion, they like what they will be, as having religion. They like religion, they like names, they like names and religion. They like it just like that."

It is best to leave the flaws of Cookout Christians alone instead of irritating and confusing them and myself about how distant the Bibles on their end tables are from them. Sometimes these people are the strongest allies for sensibility. They are a supportive group to go to when trying to find money to fight AIDS or malaria in Africa. They are just pulling for The Christians, their home team, and their mascot, the Bible, in disguise as something else. They like what they are and will be as having the Bible that is not there and the religion that is.

Even in a country where almost everyone you meet belongs to a church, where in many communities there seem to be unwritten local statutes requiring church participation, there are places for people like me who wander away from the church. There are unevenly marked tracks of thought outside of church, safe zones where you can be among the contrarians, the religiously uncircumcised, and not suffer direct persecution, although you might find yourself shortchanged if you go into a profession that is supported by people who see you as a threat to their religious or ideological bubbles.

There are precarious areas are where the grumpy children of Nietzsche wander church-less but Constitutionally protected land where they can say anything: God is dead, or God is not great, or God is a delusion—the loosely affiliated society of the disillusioned or un-illusioned, the naysaying types who crash the religious dance equipped with a tool set of rational ideas from the great thinkers to burst all bubbles and end the dance. Now I have given this job over to the reptiles, who are much better at bursting bubbles than Nietzsche ever dreamed of being.

I have walked away from the godless tribe of the naysayer, too, as I have migrated into another wilderness full of the smaller gods of my Japanese wall but absent the demanding God of Moses. I would like to reconcile with the Cookout Christians after a number of years walking the intemperate prairies of what the philosopher, Gilles Deleuze, called "nomad thought." From experience, I know that this reconciliation is just partially possible because so many Christians, even some Cookout Christians, are all or none when it comes to religion, and they cannot have their religion without seeing me thrown into a lake of fire. They can't be my friends.

I try to remember why it was that I wandered away from their churches to begin with and try to figure what role the Bible played in this exodus. I think I wandered away from church because I got kicked out of Sunday school class as a kid, and I just kept walking—just like that. Being told that we were the product of incestuous relationships within a primal, dim witted, forbidden fruit-eating, brother-killing, dysfunctional family was more sullied, in my mind, than the thought of descending from an ancient tribe of primates courageously and tenuously plodding on two legs across an African savannah. They just kept walking, something I understood.

But I was reluctant to walk away because part of me was drawn to the art of maintaining a relationship with God and church while harboring deep suspicion, even contempt, for flawed church theology. We were bound more by flaw than theology. Many people in my community, good-hearted people, the best people, retained an intriguingly quiet artistic balance between their private thoughts and their public positions in the church. There is a type of enviable discipline in living life in this flawed way.

I used to think I failed to warm up to Christianity in general on rational, scientific, and sturdy philosophical grounds, but looking back the true source of my rejection of various Christianities is far more base, even rooted in a Scots Presbyterian (read redneck if you must) suspicion of media supported people driven by money, celebrity, or power. This suspicion came from a childhood spent well outside of the suburbs and deep in the country. We did not know the Bible so well in the countryside where I grew up, but we had God. We had our religion. We had and still have our church.

Every Sunday we took the twelve-mile ride to town to go to Sunday school to join the citified others from our own tribe but from another church to learn about the Bible for an hour. Enduring this tedious hour was at the source of what led me to believe many years later that I knew the Bible when I actually did not. This hour was also what gave me a hint, even in childhood, that the Bible had a flawed relationship with the religion we were trying to practice. Bible study was usually boring—at best it was disquieting, memorably when one kid in particular fell out with his stern but well intentioned teacher.

The roughly 18.1% of the mainline American Christians still out there know the drill. Sunday school was followed by a dull, formal service that had a fine organist and inspired if not perfectly pitched choir who all tried to make the event more than mundane. But the solemn preaching and the weakly sung hymns were intractably entrenched in the long Scots Presbyterian tradition of equating the pains of boredom with the benefits of divine enlightenment.

On the up side, the ritual was followed by good food. Most of the members of the town church were suburban Cookout Christians as opposed to clueless country enlistees, like me, of what might as well have been a tree God. Looking back, they were good folks, who, once a week, because they valued reading and education, had to mediate nervously a foreign book that at once mandated crazy neighborly love and justified genocide.

As I found out as a kid, it was best not to ask too many questions about the Bible, but what I did not realize was the art involved in this non-effort for many of the adults at my church. Let's suffer through this Bible lesson, then suffer through church, then eat some good food after we've paid our dues. Let's do this because this is what we do—just like that. They were like the Japanese in this regard. Let's bore each other nearly to death in meetings for a period, then go have some fun. What I did not see then was that there was something Roman, stoic, rewarding, in a Zen-like way, in this effort, a weekly reminder that what does not quietly drive you insane might make you quietly stronger.

It was not until later that Highway Jesus Christians from God-knows-where and the once and future Hooverites, who had been in the margins for time eternal, coupled together and began their serious attempts to breach our borders and make us lament our beloved flaws. The Highway Jesus Christians were out to replace long established Cookout Christian bubbles with more fantastical bubbles, while the Hooverites were bursting bubbles with their literal and inerrant Bible. Together the mixed messages were confounding: their stereophonically euphoric and ill-tempered insistence that all was not right with our religious world. People toting Bibles and talking Jesus became more numerous on our quiet grounds, city church and country crossroads, too. They insisted that we were not close to God. We were to blame, not the reptiles.

The Bible-bangers were not all local or even from the South. Many of the Highway Jesus people and the Hooverites had their Bible-banging, old time religious roots in western New York State and other "burnt over" evangelical regions well north of us. There was also my stern Methodist minister grandfather, who was a Southerner, but who wasn't a Hooverite. He would let you know just how doomed you were if you did not straighten up and follow God's word, and he did not fire blanks when he spoke. Fortunately he lived 400 miles away and was preaching from a prior century.

There were some small wildly evangelical congregations

in cloisters around us. Many of them had Hooverite tendencies, but they were all over the map, being unplugged from the society in such ways that they would make Thoreau re-think the benefits of living in natural isolation. They kept to themselves, suspicious of modern things, which included schools and hygiene.

And there were the African American churches that we did not know much about because we were still living in segregated society. Before, during, and after that time, members of their churches were hitting the highway back and forth to engineer the Civil Rights movement, a huge and truly right-minded bubble-bursting project. This was the one Christian enterprise from that period that unquestionably achieved and sustained biblical redemption.

But back to the white folks. Suddenly the others came from beyond, with the new highways and new media and new money, and rose up from within to tell us that we were accountable for flaw. And this was a Bible that was supposed to be taken literally, but only the verses they selected and read the way they insisted the verses be read.

Although they claimed to hail back to old times, these Christians were not old time. The new Highway Jesus people differed from the soon-to-be mass organized early Hooverites in that Highway Jesus people were not that stern, at least ostensibly. They were euphoric and energetic. But along with the early Hooverites, they fueled new media movements and new therapeutic thinking with the claim to hail back to old times when Jesus was truly in control. They insisted that their literal Bibles contained secret codes that we had missed because God had never revealed them to us because we were not truly with God. I think the local Hooverites were cautious about their new friends in Christ, like two separate motorcycle clubs, and I am sure they were suspicious about why the Highway Jesus leaders and their followers looked so happy. It was not a stable alliance from the start.

In my hometown these movements erupted in modern, not old times, roughly during the 60s and 70s. Whatever links they had with the 16th century Protestant reformation, with the great awakenings in early America, or with 19th century evangelism, they found unprecedented power. It was with the use of new highways, growing T.V. and radio access, and income from a more moneyed economy, when evangelical movements from out of town teamed precariously with a certain set of local bible bangers to create a new Jesus qua apocalypse movement. They learned how to network and upgrade their provincial tent shows and marginal churches, they found media outlets, they built new churches, and they spread the good and bad news aggressively throughout our land.

Looking back, it seems that the Highway Jesus people burnt through our wilderness during the same week as the McDonald's that popped up on Broad Street and Led Zeppelin playing over a distant radio station and the marijuana burning in the parking lots of local schools. Dirt racetracks populated by the lead-footed sons of whiskey runners had already expanded into major speedways with highly professionalized and strongly sponsored drivers and race teams. They drew enthusiasts from across the country. Roughly during the same era, the Hooverites upgraded their concrete blockhouse services and went national with big preachers and big room broadcasts and big churches with firmaments built from much better materials than concrete blocks.

Excess and the excessive cure for excess came in at the same time from the same highway, along with the Bible, of course, the new iconic Bible that everyone talked about in any way they saw fit. You could never claim that *Moby Dick* is about growing up in Kansas, but you could say just about anything you wanted to about the Bible.

The percentage of people who saw themselves as Mainline Christians back then was far higher, I think, than the current 18.1%. (How can 18.1% of anything be described as "mainline?") Over the following decades many of them fell out with their original mainline churches and in with new churches in droves. Many of them felt the need, I can only guess, to either super-size the bubbles of their religious lives with the happy Highway Christians or go for the Armageddon rush by joining God's stern bubble bursting new Hooverite Army of the Impending Apocalypse.

Some went with hybrid versions of these two fundamentally different religious growth markets, while others saw to it that their mainline churches became more in step with the times by replacing boring and poorly performed old music with bad and badly performed new music and hiring fired up preachers with great haircuts who dared to preach beyond the appointed time to people who actually moved around during church services. The notion that you had to get emotional to get close to God, which is indeed old time and should have remained that way, replaced the habit of getting closer to God by practicing the highly cultivated art of napping through church sermons with your eyes half open.

These religious changes made many small town types, new followers, reformed followers, and artistic nap takers, nervous. Me included. I remember at sixteen I was invited to a meeting of a group that had been quickly formed in town, the Teen Crusade for Christ, a Highway Christian venue that offered Hooverite side dishes. I was told that I would be part of an event that, unlike the deadly boring church services we attended, had to do with us and with our adolescent needs. I went because I was heartsick over the girl who invited me, and maybe by going, I'd have a chance with her.

I was greeted by smiling people whose vacant eyes indicated to me that they were not happy to see me, but that they were smiling from an overwhelming need to prove to themselves and others how happy they were. They had found a way to manage the reptiles. This smiling lasted until the crying started, when several group members delivered sloppy, impromptu testimonies of personal failure, which signaled that it was time to worry about God, because flaw is on us, not just them, but me, too, even though I did not feel as if I had failed God. After tortuously long and demonstrably self-centered praying, teary-eyed smiles erupted. I could not understand what was it was about a routine Tuesday night that got these people so worked up.

The meeting was cultish, emotional, and weird, too weird even for me to rank being kicked out. The dramatic testimonials came from people too willing to share intimate details of their lives with a room full of people they did not know well and who did not seem stable. These were not quiet, napping Christians with their mediated, quiet flaws and doubts. These people simply presumed that their stormy come-to-Jesus stories proved that we all lacked something and that Jesus would quiet the storm and fill this void.

Fine, but I could not put my finger on what it was exactly that I lacked. I had family, friends, good food, education, radio, T.V., pocket change, and access to a fast car. What more could I ask from God? I do remember the stormy thoughts I had about the young lady who had invited me to the meeting. Was I supposed to ask Jesus to deliver her up to me?

After the quasi-Manson family meeting with the Teen Crusaders, I remember wanting to get the hell outta there, to flee back to the woods, to talk with a talking snake or confront a dog-eating alligator, or do something to realign me with the natural God of my country crossroads. I remember that the mainline speaker the Teen Crusade group rallied around was a young guy who explained that he found Jesus after living in a dumpster for four days. His addiction to heroin was what led him to the dumpster. Jesus led him out of the dumpster. He worked the Bible into his testimony about his drug addiction. Word had it that, after his Teen Crusade for Christ tour, he cashed his check and returned to his heroin—the smack addiction trumped the Jesus addiction, but not before Highway Jesus Christians presented a hard-line heroin addict to small-town teenagers as someone to be looked up to and followed. I don't know what happened to the Teen Crusade in the following years. I suppose that someone eventually cruised off down the highway with the money, and that was that.

The group dispersed and, I guess, its members went back to their mainline churches to nap or to more stable Highway Jesus groups to recharge or to Hooverite churches to reload. Maybe a few followed the leader and gave up Jesus for drugs. Many things came and went down that newly expanded wilderness highway. Eventually I took off on it.

While the Cookout Christians were quietly napping, a habit I truly believe is in concert with the divine, the Highway Jesusites and the new Hooverites were laying waste to my natural but bible-lacking God of the country and co-opting the mild suburban cookout God of the town, using, as the weapon of choice, the foreign Bible, made even more foreign by the way in which it was concocted in the prayers of lack from the Highway Jesus mind curers and self-assured evocations of mass destruction from the Hooverites.

This period is when I started, not to fall away, but to avoid falling in with new and intolerable religious movements—intolerable in that they routinely failed to tolerate. Their flaws were projected onto us as our flaws, as if we were the ones liable for the reptiles of the flawed garden. I also fell out with the boring church of the town because I was too country from the start, too in love with the divine flaws of nature to seek a cure. Add a touch of Nietzsche in college, a dash of nomad thought in graduate school, and it no longer was a resistance but a way of life.

Only recently, while thinking about the Bible, did I realize I never walked away from religion. I just slipped out the back door of the church while the sleepers were sleeping. I ducked under and stepped over new reckless religions as they flew in on new highways from outside while overgrowing us like weeds from grass root sources. I ended up with contempt for the whole lot. Much of this contempt, I understand now, was just warmed over righteousness, more mismanagement of flaw.

Getting too exposed to religion can divert you from being religious. In my backward country world we felt that we were already members of God's unruly natural community, members in good standing by right of birth, and there was not much need to get worked up over this fact. The Bible, or at least what was said and thought and taught about the Bible, jump-started the engines that powered me away. It was their Bible that kept getting in the way of the sensible, the happy, the sad, the religious, this foreign book that was not even written as a book and that was innocent of its own misuses by distant future dwellers of a spherical earth.

When I took on the task of teaching the Bible, I was not aware of the flaw of my contempt for religious practices that too often misuse people and that routinely misuse the Bible. Teaching the Bible has forced me to undergo what has turned out to be the turgid, therapeutic process of working out these emotions while staring at a Japanese wall.

The Cookout Christians are the old home team. Staring at my wall, I understand that holding out any contempt for the bubbles of Cookout Christianity is in a sense holding on to self-contempt. Though reconciled with Cookout Christians, at least from my side, I still have a cranky urge to call for replacing the Bible during Sunday school with something more wholesome. The writings of Benjamin Franklin would be a good start.

There are other groups of Christians whose views I will never reconcile with as they will never reconcile with me. I will never get over the desire to unleash the alligators of the divine marsh, via the Bible of Japan, in the halls of Highway Jesus Christians and Hooverites alike, this done as a rear guard action in yearning memory of the quiet, flawed, natural God of a country crossroads.

Free Association III:
Line Dancing with the Gods

... distrust all in whom the impulse to punish is powerful!
—Friedrich Nietzsche, *Also Sprach Zarathustra*

One wonders why Christianity and the Christian Bible have not made it big in Japan. McDonalds and Starbucks, German beer and French cafes, British pubs and Spanish tapas bars and a host of other foreign concepts in fashion, music, and culture have. A heavenly host of logos from the multinational corporate firmament light the night sky in Tokyo.

Why not Christianity in Japan? Christian missionaries preceded these corporations by many years and global Christianity is now spirited onward, like large corporations, by big money and mass media. One corporation is selling coffee for four dollars a cup, but missionaries offer redemption and the path to eternal life for free. Why are there so many pricey Starbucks cafes in Tokyo but little to no Christian heaven?

The low level of Christian belief and practice in Japan is not the result of laziness on the part of Christian evangelicals. Christian church missionaries have made vigorous efforts to establish congregations and churches in Japan. My university is one example of this effort. But when you walk the largely Christian-less streets of Japanese cities and look around, it is obvious that these efforts have failed or have had, from a Christian point of view, disappointing results.

There are Christian churches in Tokyo, but this is an area of over 8 million people, just in central Tokyo, and millions more if you fall asleep on the train and find yourself 30 minutes on the wrong side of mass humanity from your tiny apartment. In Tokyo, you can find a lot of things, even groups of polite Japanese couples who meet weekly to practice country-western line dancing. They practice meticulously, complete with cowboy hats and chaps.

But why so few Christians? Christian expansionism has often been seen as a threat by non-Christian governments, and there have been times in Japanese history when leaders or governments have purged Christian movements and have done so cruelly. But in the modern period, the government of Japan allows freedom of religion. In no way that I have come across has any governmental force that has recently tried to purge Christianity or restrict citizens from its practice.

The Japanese are open to trying out new things from the outside but rarely—maybe after a short trip to Oklahoma—do they give Christianity a go. As so many people in so many cultures, modern Japanese love variety. The curious lack of Christians might be explained by the curious presence of country-western line dancers, their method, their curriculum, and their freedom to line dance happily in a space away from the normal regimen of their day-to-day jobs.

Ian Reader observes that Christianity has failed to unify itself with the unifying tradition of Japanese religion. Except for a small number of strict adherents, in Japan there is no problem with practicing both Shinto and Buddhism (and versions of newer religions and line dancing and Salsa dancing) next to one another. As those of us from the world according to the Great-Desert-Faith-gone-multinational know well, Christianity, in its many forms, is a jealous religion. This is one real and direct connection Christianity has with the Old Testament. And the books of the Bible, throughout, insist on one single and monolithic God. Christianity, in its many forms, does not like to go out and play with other religions.

Historically, though, Christianity has managed to unify itself with a variety of cultural traditions throughout the world, co-opting these traditions into Christian practice. Japan, the land of detail, seems resistant to Christianity on other levels. The one jealous God, in the view of my exacting students, presents an arbitrary set of rules to follow, rules that are observed inconsistently throughout the Christian world. The arbitrariness of Christian practice, if not rooted in the

Bible, at least finds sources there. The Bible presents more of an obstacle than a benefit to Christians trying to spread Christianity in a culture that is so precise and methodical.

The early books of the Bible lay out fixed laws and the set rituals of worship. These religious elements, though ancient and foreign, are understandable to my students. You must be circumcised, you must carry out animal sacrifices to God in a set manner, and you must rest on the Sabbath or else be put to death.

My students are not big on circumcision and ceremonial animal sacrifices. They do appreciate the idea of a day of rest, though they would find it difficult to rest with the idea of being put to death for not resting. But the Bible later relaxes its mandates. In the New Testament Paul has a revelation that the law of circumcision can be suspended, Jesus reportedly finds exception with the hard line rule of resting on the Sabbath, and, in the Old Testament book of Amos, in particular, God seems to grow weary of the animal sacrifices he once demanded. So my students would be off the hook for circumcision and animal sacrifice, and would not have to be as restless about their day of rest. Still, they do not understand the inconsistency.

Method requires consistency. A student once asked me why God sometimes supports capital punishment, but other times he is for clemency for capital crimes. The penalty for murder is death, unless you are Cain. There is plenty of biblical support for both judgments. My student's point, one that he asserted to me privately after class, was that those many Christians in America who support the death penalty do not seem to be following their own religion. He was against the death penalty. I pointed out that the Bible has capital punishment and so does Japan.

"But we don't have Christian," he responded clumsily but poignantly.

Those who support capital punishment should steer clear of the Bible for legal precedents. Liberals who support biblical mandates should take care also. Members of the left of center religious organization, Sojourners, state that their mission is to "articulate the biblical call to social justice."

This notion is high-minded and pleasing to the ear, but one wonders exactly which biblical call, and what means or method of articulation they are referring to. Abraham nearly gutting Isaac? Ishmael tossed out into the wilderness for being born to the wrong woman? Jezebel and the dogs—Ahab, too, had a bad run in with K-9 social justice. Esau and his cheat brother who gets away clean? Uriah was killed for having a sexy wife. Adam and Eve were forever cursed for eating a piece of fruit. Women are treated badly, and slavery is just fine.

My students have problems precisely with the lack of modern social justice in the Bible. The amulets of obsequious religious convention are absent. My students do not see how out-of-context recitations can become institutionalized well beyond their biblical context. In the King James Version, the beautiful blessing from the Lord, recited to Moses to repeat to Aaron, is often delivered at the end of church services in a modified version:

> The LORD bless thee, and keep thee: The LORD make his face shine upon thee, and be gracious unto thee: The LORD lift up his countenance upon thee, and give thee peace. (Numbers 6:24-26)

This passage, with its physical God and his physical face, is the blessing Aaron and his sons, the Levite priests, should impart to the children of Israel (not Cookout Christians). It follows a series of instructions from God to the Levites on how to separate themselves from the world during periods of worship, and how to conduct sacrifices, particularly animal sacrifices. It belongs to those who practice a methodical, albeit native, religious life. The practice and method, in our time, are lost, and for good reasons.

This passage comes from a section of Numbers applied to services where first-born lambs and rams are slaughtered, gutted, and burnt at the altar, where aspiring Nazarites who have grown their hair out enter into the service to have it shaved off in what appears to be a public ceremony. The passage is beautiful, but it has little to do with Christian services on Sunday morning during our time. (But there are some deer hunting clubs in the American wilderness that follow similar rituals after hunts.)

The Bible works out internal problems with the rule of law and with maintaining an ancient desert tribe, one that is constantly under threat. Once in class I compared the quotation above with the song of Moses from Deuteronomy 32:42:

> I will make mine arrows drunk with blood, and my sword shall devour flesh; and that with the blood of the slain and of the captives, from the beginning of revenges upon the enemy.

"They love killing," Ms. Adachi said bluntly.

But my students respect the biblical view of an ancient culture trying to work out its legal and moral framework that is circumscribed by violence. These biblical characters fire wide left and wide right of what they are aiming for, which is to please an inconsistent God. They are flawed, but they really do look deeply into their own souls, at least their writers do. How do you explain the jealous God, the open-minded God, the God of revenge and the God of mercy, to students who live beyond the stormy religious deserts of the shazamed?

These students live outside the Bible's deep dung heaps dug near the holy of holies, the Bible's sacred altars next to its pissed walls, the Bible's fixed but changing moral codes, the Bible's divine judgments and the reversal of those judgments. They live far from Bible-sparked fires of analogy that rage in our separatist wildernesses of partisan and feuding Christian denominations and beliefs.

Detail is divine in Japan, and detail is the raw material for method. In Japan cultural observers note the Japanese habit of establishing the precise Way of Doing, *houhou* (pronounced "hoe hoe")—not only the way of doing Japanese arts, but just about anything. (I recently passed a Starbucks in Tokyo where they were advertising free coffee seminars with a set program that essentially focused on how "to do" coffee.) But modern biblical Christianity, taken as a whole, reflects the arbitrariness of the Bible. When viewed from within

Japan, from within my classroom, the rules and practices of one denomination or group, when compared with another, make it difficult to determine what, exactly, Christianity is. How can Catholicism, Methodism, Presbyterianism, Jehovah's Witnesses, and Mormons all be contained under the umbrella term, Christianity? Also these different doctrinal and theological groups, presumably all within Christianity, are long on theology and short on a consistent method and curriculum for practice. What, really, is the method of the Methodists? Line dancing has a set way of doing, a course to follow, but this way of doing is lacking in Christianity, in its many forms, with its many different views of God, arguably with its many different Gods.

This problem of doing Christianity presents itself early on in Christianity, in Paul's writings, so much of which are dedicated to the idea of how to *become* a follower of Christ, but little on precisely how to *do* Christianity. Pauline Christianity focuses on conversion. First you become a Christian, but then you are in a world of various practices and disagreement over what those practices should be, a problem addressed by Paul in his letters to the Corinthians and elsewhere.

It is a curious element of Western religious thinking that you become a Christian before you have practiced Christianity. You cannot become a high school graduate before you go to high school, you cannot become a member of a profession without first being schooled and certified. In Japan, or anywhere else for that matter, no one would identify himself as a martial artist before practicing the martial arts, or as a certified practitioner of *ikebana*, or flower arranging, before studying ikebana, or as a country-western line dancer, without rehearsing the art of country western line dancing. The Bible itself, with its one, often angry and always jealous God, with its arbitrary messages on how to worship this God, may be at the source of why Christianity has made so little headway in Japan.

Arguably, mainline Catholicism, with its historical de-emphasis on the Bible and its focus on set ritual practices, would seem better able to handle the needs of people who go about becoming line dancers by learning the precise method of line dancing. Catholicism should be able to instantiate its saints among the many *kami* of Japanese religion, even push through ubiquitously the idea of the one true God as it has done historically in so many other cultures. Still, you must be a Christian first before learning the way of doing Christianity, and I think this is an oxymoron in Japanese thinking. And, let's face it, this Roman institution cannot be unified with Japan precisely because it is a Roman institution. Neither side, Rome nor Japan, has enough flex for the widespread assimilation of two powerful forces, one of which is foreign and Western—not Japanese—and therefore generally eyed with distrust. Wrong passport.

The Bible occupies center stage in Protestantism, but Protestantism at the outset has admitted the shortcomings of the Bible with its need to codify religious practice outside of the Bible. The *Book of Common Prayer*, the prayer books, the hymnals, the many guidebooks and guidelines, the copious, endless biblical commentaries are the lasting legacy of the Protestant Reformation, the move away from the Pope and toward the text as guideline. Still, the emphasis is on becoming and being a Christian before *doing* Christianity. Not one single and clear methodical way of doing Christianity has emerged.

A friend of mine once asked me, while visiting Japan, why I did not use my Bible classes to encourage conversion to Christianity. He is a mainline Methodist, a Cookout Christian whose wife is a Methodist minister. I had no quick response for why I would never take on such a mission, so I answered that we were close to a fine Thai restaurant, where we could talk more about the subject, which we never did. Food trumps religious debate in Cookout Christianity.

The quickest answer I can think of, one that my friend would find rude, is that one could never take on the task of trying to convert Japanese people to Christianity by using the Bible. It is not the right text. One would need a better manual and a curriculum of practice that does not exist in the Protestant world. The manual would have to set the course for becoming a Christian rather than allowing that one becomes a Christian first before learning the practice of Christianity.

Without a Christian foundation in their thinking, my students see no signs of my private, Jacob-like wrestling match with non-methodical Christianity and the post-facto ambiguities of Christian practice after conversion. They certainly do not see me as I stare at my neighbor's wall while I remember the happy food that followed the nervous, haphazard study of the Bible that was not there in times past. I cannot explain the nervous wholesomeness of my own faux-biblical learning.

As for Highway Jesus Christianity, the biblio-charismatic pastiche orchestrated by these followers is religious free form that flouts the idea of a detailed manual or a set religious curriculum or practice. They flee from method. Instead of establishing a way of doing, this type of Christianity promotes an improvised way of not doing. One must follow Jesus without any clear instructions on how to do so, except that, depending on the congregation or arbitrary circumstances, we are no longer to engage in unruly behavior. The unclear path to not doing would not sell in my classroom, and rarely does it sell in Japan. There is no clear method in embracing abstinence while channeling one's desire for excess into a love for a human incarnation of God. I still do not understand why Highway Jesus Christianity sells anywhere else in the world, but for the fact that consumerism thrives on creating a sense of lack, and Highway Jesus Christianity thrives on lack.

I think that in typical Japanese culture Christian prayer could not truly be actualized without a detailed and pertinent way of doing prayer. And the Christian world on the whole, particularly the impromptu and inspired Highway Jesus world, has never agreed exactly, precisely, on what prayer is and exactly, precisely, how, where, and when it should be carried out. Many Christians want prayer in public schools, but they do not present one precise way of doing prayer, and they do not seem to have a concise idea of what prayer is. In the Shinto tradition it is good enough to clap your hands a couple of times, beckoning a kami for good fortune. This is a small prayer—perhaps all prayer should be small, simple, and firmly set.

The hard-line Hooverites try to preserve a way of doing by way of retaining the concrete physical cosmos of the Bible. In their world, one still goes up to heaven. But the

God in heaven is fearful—the Bible supports this notion. Once converted, one should be driven to convert others with fearful warnings. The Seventh Day Adventists have made some inroads in Japan, probably because their members follow a regime of knocking on doors and offering personal testimonies to the poor souls who elect to answer their doorbells. Their testimonies are backed by printed information, which they are trained to explain. I am speaking from experience when I say they can be a methodical and tenacious lot.

Some of my students are vaguely familiar with this type of Christianity. The central and highly abstract Hooverite concept of the *Rapture*, popular and widely believed in America, bleeds into my classroom through the veneer of Western Christianity. Even those of us from the Christian world who keep the Hooverites at a safe distance know the Rapture drill because we have had the experience of pressing the wrong buttons on our remotes and ending up mesmerized by a T.V. evangelist who overtakes our living rooms from another world. He has a stern face, insincere in its grave sincerity.

We are told we need to trust in God, to trust in "him." The word *him* is pronounced, in at least one case that I can document, *heeee ma*, in an effort, along with the entranced look of the speaker, to convince us that the spirit of God has possessed the speaker and with the assumption that the spirit of God would have trouble pronouncing English words. This speech-impaired projection of God is much different from the God who is a straight-talking and familiar fellow that dickers with Abraham after Abraham sees him standing under a nearby tree in Genesis 18. The God-stricken speaker on television continues by telling us that if we believe in *heee ma*, then we will be included in the rush when all real Christians, living and dead, are sucked up into the firmament.

If we go with the advice of the gentleman on television, via his robotic pronunciation of English words, we will enjoy bliss in heaven, where we will get to linger for eternity with unpleasant people like the speaker, crowded in with a perpetually unpleased God, who is accompanied by his son, the kind, but humorless rabbi. I prefer the fellow under the tree.

Perhaps the Rapture does appear in concept in the Bible,

depending on how freely one associates biblical passages with latter day ideas, but the word, rapture, never appears in any English version of the Bible that I have searched in relation to the last days or to the offhanded notion that the righteous will be sucked up into the firmament. Adding to the confusion is problem that *up*, for the American Hooverite, is *down* for my students on their side of planet earth.

Most of us from the Christian world have come across talk about the writings of Revelation and the fact that many believe there is an approaching Beast or Anti-Christ. The idea appears notably in Yeats' apocalyptic and stunningly acute poem, "The Second Coming." But I cannot find the word *anti-Christ* in Revelation. It appears in the John books before Revelation. The anti-Christ in John is anyone who does not acknowledge Jesus as the Christ, not a singular beast of destruction.

The desert storm of free association! There are various beasts presented in Revelation, horrid images to engage Hooverites through to distant future eras. In Revelation, we are told that:

> the stars of heaven fell unto the earth, even as a fig tree casteth her untimely figs, when she is shaken of a mighty wind. (6:13)

Figs falling from a tree in a storm—my students understand this image. It belongs to a region that has storms and that exports figs. They are confounded by the image of stars falling from the sky. Combine these falling stars with lakes of fire, monsters in the air, and other monsters in various disguises, say, as a leader of a nation or race that the gentleman who wrote Revelation did not like. These images bubbling up in the air beneath God's firmament leave me with a lot of explaining to do in my classroom when the eternal question comes: "Do Christians believe this?"

How do I describe the odd way people handle the incomprehensible passages of the Bible on the stormy side of the religious world I am from? How do I explain that in some circles of Christianity ideas are just brewed up before stirring in a few vague references from the Bible, but in others, Christians just hang back in silence, hoping not to disturb the reptiles.

The Japanese can blow up their own big ideas from vague references in their culture, too. But we are talking about the Bible. Any religious group seeking to Christianize Japan should leave the Bible at home and show up instead with a detailed program, one that dismisses the power-hungry condemnations of the Hooverites and instead promotes self-improvement daily through affirming group activity, practice, and study. The face of Christianity should not be that of the gentleman who barges in to implant scary thoughts in the minds of people trying to enjoy the comfort of their homes.

Method. The transitory notion that it is time to love and trust God while we simultaneously huddle up and brace for his catastrophic destruction of the world just does not sell in a corner of the world where people vigorously go about their daily business fully aware that the great catfish deep underneath may at any moment stir and destroy life on a massive scale. My students get confused when they come across the rigid, frightful, post-lapsarian thinking of Hooverite Christianity. I still do not know how to explain to my students that, in America, Hooverites thrive underneath a sturdy stratum of well-adjusted people who are generally tolerant and sensible and kind and completely unable to comprehend how much power the coarse cable channel mystics can garner and how strong a hold they have on American consciousness at influential institutional levels.

Hooverites hold loose alliances with various Highway Jesus Christians when it suits them and even garner modified support or, worse yet, compliance, from right leaning Catholic and mainline Protestant groups. They have shown that they can weigh-in heavily in American political debates and elections, and they have a despairing amount of well-documented influence inside a number of local school boards and within the American armed services.

Hooverites are the most vociferous about the idea that those beyond the borders of their Christianity, as well as many within their borders, are doomed to be tormented for eternity in the afterlife. This medieval vision statement, when heard abroad, does not go over well with so many billions of people who cannot imagine themselves born into a cosmos that is supremely powered by a fitful single parent who wants to perma-fry them.

I think the Hooverites are energetic enough to take over the world completely—always have been, since their pre-medieval beginnings. They would have and would do so still were it not for the fact that they so badly need what is not them to charge and recharge them emotionally. Fearsomely powerful in spurts, they remain huddled within narrow margins because they must feed on that which they imagine to be outside those margins in order to secure and sustain what they think they are. They cannot save themselves without the idea that most are damned.

I teach in a culture that respects training and method but that is entirely untrained in the non-method of generating what can be oxymoronically described as the concrete abstractions drawn haphazardly from the Bible and defended chiefly by Hooverites, who claim interpretive rights that they seek to forbid among others. In the Hooverite world, now in our world, too, we can take the word *Armageddon*, a single word, a place name, a word that appears exactly once in the King James Version, and blow it up into a threatening zeppelin that hovers over the Christian imagination.

But who can get away from abstraction? I thought while looking at the ink blots on my neighbor's wall, *Who can get away from non-methodical free association, from projecting our own circumstances by analogy onto the ink blots of the Bible when thinking about the Bible?* How is it that, sitting in my apartment, I suddenly begin to relate a thrown rod in a car engine with the rod of Moses or with the rod of correction that the book of Proverbs instructs us to beat our children with?

Japan has a number of religions and a number of people seeking spiritual enlightenment. Japan has its share of people bubbling up with new religions, sometimes extreme ones, so extreme that one marginal group, in 1995, launched a deadly sarin gas attack on the Tokyo subway system for religious reasons that were never clearly articulated. Japan has its share of abstract thinkers. But my polite, middle-class students just cannot figure out how you get from the Bible they are getting to know to falls of man, dinosaurs in Eden, and raptures. We can argue until the second coming about the validity of these ideas in any society, but in my classroom, these are ideas that do not belong to, or even start with, the Bible.

From Alpha to Omega in Christianity, there is little method, no agreed upon way of doing, and little in the way of regular and disciplined understanding of the fundamentals of practice that Christianity would need to thrive in Japan. Exactly, precisely what do you do to follow God? Is there an exercise program, maybe some yoga? What drinks to drink, what foods to eat? In my classroom, when I announce the forthcoming day of the test, 99% of my students pull out their day timers, their *techou*, and write down the date and then wait for me to confirm said date. They are Japanese. They follow their techou religiously, their holy notebook, and this habit is part of what makes them Japanese.

Beyond the many laws of Moses, few of which modern Christians know or follow, the Bible is short on what the average child of God should do day-to-day and long on what the chosen and saved should not do in general. Pray. Fear God. Follow God. What is the exact, precise way of doing these things? Even the chosen people had trouble with the details of following God.

The desert storm: By analogy it is not us, and by analogy it is us—the Christianized, whether Cookout Christians, Highway Jesus Christians, Hooverites, Humanists or Heretics. And it is the Bible itself, the bound series of ancient books that we are given the charge to know, but that are—in the very multiplicity of their composition and arrangement and translation and reception— eternally unknowable.

I was brought up as a shazamite, so I understand—somewhat— the methodologically impaired essence of the many Christianities. Our non-methodical free association takes us everywhere and nowhere, but somehow we always make it back to the Bible, back to stormy Babylon. The God of the Burning Bush calls out to Moses, and Moses says, simply, "Here am I." So *here am I*, in my little apartment deep in Tokyo, staring at my neighbor's wall, lost in my own non-methodical wilderness, camping on my tiny cut of dry land and sky, sitting still in the airy void of the Gods.

Free Association IV: The Problem with Pronouns

Have you ever inserted your name as you read the Bible to make it more personal?
    —Catchphrase from "The Personal Promise Bible"

    I learned as a Boy Scout that you have to set up markers in order to find your way out of the woods. You notch trees, or tie cloth around brush. You keep track of your tracks. Markers do not show you the right direction; they show you that where you have been, the wrong direction. My Japanese neighbor's wall is a marker, and I wanted to find my way beyond its reflections of where I have been. I needed to set a course off the reservation and out of the wilderness, not out of Japan, which is its own wilderness, but out of what I was beginning to think was the biblical wilderness in me, the stormy old religious home front of my upbringing.
    One marker, one wrong direction, is the direction you take when you get too up-close-and-personal with the foreign terrain of the Bible and its characters and its God. Deuteronomy (32:10) tells us that God finds Moses "in a desert land," where "In the waste howling wilderness; he led him about, he instructed him, he kept him as the apple of his eye." This is a physical god who watches Moses closely.
    A pious soul might replace "Moses," leader of twelve giant tribes, with "Me," the leader of no tribes, and hope that God will keep Me as the apple of his eye during My trials in My own personal wildernesses and that one day Me will be led out by a God who loves and protects Me just like he loved and protected Moses.
    Our religion allows us to take a giant proper noun from the Bible, Moses, and substitute a tiny pronoun: Me. I can only give

hearsay examples of this habit, but the trials of any biblical character, in my church experience, are often reduced to a comparison with our own trials. What is the point of the Jonah story? Jonah could not hide from God. The real point is that YOU cannot hide from God.

In my recent reading of the book of Jonah, the story has more to do with Jonah's disdain for the people of Nineveh and God's short anger management talk with Jonah about separating what is important from what is not important. This is a subject more complex and engaging and humorous than an unvarnished tale about ME wanting to run and hide from God.

These pronoun substitutions create false markers, deceptions. There is nothing wrong with believing in a God who comforts and protects you, but the God of Moses is not the right god for this job. In the verse from Deuteronomy above, God is talking. He has eyes and can see you. He protects Moses for a time in the desert. At other times God does not like Moses, and he is not so willing to protect him. God snaps at Moses when Moses asks God his name. God jumps Moses and tries to kill him for no stated reason near an inn in Exodus 4:24. God punishes Moses harshly for the minor infraction of bringing water to his people in the wrong way. "Why is God so angry?" Ms. Sato wants to know.

An electrical storm approaches while you are playing the back nine on a golf course. If you think that you and the God of Moses have roughly the same relationship as Moses had with the God of Moses, then you might have it in your head that God will protect you like he did Moses, might keep you as the apple of his eye. But God did not always protect Moses.

To my students the desert storms depicted in the Bible are about those people, not my students. Mr. Itoh does not have the thought tools it takes to put his own life in the place of giant Moses. As much as the story of Moses might interest him, he does not feel much of an attachment to this character. He does not like Moses, or the God of Moses, for that matter. Both male figures are distant and harsh. My students cannot draw from a Bible story about God's relationship with Moses that God will protect them. The story is about more than protection, or about ME. The story is about God and his frustrating relationship with his stiff-necked people, who are not we.

My students are not trained culturally to replace giant proper nouns from the Bible with tiny pronouns of self. They see desert people who were not *lost* in the desert. These people knew where they were. They had to wander the desert because a God too quick to anger was angry with them because these desert people complained, and they were scared. In the view of my students these people had a right to complain because they had been, manna or no manna, living in godforsaken sandy oblivion for a long time. Moses was not protected in the end, something that even the writer of the beautiful passage in Psalm 17 seems to miss purposefully, when the speaker, in an obvious reference to Deuteronomy, humbly asks God to keep him as "the apple of the eye," to hide him "under the shadow of [God's] wings." This loving god, with his protective wings, has taken on angelic features that the angry God of Moses did not have.

Moses died in the wilderness and God was obliged to bury him nearby. Moses never made it to the Promised Land. An entire generation of Chosen People also died in the desert, unprotected. They doubted God. Aside from their angry God, who could blame them? They had been brought up as slaves, not career warriors, and were understandably horrified by the idea of wandering into any foreign land, promised or not promised, and fighting large numbers of people, who, given the scouting reports, were huge and powerful.

Thank God we are not Moses or God's chosen in a real ancient desert. I think I am right in saying that it is an old Jewish prayer to ask God, please, to choose someone else.

Those pious golfers who think that they have by analogy the same relationship with this mountain God as Moses had should get off Number 16 and make for the clubhouse post haste when the electrical storm comes in. Moses never made it out of the wilderness.

The writers of the books of the Bible had their own storms, their own wilderness of human experience to write their way through. It takes a large ego to cut and paste ones self into this grand biblical narrative, though this substitution is habitual in the under disciplined religious culture I grew up in. This substitution turns a big story about a powerful mountain God into a little story about a little voice talking inside your head. Nor does it seem anything but absurd to draw analogies with Moses while staring at my neighbor's wall among millions of people who would rather eat raw fish than try to reckon their relationship with an ancient mountain God who strands his people in a stormy wilderness.

Some might think that the correct pronoun is *We*, and not *Me*. *We* are the races of people who insert ourselves into Bible stories that were not written for us. *We* are all in a desert storm, together in our desert wanderings. Maybe I can show my students how this thinking keeps the Bible pertinent in Christian culture, even now that we know the earth looks more like an orange than like a coffee table. The pronoun *We* has resonance in Japanese culture, a culture that values group cooperation.

Isaiah has a vision that Babylon will be conquered:

> As whirlwinds in the south pass through; so it cometh from the desert, from a terrible land. (21:1)

Whirlwinds—a storm in the desert heading towards Babylon. The Hebraic struggles against Babylon in the Bible, by wayward, stretched analogy, might be something like our recent struggles in Iraq. This biblical reference parallels our own wars.

"Can't you see how this connection and other connections are made?" I said to my students once. Judging from their faces the only thing they saw was their teacher saying strange things about their textbook. To them, the American hope to bring democratic freedom to Iraq does not seem a bit similar to the hopes of ancient desert tribesmen to conquer Babylon. The Chosen, of course, are the Israelites—an Israelite is a desert tribesman, turned slave, turned warrior, turned slave, warrior, slave, warrior, slave, turned middle-class Army recruit from Dayton, Ohio, turned Christian Baptist member of the Alabama National Guard—wait, this analogy doesn't work. No wonder my students did not get it.

Saddam called himself the Son of Nebuchadnezzar,

but he was a crazed dictator. We are too even-headed to make associations between ancient dynasties and our modern democracy and use this association as a precedent, as a supplemental justification for war. Only someone crazy like Saddam would free-associate so wildly across time and circumstance. What sane American would think in this way?

On his website, Pat Robertson, in a defense of Israel that I do not think anyone in Israel asked him for, sees the second Iraq war, though, as the American fulfillment of biblical prophecy. Here is an excerpt of Robertson's interpretation of Daniel's interpretation of the dream of Nebuchadnezzar:

> How does America fit in? Well, we are the heirs, in my opinion, of Rome. We have a lot of the Roman culture. Britain was taken over by Rome. Our people have come from Rome. So what has now happened? But look at this. I think it's very interesting. Babylon is the head. This is the first major empire, and it's gone all the way full-circle back to Babylon again. And who brings it back to Babylon? None other than the continuation of the dream of Nebuchadnezzar. We now control Babylon.

There is an expansive biblical wildness between Pat Robertson's Bible and the one I am trying to teach in Japan. Who controls Babylon or Iraq? No one Pat Robertson names as We ever did or ever will, but this is not my stop, not my train station.

More pertinent is figuring how Robertson associates, let's say, Native Americans or African Americans or Asian Americans or for that matter Americans who immigrated from Ireland or Scotland or England, how he mixes all of the Europeans together, adding, by historical default, Angles plus Picts plus Saxons plus Celts plus Jutes plus Normans to equal Romans and made them and all of Us, whoever Us are, the biblical descendants of Nebuchadnezzar's dream. Saddam isn't the son of Nebuchadnezzar—WE are—all of us who control Babylon and who Pat Robertson deems to be part of the WE.

And in Pat Robertson's world—a world that intellectuals usually brush off as low brow but a world in which a Yale Law School graduate founded another law school whose graduates heavily populated the American Department of Justice during the Bush administration and a world that is big and status quo if you are in it—in Pat Robertson's world, by God, We are the Romans.

If we can insert ourselves into the category of the We Who Are They—something my students cannot do—We are Romans and the Children of Israel and the sons of Babylonian kings and anything else we want to be. We are ultimately the children of God, and God is the great moving target of our free associations with various ancient civilizations. It is so clear and innocent and childlike, this method of pretending.

Pretending is a habit we encourage in children. When the Bible is thrown in the mix with modern adults pretending that they have special connections with ancient people they do not have special connections with, then all involved sound like they are crazy. White Hooverite and evangelical ministers publicly defending Israel even while they maintain that the Jewish religion is dead wrong: This duplicity does not speak well for people who are believers, because at the core of this belief is saying things you do not believe.

But Pat Robertson seems to believe what he is saying. I wish biblical free associations were harmless, but they are not. People get hurt because there are no traffic signals in the heavenly kingdom of free association and pretense, and there are wrecks with other heavenly pretenders. The Middle East is often the site for these collisions. Children also get misled. *We have a lot of the Roman culture.* This is something a Sunday school teacher might say to a child. Children might even buy into the childish adult idea that, along with being members of their hometown American church, they can also be Roman. Cool. But kids are not so easy to fool. A child might have a clearer view of the boundaries of pretense than the brainwashed, adult spokesperson for the We Are They. That child might ask, "didn't the Romans have a hand in killing Jesus?" No juice and cookies for that kid.

And the We Are They preachers have to pretend that the Bible is not as harsh as it is. Who among the We Are They believe that they would sacrifice a child to God on God's command? In softer language designed for children, a Sunday school teacher might say to children in class that God asked Abraham to give

Isaac back, rather than saying that Abraham heard a voice telling him to dress out his son with a large knife, as you would a wild boar, and then cook his child on a large outdoor grill.

A child, who can pretend seventeen hundred times more than the pretending adult teacher, can quickly make the leap of imagination it takes to fill in the blanks. Not all pretending is happy pretending—any child knows this. Sometimes there is a monster in the closet of your bedroom, and sometimes he looks just like that bearded man in the Bible with his large knife who was about to gut his own child and serve him up to God. Then you have to wonder about the people who brought you this unsettling ancient story, your Sunday school teacher, or your preacher, who might look at you in a strange and fearful way one day after they have done a pronoun substitution with Abraham and begin to pretend that they have gotten the message from God to give you back.

As a child I wondered about what you had to do be given back to God. There was a fearful vagueness in this expression that incites wonder, even excitement, if you are not the one being given back. Occasionally, while on the expansive wilderness of the Tokyo train system, your train stops. You hear an announcement that there will be a delay due to a *jinshin jiko*, or, literally, a human body accident. There are those on the stopped train, including me, who pause for a moment of childlike wonder during the delay.

Maybe someone was just given back to the Train God. Or he gave himself back. Maybe it is another desperate company man leaping in his dark suit from the platform into early retirement, a short moment of flight into the tunnel of air forced forward by the Rapid Express to Takao. Some grumble at the delay; others are oddly amused by the thought. Brutal stories about someone else's bad fortune can be both scary and amusing. The Abraham and Isaac story became brutally clear to me one day when, as a child, I ran across and thumbed through a picture book of Bible stories. I saw in graphic artistic detail a picture of Abraham holding a long, sharp dagger over his son, who was tied to the desert altar, looking at his father with fearful, wide eyes.

The artist, who had probably been inspired by

Caravaggio's graphic depiction of the same scene, had not collaborated well with the Sunday school teacher at my church. We all enjoy God's grace. This was the party line, but the artist captured what the story was about. Dad and God can team up to kill you, and for no good reason. I remember looking closely at my father that night during supper as he ate, stoically lost in thought. I wondered if God was going to tell him to give back one of my brothers, or me. My oldest brother, the first born, was the first candidate for giving back. He was good kid who behaved in school and did his homework, so I figured we were safe for the time being.

It is difficult to know how my father would have responded to being told by God to sacrifice one of his sons. There were a couple of incidences that occurred among my brothers and me that resulted in severe property damage, and there were also countless human body accidents. At those times he may have been inclined to give all of us back. Maybe he tried to, but God would not take us.

I don't think so because my father was too rebellious himself, too well aware of the fact that those people in the Bible were not us. He taught adult Sunday school for decades and often found himself on the wrong side of some of the members of his class. He was too graphic in his frank, adult, non-pretending descriptions of the destructive instincts of Old Testament people and their Old Testament God. Like my father before me, I have trouble with the idea of cleaning up the brutal stories about the big, angry God for nice, middle-class students so that we all can pretend that We are They.

As for us, the WE of Pat Robertson's vision, we should be the pretending Children of Israel, the once and future children of Rome and Babylon. WE are the Chosen. To those of us who are now adults, this pretend world, even with the darkness and anger and destruction that belies its cheerfulness, can be better than Happy Hour at your favorite bar on payday. This is free association heaven with the Bible: It takes you so many interesting places, and, by spasmodic analogy, you can pretend to be anyone you want to be.

You, too, can be Roman. This approach might work

when you say hello to the suddenly artistic looking blond, who smiled at you from the corner table, or at least you pretended she did. You don't have a chance, but you approach her anyway one fuzzy hour after Happy Hour. You can tell her that you are anything but a nihilistic college English professor who can't afford to repair his old truck because you spent fourteen of the seventeen dollars you made that month on rent, the rest on booze—anything but a college English professor, eternally sentenced to poor-wage hell by the Cookout Christians who cut your checks—anything but a college English professor because at that moment, transported by the power of fermented hops and self-deception, you are at the peak of your faith-based powers to transform yourself into anything and everything you are not.

  The train is breaking, and I am jarred awake from a dream of life in the States, before Japan. Everyone is speaking Japanese, and I have been slobbering on the shoulder of the horrified grandmother sitting beside me, and my station passed us 17 stations ago. I am headed to the end of the line. Takao, the last stop, where at 1:00 am there is no return. I have perfected—almost—the Japanese art of train sleeping. During regular hours, my train-riding colleagues and I, if we're lucky enough to find a seat, know precisely how to sleep through the stops until we hear our station called out. Add two beers or more to this sleeping art, and all is lost. You might find yourself stranded in the freezing cold on the west side of hell: Takao.

  I almost slept to where there is no redemption. I am crossing the platform, heading back through the dark, long tunnels of the Tokyo night, back the long way round through the ghosts of rapid air pushed ahead by rapid trains to my tiny apartment and, if I can avoid a human body accident, back to my reflecting wall and to thinking what would happen if I were actually able to teach my exacting students how to play pretend, Pat Robertson style, with the Bible.

  If I could do that, then my students and I could have a blast returning to the pretend world of childhood. No more vexed Bible reading. We would give ourselves back to

God, who is anyone we decide we want him to be, and we can be anyone be want to be in the Good Book. We could reduce the whole Bible into one big, kiddy picture book and sing together as we watch re-runs of Barney the Dinosaur, who'll be frolicking with Adam and Eve, just like in Kentucky. Barney's good friend, Little Tommy Rex the Behemoth, is hanging out just east of Eden, and he wants to give us all a big hug before we hop on his back. He and his hug buddy Puff, the Magic Leviathan, will hump us all safely through the wilderness where we can all join our happy Christian Roman Hebrew church family for a fun war in Babylon.

Free Association V:
The White Lines of the Freeway

Hey Momma, Look At Me
I'm On My Way To The Promised Land
I'm On The Highway To Hell
—AC/DC

Down the road from Babylon is my own childhood home in the American South. In my small apartment staring at my neighbor's wall, I returned to the image of Desert Storm and to the place where people scratch their heads over open car hoods, where people are supposed to be genetically familiar with the Bible. I remembered that I was returning home after teaching a college class in a university near where I grew up. I was driving west through the swampy wilderness of Interstate 20, somewhere between Florence and Bishopville, South Carolina—in the Year of Our Lord, nineteen hundred and I forget—but it was during Desert Storm, and I think it was February of that year because I remember they waited until after the Super Bowl to start the war, so that the light shows, the first bombs and missiles hitting Baghdad, could get their props on cable news.

A pickup truck came up behind me going at a good clip. I passed the next car and eased over to the slow lane. The driver gave me a wave as he passed, index finger and thumb extended as he cruised by. On the back of his truck was a big wilderness marker, a bumper sticker that read, "I Support Operation Dessert Storm."

Anti-war humor? But the driver, his truck, his wave, the gun rack with gun, his 24-inch neck, the baseball cap with the words, having reversed the letters previously from my rearview mirror, that said, "Eat Me," didn't signal the type of guy who would make anti-war jokes. I do not doubt that big sumbitch was transporting more issues than dessert storm with him while barreling through the wilderness in his pickup truck.

Eat me, Dessert Storm, I thought. The pick-up truck driver, given the signs that led me to think that he had never been the nerdy know-it-all at the front of his English class, did not notice the difference between the spellings of desert and dessert because spelling had never been a priority for him. We have all made spelling errors and have come short of the glory of our middle school English teachers.

But now free associating about other markers, about the 17 billion spelling errors I corrected in the billions of freshman compositions I had to read where I was teaching nearby. I was in my first job at a college heavily salted with "I'm a Christian," Christians—the type who tell you that they are Christians every 5 minutes as if you were the one wracked with doubt—the college I had to commute 17 billion miles to every day in order to get paid seventeen dollars a month by the Cookout Christians. I was teaching kids who hailed from the Bible Belt, many of whom cited the Bible, or what they thought was the Bible, as a source for things they said in their freshman compositions.

But they rarely quoted chapter and verse, which is good, because people who quote select chapters and verses of the Bible in support of various modern agendas (see Pat Robertson and me above) are more annoying than people who don't bother. But many of these students, the children of the swampy wilderness, typically drew a blank when I brought up the book of Job.

At the beginning of Job, God allows his advocate, Satan, to kill the children of Job in order to up the ante on God's bet with Satan that Job will remain loyal to God. Job's children are killed (given back to God?) and Job loses everything he owns. And this is for starters. Job is an all time favorite. It is a superb story, complete with stark, brutal images of death and disease that will give you nightmares as you re-read it wide awake, heading west out of central Tokyo on the Chuo line.

I thought about the book of Job a lot in those days because I felt at that time that I was living it. Well trained to stretch analogies, I took the big noun, Job, and substituted the tiny pronoun, me. Lost in the wilderness, teaching in a small college in the Bible Belt, a place where bible-talk was ubiquitous but where Job was curiously absent, in a system where highly-paid, good Christian administrators, some of whom, I think, were secretly Hooverites, were dismissive of teachers and their place in the food chain of education.

Reading freshman compositions, similar to reading the book of Job, will trouble your sleep. Then while staring blankly at my neighbor's wall with no writing on it, a blinding light came through the window and a sad melody sounded from heaven. I realized, suddenly, horribly, that I could remember every freshman essay I ever read.

Stories are more interesting when you go over the top in their telling. Ask any storyteller, or any of the gentlemen who wrote the books of the Bible. Actually my neighbor turned on his outside light because it was getting dark, and, in Japan, public address systems play a sad tune throughout the neighborhoods each evening to let children at the park know that it is time to stop playing with the dinosaurs and return home for supper. I was only struck with the memory of one freshman essay, which was retribution enough, or maybe no real retribution at all, given that I am not certain the God of Moses would want to punish a reformed nihilist who advocates close reading of the Bible.

This student, who was a good writer, argued against abortion. While reading his paper I was angry with myself for assigning a paper on abortion. I was running short of topics. Normal people are uneasy about the abortion issue. Many of those who drive themselves crazy being pro-life have chosen abortion in the past, and most of those who are righteously pro-choice have never been faced with having to make such a weighty choice. The rest of us would rather not talk about it.

The pro-life writer was well on his way to making an "A" on his paper, doing a good job of faking his way through his position on a topic I am sure he did not care to write about. He got to the Bible, stating, along with many of his less talented classmates, that the Bible is against abortion. He did not give any supporting evidence from the Bible because in that world you do not have to. He finished by proclaiming that abortion should be outlawed, "except in cases of rape, incest, and sodomy."

I was recently divorced from a woman who understandably did not want to be married to a man who only made seventeen dollars a month after taxes and a man who was often in a bad mood after reading billions of essays on bad topics of his devising, after being lectured to by a young writer on the biblical virtues of going through with a pregnancy, even if the pregnancy is the result of sodomy.

The woman had insisted in the early, halcyon days of marriage, the days before bad topics and poor pay, before the wilderness, when she and the man were happy students, that the man's old but perfectly reliable car should be sold because her rich father was going to give them a nicer car. But the rich father, after the marriage went sour, insisted on getting his car back, complete with its healthy head gaskets and well-oiled rods. This left the man, who was poor and typically in a bad mood (see above), with only enough money to buy a small paint-less pickup truck made in the 18th century that could barely go the speed limit on Interstate 20, even with the pedal to the floor, a floor you could see through in various places. This is why the man was easily passed on the highway by the guy with the 24-inch neck who could not spell very well but who had a far nicer pickup truck.

No wonder the dessert storm man gave the paint-less pickup man a friendly wave when he passed. He felt sorry for the guy. Maybe he even felt a kinship with his less fortunate brethren of the wilderness, the man whose rusty bumper alone stood as his bumper sticker, his sign of many other issues in transport, including a soon to be fried head gasket and rattling rods to be thrown, a tired man in a tired truck struggling to make a buck in his religious homeland. This was good raw material for a country-western song, one in which a college English professor thinks the joke is on someone else, but it is actually on him.

And the joke is not on Pat Robertson or religious

Hooverites making wild, spasmodic, and free associations. It is on the intellectuals, just as guilty of making our own free associations but we have not figured out a way to make a decent living with them, have not figured out how to make people around us feel better about themselves.

It was time to decamp from the great Babylonian trek, take up line dancing on the Pacific Rim, where our pals will be glad to see us when we show up on Tuesday night at the Home on the Range Club, Shibuya Branch, in our cowboy hats and chaps. I think the train passed my station a few sentences ago.

My narrative comes nowhere close to the suffering of Job. But my point is that this story may explain why the man in the paint-less truck, in good biblical fashion, went into exile from his religious homeland and ended up teaching the Bible in a place where people do not know the Bible, where they do not feel they know the Bible, where they do not freely associate the Bible or what they think is in the Bible with anything they happen to be staring at, a land that has become this man's land of milk and honey, that is, if you substitute the words *sushi* and *sake* for milk and honey.

The land where the apartments are small and the walls speak back to you by not speaking at all. The pay grade for professors is much bigger, set by not-Christian folks who view teachers as *homo sapiens*, fellow bipeds in the methodical walk of life. The heathens who now surround this man think that college English professors are a little upscale. The post Happy Hour artistic blond isn't a blond anymore. You do not have to lie or pretend, not as much. You leave the venue late and alone and hail a cab because there is no way you would wake up before Korea if you took the train. The cab will cost 17 billion dollars, but it doesn't matter because the great thing about Japan is that drinking makes you rich.

No tsunami, not yet, no reptiles, no raptures, no beasts, and the dinosaurs and Godzilla and the Great Catfish are sleeping for now, and the world is safe and shallow and the lights of Shibuya are line dancing with the white lines of the road home. The not-Christian taxi driver speeds through the concrete desert to your tiny apartment buried deep in this concrete. You mumble convoluted instructions in Japanese for him to find Itsukaichi Road somewhere on the south side of West Ogikubo. "Then," you say, "head straight, and wake me up when we get to the Subaru sign." He sings "Yesterday" with you part of the way, even bows ironically to his steering wheel when he learns you are *Sensei*, miraculously finds your apartment, and wakes you up politely and never overcharges you. Big and small in Japan.

Tokyo's immaculately conceived taxi service, the driver's perfect cap with its shiny bill makes you think again of pronouns and bumper stickers and homeland and the biblical markers in that old wilderness. The posters and billboards that zip by in Tokyo transform from the tic-tac-toes of Japanese to the Roman letters of English. *We have a lot of the Roman culture*, big markers in the wilderness pointing in the wrong direction, signs that insist so strongly somebody else's God must also be your God. I cannot shake from memory the back road billboard advice I saw in the most profound Pee Dee region of South Carolina after a wrong turn: "Love Jesus or Burn in Hell." Wouldn't it be more accurate to say, "We Hate You—and Don't Much Like Ourselves"? But my contrary ideas for religious signs would not be much more alluring:

> *Moses never got out.*
> *Give Job a Break.*
> *Free Associate This.*
> *I am a True Believer—I Think.*

Better than these is the "Eat Me" baseball cap, which is much more to the point and even something that Jesus would say.

The absence of such billboards, plus the sushi and sake and biped pay grade makes my little rabbit hutch of an apartment comfortable, but this is not where I am from. I am from that little country house beside that old, vast, smoky, stormy wilderness highway of free-associating Christians. The Bible took a detour from that highway and found me here, living among the non-shazamites, in this heathen wilderness of small things, where I am not lost but where I keep missing my station because I get lost in thought or fall asleep on the train, where, even now, I find myself staring at the neighbor's wall in a Zen trance. The penalty for pissing on it wouldn't be anywhere near as severe as it is for pissing on the walls of old Jerusalem. And that's another good thing about Japan.

I am a living composite of this imaginary biblical world of childhood and beyond, and also neurologically tied to it, and it makes me nervous when I shouldn't be nervous, to have the Bible-that-is and the Bible-that-is-not find me here in my adopted land. I am Jonah, attempting to run and hide from Pat Robertson. Pat and his pals have found me here and have put me, at various times, under house arrest, or tiny-apartment arrest, where I catch myself staring at the wall that I've gotten to know far better than my neighbor will, or will ever want to.

They want me back home, with their out-of-context verses, their nouns turned pronouns, their *they*, the Satans, the devils, the evil ones, the other enemies we often have trouble naming, being fought by the *we*, the Roman Christian Jewish Babylonian sons of Nebuchadnezzar with our biblical billboards and bumper stickers—the desert warriors. The image, now coming online in my head, of a more recent war fought on biblical turf, financed from newer stormy wildernesses across the world—back to Babylon.

This blended with memories of young American college students who seem pre-programmed to relate the word *Bible* with the word *abortion*, a word that I can't find in the Bible. The biblical memory of a student against pregnancy by anal sex.

More select memories of that particular tribe of young students back home, not the party types but the serious-minded kids who are now twenty years older. These children are now all grown up. Some of them joined the Cookout Christians. Some fly intermittently with Highway Jesus, while others inherited the mantle of the Hooverites of the desert storms of yore. The old Hooverites are still out there, carving out new pretend subdivisions for their flocks with Pat Robertson and always heading toward a new Babylon. In the old days the wilderness was well populated with Hooverites, and, alas, it is now even more populated, regenerated by a new, larger bloodline of lovers of over stretched and brutal free associations. The next generation joins the old guard.

These are the generations of pronoun abusing, free-associating once and future Highway Jesus Christians and Hooverites from the Bible Belt and far beyond, who piss you off because they have sandwiched you between their own adamantly abstracted generations, who piss you off because they have renewed in you the old biblical burden of profound and lengthy cursing, who piss you off because their wilderness scouts have caught up with you and Hoovered you back in from the other side of the earth, back to a wilderness you can never escape, who piss you off because they are with you even as you blast into western Tokyo down the Chuo Line into the small lights of 17 billion tiny apartments embedded in a desert of not Christian concrete, who piss you off because their pretend Bible denies you a portion of the sweet side of bittersweet exile, who piss you off because these people, in your perpetual efforts to reject them, are you. Their wilderness is forever your wilderness. Regardless of what wilderness you try to escape from, you are still barreling with them down that free associating highway of total recall, heading due west, through the desert and into the storm.

Section Three: Creating Gods In Creation

For, dear me, why abandon a belief
Merely because it ceases to be true.
—The preacher speaking in Robert Frost's
"The Black Cottage"

The Curse of the Colonel

It's just another weeknight in *Yurakucho*, an enormous commercial district in central Tokyo. The company people are drinking *nihonshu*, Japanese whiskey, and eating *yakitori*— meat and other things on a stick. And talking it up. This is where the mid-level company guys—the backbone of the Japanese economy, the enduring men and women of the economic miracle— come with their groups after work. It's close to the station. If you're a Japanese salary man drinking after work, the station is like first base: You don't want to be caught too far away from it. You have an hour, maybe two, on the train, ahead of you. You'll get home late, but you have to make it home. It's a rule. You're drinking for a couple of hours, maybe more, with your colleagues after work because—well—because it's a rule. There're no less that 17 million small *izakaya*, little bar/restaurants, to chose from, most of them lined up and packed under brightly lit red lights in a long, long line under the *Yamanote* train line.

Yurakucho isn't my style, but my buddy, Wayne, wanted me to see the event. It's not Christmas, or July 4th, or a special Japanese holiday or any other official celebration. It's just another night. But every work night office people convene for the religious celebration that follows the sanctified act of plowing your way through another day of work in Japan.

We take our seats at one of many indoor-outdoor joints and order beer and food. The folks at the surrounding tables are feeling good—everyone is into their cups. The whiskey and the food are just too good after another stressful day, and the rising smoke from cigarettes hints that the night is spiraling to a close. The train time cometh. Rumbling the ground from above are the final trains sweeping through the air, their horns blow through like so many ominous trumpets.

Everyone is friendly to the two gaijin intruders in a glassy eyed sort of way. Our drinks come. A guy from a table, catty corner to ours, suddenly points at me.

"*Baa-su! Baa-su!*" he yells out, pointing at me. His friends look over. Another guy says, "*Kaaneru Sandaasu niwa nite nai yo.*"

I don't look like *Kaaneru Sandaasu*. Who? Everyone laughs. The pretty office lady, a stock addition to any group of working men, gives me a wave, a polite way of saying that her cohorts mean no harm.

"*Baa-su! Baa-su!*" the guy hollers agains. Then he falls backwards from his flimsy chair and rolls into the street, but not before his foot hits the flimsy table, sending everything on it, glasses of whiskey and all, shattering to pieces on the concrete floor. Everyone pauses—no one gets upset, not even the owner, who quickly appears. Now there's a job to do, and company people and bar staff on cue get busy doing what, in Japan, is the empowering, even exhilarating act of cleaning up a mess. Nothing brings more meaning to these ordered lives than calamity.

"Any clue what that was about?" I say under my breath to Wayne.

"You don't know?"

"Give me a hint," I say.

"You look like Randy Bass, but you don't look like Colonel Sanders."

"Kaaneru Sandaasu. Okay, I get it. Baa-su, Bass, I get it. Who's Randy Bass?"

"You don't know?"

"Give me a hint."

Wayne then gives me the abriged version of one of the most spectacular chapters in the history of Japanese baseball. He's logged more Japan time than I have.

As it turns out I look like the legendary gaijin slugger, Randy Bass, at least that night to a cross-eyed drunk guy who saw me from 15 feet away before he tumbled, suit and tie and whiskey and all, out onto the street.

In the mid-80s Randy Bass played for the Hanshin

Tigers in the Kansai (Osaka) region of Japan, a region second only to Tokyo in being able to pile mass humanity on trains daily. Much like the Boston Red Socks of the 20th century, the Tigers were the established underdogs of Japanese baseball, and had to live in the purgatorial shadow of the Yomiuri Giants of Tokyo, who have historically dominated Japanese baseball much like the New York Yankees in the States. The Hanshin Tigers have always had devoted fans, notoriously zany and known throughout Japan for being unmatched in their ability to cling desperately to the perennial hope that their team will be champions.

These fans lived under their own Curse of the Bambino for years until the magical season of 1985. To everyone's surprise, particularly to the astonishment of their own fans, the Tigers, led by star American slugger, Randy Bass, made it to the championship series where they held off the powerful Seibu Lions and won the Japan Championship.

The fans went nuts, and a hoard of revelers congregated at *Ebisubashi*, literally, the bridge over the river of the happy God, Ebisu, in Osaka, to carry out a strange ritual—maybe strangeness is what makes a ritual a ritual. Each fan who had been selected as best resembling a player on the team was to jump from the bridge into the river below when his player's name was called. And so they did, plunging into the water below on cue and then swimming their way out. Scary, but at least no one drowned, at least not on that night.

So far so good, as far as drunken baptismal sacrifices to the gods of your local baseball team are concerned. The only problem was that no one remotely resembled Randy Bass.

As the story goes, someone in the congregation figured that the plastic statue of Colonel Sanders outside a nearby Kentucky Fried Chicken was the closest thing that anyone at that undiscriminating hour could find that looked like Randy Bass. The happy *ojiisan*, the smiling grandfatherly image of the Colonel, commonly seen in front of Kentucky Fried Chicken outlets, is famous and even beloved in Japan—it's one of those heathen religious things, honoring, celebrating old age.

But Colonel Sanders is still, after all, a gaijin, and, like Bass, he had a beard, so for that night, at least from yards away to the cross-eyed drunken revelers, the image was likeness enough. He'd have to stand in for Bass. The effigy of Randy Bass, the distinguished Colonel Sanders, was shanghaied and then launched into the river.

You wake up sober, with a headache, and then start thinking about the mistakes you made the night before. You think about the difference between the new God, or *kami*, Randy Bass, and the Colonel, who was already a kami of sorts. Maybe this sacrificing one God to another was a little out of hand. Maybe you took things too far. What a calamity.

The Hanshin Tigers resumed their normal habit of losing games the next year. And this was the beginning of "The Curse of the Colonel," the era of no more Japan Championships, because the Colonel is angry about being thrown in the river. Searchers were dispatched to the Ebisu river to find the Colonel and restore him to his former majesty, but with no luck. Recently, well after two decades, the Colonel was found by accident. He was pulled from the river and put on display again. He looks like a post-modern male version of the Venus de Milo. At this writing, the Tigers haven't won a Japan championship since 1985, and legend has it that they never will as long as the Colonel remains angry. Given the way he looks, this may be a long time.

I recently visited Kobe. In 1995, Kobe was the site of the great Hanshin Earthquake. The Great Catfish stirred and the resulting quake destroyed the town and took the lives of over 6,000 people. Kobe has been rebuilt now, restored to its former majesty by the sea, repaired more quickly and completely than the damage from the Colonel Sanders calamity. Kobe is also Hanshin Tiger territory.

At the bar in the hotel where I was staying, I got into a conversation with a couple of locals. Happy, distinguished, grandfatherly guys. One of them says in Japanese, "You look like Randy Bass."

I paused, "but do I look like Colonel Sanders?"

They broke out in laughter. The guy says in English, "Randy Bass is a god to us." He looked at me admiringly.

I like resembling one, maybe two, of the honorary gaijin gods of Japan. I like the innocent notion that you need no more pedigree than to resemble a god to become god-like. Maybe resemblance itself is godly—there is even a biblical precedent for this idea. We, too, hold the great God-like power to destroy all, as those who continue their struggles in Fukushima and northern Japan know too well, those whose world was shattered on March 11th, 2011. In this case the mess made by the gods has proven easier to clean than the un-godly, man-made mess made from shattering atoms into pieces. This is a calamity indeed more intractable than the curse of the Colonel, one that will outlast even the enduring curses of the mountain God of Moses.

A simple Buddhist chant is more fitting, here in the land of the smaller gods, than a high and mighty Christian benediction: "*Yonaoshi, yonaoshi*. May the world be repaired, may the world return to normal." What meaning can be gained from calamity, but that calamity is meaning itself?

In Search of the River God: Part I

In a dark time, the eye begins to see.
—Theodore Roethke, "In a Dark Time"

We will have our gods. But where is our happy God, our river God, the God of the rivers we know, the God who relieves us from the fearsome God of the unknown desert?

The New Testament, good news though it may bring, is not a happy area of the Bible on the whole. As in so much of the Old Testament, there are the mass slaughters—Herod's slaughter of the children, the lake of fire that so many will be thrown into the Revelation. There are killings—John the Baptist and Jesus and Stephen. There are beatings and torture. And stories of despair. The New Testament is one of the few places in written history where a reader is left feeling sorry for a rich man. The Jesus narratives, with their prominent calls for all-embracing love, still leave us with one of the great textual sources for anti-Semitism in John, where "the Jews" are represented as the menacing other. We are given a chance for eternal life—which is literally uplifting but completely mind-boggling.

Maybe the most under-considered feature of the New Testament is the example of courageous or crazed souls revising and then outright rejecting long established religious dogma. My students see this feature, and of course the questions come about how Christians deal with a Bible that, in its entirety, rebels against itself.

The spirit of the rebellion is carried forward on several fronts in the New Testament, the most obvious being word of mouth teaching and preaching and then the establishment of alternative church groups. Less obvious, but more important in the long run, is the fact that members of this renegade religious sect had the sense to record and preserve their writings. But these writings would have been of little consequence to the generations that followed if they had not been informed by close interpretations of specific Old Testament writings, if they had not been linked to the long standing tradition they were rebelling against. The writers knew that in any lasting attempt to free yourself from religious dogma, to undo the many shazams embedded in your religious tradition, to find your own God, be it Jesus or the River God of your own river, you have to start by reading and writing your way out of the established written tradition.

The rebels who wrote the books of the New Testament had a powerful sponsor. Their liberation was not exactly liberation but a radical shift in allegiance. The movement needed a new Messiah to carry out the interpretive rebellion, and the new Messiah, be he Jesus or the Pope or Mohammed or Martin Luther or the Archbishop of Canterbury or Joseph Smith et al., will not free you, in the end, from the Bible any more than the New Testament Messiah freed Christians from the Old Testament or its God.

Circumcision is important in the Bible. It was the ID card for the Chosen. There is a Japanese word for circumcision, but my students do not understand the circular meaning of the Japanese word, a word that, like circumcision, does not explain precisely the delicate operation that Japanese men do not usually undergo and that no man that I have met feels comfortable thinking about. I explain circumcision on the chalkboard.

Polygamy is another difficult concept for my students, why polygamy was fully accepted in ancient biblical culture and sanctioned by God. That was then, but when asked about how circumcision and polygamy play out in the modern Christian world, you have to say that, yes, circumcision is still fashionable for men in the Christian world. It is seen by many as good hygiene, but not a marker for being chosen. Polygamy, in most places, is against the law of man. And, if you leave off the Bible, you can argue that polygamy is against the law of God. But polygamy still exists in the Christian world.

I am not looking for a fight with any modern religious practice that claims to ride smoothly on the bumpy road of the

Bible, but with my students looking on, I do want to secure my place in a belief system that unhinges my own practices from ancient practices that are no longer necessary or have become immoral in our time. This is our time, not theirs. I reject the practice of polygamy, and I do not think there is anything wrong with eating shrimp. But the River God I am searching for, happy though he may be, is no Messiah, so those who agree with me are vulnerable, being left with no tradition to reform to our own positions while we search for a new champion.

Let's learn from experience, drop the failed teaching modules that I tried early on, and just read the text closely and critically—beyond Christianity. This route works best, though it isn't always well paved. Returning to the opening chapter of Genesis, let's try to illuminate as much as possible the dark time of God, when God began to see, a time long before Christianity.

> In the beginning, God created the heaven and the earth . (1:1)

This famous topic sentence holds the two primary areas of existence: the heaven and the earth. There is no planet Mars in this world or planet earth. In this version the word is heaven, not heavens, because heaven, in the Bible and long after the Bible, begins as a physical place above. Earth is not a sphere, but flat dry land surrounded by life and death giving water.

> And the earth was without form, and void; and darkness was upon the face of the deep. And the Spirit of God moved upon the face of the waters. (1:2)

The formless void is the watery deep that will have to be parted to make room for God's physical creation. God first makes light and then parts it from the darkness:

> And God said, Let there be light: and there was light. (1:3)

All things made by God are good. Light is good. God created it to offset the dark, watery void.

Some take offense when you refer to the writers of the early books of the Bible as primitives or even ancients. But they did not have electric light bulbs, or even flashlights. For us the primal importance of light is not obvious, that is, until our lights click off during a power outage. Pitch darkness and creation are opposites.

Light is good in a world where people lived closer to the unnerving encroachment of darkness than we normally do. In my class I turn off all the lights in the room while teaching this verse, a low tech teaching aid. But not for long, because having the lights off makes my students nervous. There is something disquieting about sitting with others in the dark.

After God makes light in the dark void, he separates light from dark (1:4), dividing, naming. Light makes Day possible. Day gives us Time. The work of the first day is to make Day, by naming and separating day from night, a time of light, and so that we have Time itself. When evening and darkness come, followed by morning, is a unit of time: One Day.

And the evening and the morning were the first day. (1:5)

The first day ends the morning of the second day. A new day technically starts for us at 12:00 am, not sunrise or morning, but we have digital clocks—along with our man-made lights.

With light and time in place, God begins serious construction work. He makes the firmament (1:6) by parting the waters of the void, "under" and "above" (1:7). The firmament is the most important physical construct in Genesis and in the Bible. It is the place God names Heaven (1:8), the physical area that holds back the watery void and that makes room for sky and air. It is in the distance, but not that far away. The idea of heaven is still intact in modern Christianity, but it cannot be the awe-inspiring firmament of Genesis, the place where God sits.

We are the children of Copernicus. We take light for granted, and we have lost the hard-domed ceiling overhead. Science and technology giveth, and science and technology taketh away. The earth or dry land under the firmament in Genesis is a flat area, with mountains. This land and sea is the area covered by the firmament, the dome, the heaven.

Dry land is a far smaller area than the continents of Planet Earth today, although the region, for those who had no flashlights, no cars, trains, or planes, was big. God's roost in the firmament places him in a physical Heaven. This is a powerful, material cosmos constructed by a powerful being, the ceiling of which holds back enormous amounts of water, a universe far more local, but magnificent and real, more real than in the abstract amorphous heavens where this God must be placed today. This Genesis firmament is where God looks over them—in the mega Hoover Dam of the grand expanse of sky. God creates this real, physical place on the second day.

God gathers and parts the water below Heaven (1:9). He then gives the land grass—vegetation or food. He follows by producing herbs and fruit bearing trees—more food, important because it is free. These natural things are created "after their kind," a phrase that is difficult to understand but that points to the happy fact that the grasses, herbs, and fruit in turn produce their own seeds, so that they replenish with more of the same kind of good food freely. A fine system, one inserted into the Genesis biosphere, the new enormous complex about to be completed before the management team arrives. Day Three.

Day four presents another challenge in Genesis. Light and Day and Time have been made, but not the things that give light to the new development called dry land. The house is wired for electricity, but it still needs light bulbs. So God hangs the big lamp, the sun, and the lesser lights, the moon and stars. The sun is not a separate planet but the largest light among the "lights in the firmament of the heaven" (1:15). The sun, or "the greater light to rule the day" (1:16), the moon or "the lesser light to rule the night" (1:16) and the stars are the rotational light bulbs in this firmament. Light rules.

If you add the elements of this domed sky that are not mentioned but that are also physically present—the rain, the clouds, the lightening, the occasional meteor showers and comets, in sum all of the elements of sky are manifestations of a physically powerful God. Together, these elements of sky are wondrous and close physical evidence of God's existence and his sweeping control of this local and material cosmos.

On dry land, the "four corners" of a smaller section of land in the biblical world, those people think that going to a mountain top puts them closer to God, not only spiritually, but physically—both in one. You see why, later in Genesis, a group of people might venture to build a tower to reach heaven.

More creatures are created on day five. This grouping is more elusive than the plant life. The "moving" creatures, the birds of the air and the whales and fishes of the sea seem a strange grouping of unlike creatures, but the Genesis writer is making a distinction between migrating creatures of the sea and air and landlocked creatures—like cattle—that do not move around as much. This idea presents no problem in my class. The word for animal in Japanese is *doubutsu*, which, in kanji, could be read as "moving things." And creatures that move around too much and beyond our means to contain them cannot be owned. On the fifth day, we also see creatures that reproduce themselves differently from the plant life of the third day. These creatures are charged to "be fruitful and multiply." Procreation is encouraged in the new creation because procreation in animal and, later, in human species, is abundance, the good life, wealth and security.

Day six brings the cattle and the beasts of the field. The big animals are created along with the creepy crawling things on the ground—the land animals. Day six also brings mankind, men and women in separate forms, parted and categorized just as the water is parted from dry land and each part of nature is made after its own kind. Men and women, in the plural form, are created, and are able to recreate themselves.

Just like that. All are told to be fruitful and multiply by a happy and self-pleased God, a jolly God who in verse 29 even sounds like a vegetarian, with his talk of providing herbs and fruit for "meat." The Bible starts well, with a powerful but happy God who is the type who might like to have a beer with his good natured, but lesser friend, the River God. This marvelous state of affairs will not last for long. There will be blood.

In class, during our reading of the early verses of Genesis, students are initially confused by descriptions that are, indeed, confusing to people who live on Planet Earth. They are also confused about the style of biblical writing, so familiar to me, so alien to them. The most prominent stylistic habit of this writing is repetition. The phrase, "it was good" is used six times in the King James Version, Genesis 1, followed, finally and in sum by, "it was very good." Seven repetitions, seven days—seven is an important number in the Bible. There is a chanting repetition of creative acts described in this creative writing, including a short poem toward the end of chapter 1:

> So God created man in his own image, in the image of God created he him; male and female created he them. (27)

This repetition and chanting, a feature found throughout the Bible, smacks of the type of training salespeople get. The aspiring leader of a new cult understands the value of this habit naturally.

But the Bible should not fall in with bad company here. The repetition and chanting belong to a teaching and preaching style found in texts that are crafted to be spoken rather than read. During its time and for many centuries later only a relative few would have access to these words as a text that could be read, and few could read. Far more could listen to it being read. These writers did not have the luxury of making copies or print outs for audiences, like I do for my classes. They did not have the luxury of literacy.

They did not have readers. They had listeners, and they wanted their listeners to remember as much as possible. Repetition. The common protocol in church services to this day is for members to listen to preaching, often hearing the oral cadences of repetition in the Bible. Any good preacher knows, any good teacher knows, indeed any good sales person knows the value of repetition in driving ideas home to an audience.

If we listen to the Bible, if we back away a bit from its drum banging and look at the great domed world described in Genesis 1, we can see them vigorously reckoning with their cosmology and environment. In the beginning, all is happy and good. We see, potentially at least, a call to have a thankful relationship with the powerful creator of this abundant world. In the beginning, the parameters are laid out. There is the domain of God, the firmament or heaven, and the area inhabited and dominated by man, the dry land—then the free, self-sustaining and life-sustaining food given to them by God. The simple children's prayer before meals is a perfect summation:

> God is great, God is good,
> Let us thank him for our food.

We imagine how they saw the expanses of water on their coastlines and the rivers, we learn how, for them, the rainwater pours from the firmament, when the "windows of heaven" are opened, we read, later in Genesis, about how much water they had underneath them in the "fountains of the great deep" (7:11), then we understand why the writer and many among his people felt that water was the primal element, "the deep," that preceded firmament and dry land, and we understand why they felt that God first would have to separate water from water, above, below and to the sides, to forge a space for his abundant creation.

What a great God and what a great sustainable place he made. He is indeed much better than a simple river god, that is, until you get him angry. He then un-parts the water from above, below, and to the sides of your world. You are, after all, only tucked inside the massive dark, soon-to-be wet void of the nothing that is there and the nothing that is not there.

In Search of the River God: Part II

*I said, "It's certain there is no fine thing
Since Adam's fall but needs much labouring."*
-W.B. Yeats, "Adam's Curse"

My students find it odd that Genesis 1 finishes on the 6th day. The first three verses of Genesis 2 end with God blessing the 7th day as a day of rest, but these verses fit better with the narrative of Genesis 1. This abrupt division stands out because verse four of Genesis 2 begins a new story, one that really does not settle with the accounts in Genesis 1. The Genesis writer or writers did not have a Genesis 1. And this is precisely when, early on, new and large troubles begin, namely the problems that arise when charting your way through the murky void that is the textual history of the Bible.

Any discussion of textual history puts students to sleep, just shortly after confusing them, and me. I know this from experience, but textual history is important, even though this search will fail to bring us any closer to anyone's god.

(1) There is no use in talking about how the individual scrolls of the whole original Bible looked. Aside from fragments of early Biblical writing, there is nothing that could be called original full manuscripts of any of the earliest books of the Old Testament in our possession. Any full or almost full text in Hebrew or Greek, any snippet of Aramaic that has been consulted to translate from sources close to the original languages were preserved hundreds of years after the books of the Old Testament were written.

New Testament texts are another matter, but they too emerged well after the fact. Certain religious speakers argue vigorously that now lost source manuscripts for Bibles were perfectly or nearly perfectly preserved over time and copying and re-copying. But we cannot be sure what changes are made in copied manuscripts we no longer have, manuscripts that arose long before the printing press, manuscripts that were copied and translated by hand again and again over hundreds of years. My students, having had the grueling experience of learning Chinese characters by hand through rote practice in grade school, could not agree more.

(2) What we do know is that the books of the Bible were divided into chapters long after the early Christian era. There was no Genesis 1 until someone other than God created Genesis 1 a long, long time after the writing on the scroll.

(3) The verse numbers of the King James Bible were taken from the 16th century Geneva Bible, which was the first Bible in English to have verse numbers. So the verses for Bibles in English were added a long, long time after the era when Genesis was first written. These verses were added by man, not God.

Lopping off the last portion of the Genesis 1 story and placing it at the beginning of Genesis 2 looks to be an attempt to give the reader (not the listener) a sense of unity between the first creation story and what follows—another creation story. Genesis 2:4 begins another account of the "generations of the heavens and the earth," the famous green story of the Garden of Eden. This story, too, begins happily with God creating, in reverse order "earth and the heavens." The King James translators have now settled on the plural form for heaven. Maybe all of the new bright lights give the hard firmament the image of having multiple levels. But, in Genesis 2, there is no talk of light or day (Day 1) or parting the waters to make the firmament (Day 2) or dry land with vegetation, herbs, and trees (Day 3). The second story quickly focuses on the vegetation, which is not on earth yet because there is no man to till the soil. In Genesis 1, the vegetation, herbs, and fruit trees sprung forth before any man was in sight.

In the second creation it is a man, one man, who is created from the dust. This man is created before the vegetation and all else on dry land. Now Ms. Haneda is confused, "Didn't God create people last? Didn't he create a lot of people?" she asks.

Of course the answer is yes, for Genesis 1. Men and women were created last. In Genesis 2, man comes earlier, and only one man, whom God brings to life by breathing into his nostrils. Then God plants a garden complete with vegetation and fruits trees, notably the forbidden tree of the knowledge of good and evil. The first vegetation, the first trees, are clearly brought forth after the man is created. The garden is planted east of Eden, and he places the man in the garden. At this point God seems like a child doing an arts and crafts project.

In this narrative the focus is not on the cosmos, but on a specific geophysical area on earth, a place that, at least according to the brochure information we are now given, would make a fine location for a retirement home. Water is important, although not in the same way that water is important in Genesis 1. For a few verses, we have a happy River God in the making, with the pastoral description of the river that flows from Eden and breaks into four branches, each branch bringing life-sustaining water to the regions that comprise their desert world. The tone is of a writer who assumes his reader, or listener, knows about the locations to which all the river branches flow. We are not they, so these verses are obscure. This was their turf, their geography, the dry land of their belief, whether or not it proves accurate to the particulars of modern geography. The source of their rivers is the earthly paradise of God, a real place, but one that cannot be entered by men because of what happens later.

Adam is given the good life in the lush garden, which he is to "dress and keep," a pleasurable assignment. He can eat from any tree, except one. Life is good, albeit boring. God makes other creatures so that Adam does not have to live alone. We are told that God makes the beasts and fowl for Adam, so that Adam can enjoy giving them names.

Ms. Haneda puts on her perplexed face. "Of course, Ms. Haneda, in Genesis 1 the beasts and fowl were created before any people were made. But this is Genesis 2. It's a different story."

"But why two?" she asked.

"I don't know."

I push on. God made time in Genesis 1, so now I live

in a world of time. Only a few minutes to go, and I have to get through Genesis 2 before the end of class.

Beast and birds can only go so far to keep a single man company, so God puts Adam under and pulls out part of his side, and uses that to make woman. After the woman enters the story, life is not boring anymore. The chapter ends with the pronouncement that man and wife are one flesh. Adam and Eve are naked and unashamed in the Garden of Eden.

The chimes sound (Lead me Lord) just before I finish. I hurry off to teach another class, but I am apprehended by Ms. Haneda, and her friend, Ms. Aoki. She points back to Genesis 1, to the part where God tells people to be fruitful and multiply. "Why not Adam and Eve?" she wants to know.

"It's a different story," I say as I hurry down the busy hallway. "And next week we'll be thrown out of the garden."

Several students passing by give us strange looks. "What do you mean—*we* will be thrown out?" Ms. Aoki asks.

In Search of the River God: Part III

*There are more things in heaven and earth, Horatio,
Than are dreamt of in your philosophy.* —Hamlet

The Garden of Eden story, the second creation story, does not settle well with the first creation story, but this is religious thinking. Religious thinking provokes contemplation. And contemplation involves both acceptance and dispute—both at the same time. Maybe this is an early, maybe the earliest version of what you could call a Hebrew compromise. Two groups of Hebrew priests meet to discuss two inspiring but different versions of creation. They argue bitterly over which version best serves God and the needs of their people. After an exhausting dispute for days on end, the head priests from both sides decide to settle the matter. One says, "Can we agree to disagree?" The other says, "Only if we can meet regularly to argue this matter further." The first says, "Done, but we must agree to write down both of these stories so that we and the generations who follow us can dispute this matter—"

All from both sides finish the sentence, strongly in unison, and chanting, "*until the end of time.*"

The compromise in place, members are barely able to contain their joy over the outcome. They have created something more than the creation. They have created a creation debate that can be fiercely and joyfully debated forever. They break for tea. The head priest from one group puts his arm around the head priest from the other group. "Now Josh," he says, "tell me—how many goats do you have now? And the wives—are they still producing sons for you?"

Religion involves contemplation and contemplation involves acceptance and dispute. Many want only the acceptance part, which arguably is not religious, given that Christianity and other religions, too, are the sum total, not only of their histories of acceptance, but also of their histories of dispute. Still many are uncomfortable with inconsistencies. They ruin the joy of dispute with the unilateral proclamation that the Bible has no inconsistencies at all. Say it, repeat it over and over. When the textual evidence to the contrary threatens to be heard, then shout it down.

In Japan, we of the happy River God search find meaning in both Genesis 1 and 2. Best to enjoy inconsistency, the nature of creation. The creations, other Bible stories in my not Christian environs, turn me away from obstinate false harmony and lead me to the retired, rearguard search for who we inconsistently are. River God searchers must learn to enjoy disputation—such might give new life to the divine rather than etherizing it. Disputation just might keep us from getting bored, from becoming old and soft as we share our disputes with the priests who created the creations.

From a River God searching view, Genesis 1 sets up the God of the firmament, the heaven. He is the Sky God. Given the physical description of the world in the beginning, one of the challenges for the writers of the Old Testament was to draw readers into a physical understanding of this powerful Sky God, a God who lights up the world and creates the wondrous self-replenishing system for plants, animals, and humans. This God of the marvelous heaven is close by, but still in the distance. The charge of this happy story is to be thankful to the creator. We are not yet to the part where this highly self-pleased God turns from creator to destroyer, but we are well aware from the beginning that he is capable of letting go of water, lots of water, if he so wishes.

The God of Genesis 2 is not a sky God. He likes earth and working with earth. He is the hands-on God of the garden, and the potter, forming Adam as he does from the damp, misty earth. He creates plants for Adam's comfort and birds and animals to relieve Adam from boredom. This God, you suspect, had been bored himself. It is certain he likes company. Unlike the Sky God, this God of Earth walks closely with his creation.

This is a special garden in a desert terrain where gardens are special. The garden gives sensual pleasure; it is a godly place with easily obtained food and shady comfort. It exists in polar opposition to the toils for food the writers and their kinsmen experienced in the harsh desert. Even with its talking serpent, the Garden is not a place you would want to be thrown out of.

Most of us know what happens as we move into Genesis 3. We are introduced to the serpent. Adam and Eve eat that fruit, and all is lost. No happy River God here. In the end, we have a highly displeased God of the Earth. But the second creation story fills at least three gaps in human existence that are not covered in Genesis 1.

(1) The Garden of Eden provides a geophysical source for God's natural abundance on earth. Unlike the Heaven of Genesis 1, which at this point is God's domain and God's domain only, the Garden of Eden is an earthly paradise that could be physically inhabited by God and man alike, a heaven on earth with God, a paradise that could have been possible. As we move through the Old Testament and into the New, this God is willing to change his mind and let people back in, should they learn how to follow him.

(2) The Garden of Eden brings sin into play. The story does not explain evil, but it does show where evil or wrongdoing started. The explanation is weak. A snake sparked all this? But the God of the Earth seems much weaker than the Sky God. Everything about the Garden story is fragile, a try at perfection that was doomed from the start. This God is more whimsical, not the magnificent structured creator of the Genesis 1 world, whom we seem to be back with around the time of Noah. He will wipe out everything and just start over.

(3) The Garden of Eden story attempts to explain why life is hard and why we have to die. Genesis 1 leads us to believe that living can be easy, and we know better. Life can be hard. Why is it hard? It is Adam and Eve's fault and by a proxy that I have never understood, it was also the fault of all of those Hebrew tribesmen, and by yet another proxy in modern religion, our fault too.

The two stories need each other. They are contradictory, incompatible, but they do stand in for each other, where each fails at explaining the basics of life and world. In the beginning, God is both distant and close. Two different fellows, both set up to be the one and only. My students understand, but they see too much they understand, and what they understand does not fit into a whole part. Two creations stories—isn't this one too many? I am arrested by the faces of the deep.

Genesis searches for firm ground on which those people could position themselves in their world, even if they had to do it with two creation stories and, if not two Gods, at least two very different concepts of God. Maybe they felt that unless they could make some sense of what their physical world was, how and why it was shaped, then they would never come to understand where they came from, and if they did not know where they came from, it would be difficult to determine who they were and if they did not know who they were and why things happen the way they do, then they would not know where they intended to go. If they did not know where they intended to go, then they could not function together as living human beings.

They would not be able to survive as a people in a world where plowshares often had to be beaten into swords. The Bible is, from the start, a survival manual. The first two chapters address, brilliantly, the primal need for cosmic and personal identity in order to survive from generation to generation.

Like God after the first creation, I feel very self-pleased with this explanation.

"Why two stories?" Ms. Fujimoto, yet unsatisfied, asks as the chimes sound.

The Bible of Sky and the Bible of Earth

And the sun stood still in the midst of heaven, and hasted not to go down about a whole day. —Joshua 10:13

My students of the River God see two creation stories in Genesis and cannot forebear the anti-mathematics of making 2 equal 1. Again, you cannot breeze through these biblical incongruities in Japan. You run against a Japanese wall, one taller and much more durable than my neighbor's wall. Those who believe that the Bible is inerrant and consistent have built another great wall, one that protects their belief even from the Bible. They are by virtue of their inerrant position—inerrant. But let's leave the narrow bookends of this logic aside. Throughout the Christian world there is a strong sense of the Bible as a unified, harmonized, carefully planned book, a book that has a separate existence even from its own texts. Even Cookout Christians—those who might have an open mind about the Bible being something other than entirely and completely inerrant—hold a great sense of respect for the Bible as book. As a book, yet unread, it is a holy, a Godly object.

A Methodist minister friend of mine told me a story about this phenomenon. He was preaching a sermon to his moderately conservative congregation, a sermon in which he insisted that peace on earth should be a real mandate for modern Christians. He quoted Paul's call for the same from the Bible. While making his point with Bible in hand, he asked his congregation if this call for peace in the New Testament should be ignored.

"Should we simply throw it out?" he said.

He made a throwing gesture, Bible in hand. Lost in emotion, he lost his grip of the Bible, and the Book flew from his hand and over the heads of those in the front rows of the church. It somehow got wedged at the roof of the church between one of the rafters and the ceiling.

When the book left his hand the entire congregation in unison craned their necks and followed its flight through the air. Everyone gazed at it in amazement at the place where it got stuck. Time stood still while all were transfixed by the sight of the Bible wedged in the ceiling of the church. After the service, a long-standing member of the church met him at the front door.

"Pastor, that Bible kindly got away from you, didn't it?" she muttered.

My students do not live in the world where the Bible itself, the bound book, is a holy object that should not be thrown. They do not understand how the Book, just the Book, the binding and pages, reinforces belief and faith to so many. To so many the bound book is the hope chest of God's infallible will. My students do not know that they are reading what the Christian world holds as the Holy Bible, the Word of God. They do not comprehend why it is necessarily a unified Bible. The Bible—the physical book. It stands as mighty as the firmament stood to its creators in its magnificent strength to hold back the deluge of its own words. It is the word *Bible* that has the power to make time and thought stand still.

This is the all powerful Bible of Sky. It is as commanding as the Sky God fighting from the Heaven with Joshua. The Holy Bible, the greatest mass-produced holy relic on our planet. In times and places, you put your hand on it when you swear to tell the truth, even though it contains the original fish story. It is the object carried conspicuously by the young evangelical to bolster his credibility, even though Jesus reportedly despised public demonstrations of piousness. It is the object with the soft black leather cover with truth in print too small to read. But holding it and holding it alone is enough. Often it is neither hardback nor paperback, exactly. It is produced to look and feel unique, different from a normal book, more than a normal publisher and press would afford. When held in its smaller, thin-paged versions, it is fragile, a victim of its own delicate production.

But it is also the large book with the velvet page marker on the lecterns of so many pulpits in so many churches. When read from the pulpit during services, its words are treated as sparingly as holy water. Just a sprinkle of these words during a sermon can bring a roomful of people closer to God. Throw it, and watch the central nervous systems of these people go kindly into suspended animation.

The Bible of Earth is different and rare. Another under-read but magnificent book was written some years ago by Bernhard W. Anderson, ambitiously entitled *Understanding the Old Testament*. When covering the textual sources of the Pentateuch, or the first five books of the Bible, Anderson remarks in passing that their are "evidences of disunity" in the early books of the Bible and goes on to diagram the cut and paste method by which many Bible scholars think the first books of the Old Testament were put together.

Evidences of disunity? In my Sunday school training, which was scattershot but status quo, the words, disunity, and, Bible, never kept company. Here is Anderson, once Dean of Theology at Princeton, who, in this 1975 reprint of his 1957 first edition, speaks openly about the relationship between the Bible and disunity, writing within a respectable community of America's top theologians as if the notion of biblical disunity was widely held as old news.

Scholars at distinguished universities have been discussing biblical disunity for some time. But they are closer to the flawed Bible of Earth, the Bible you have a conversation with, the Bible that demands precision in study. But mainstream churchgoers hear little to nothing of the Bible of Earth while they hang with their Bible of Sky, their high-flying Bible. Even in mainline Cookout Christian services, the Bible is highly unified. Unified, perfect, static, and fragile in the very properties of its strength: The Bible should never be thrown like a Frisbee.

My students understand the hard biblical rule that you cannot work on the Sabbath. Resting on the seventh day honors the principle of God's recognition of his own day of rest on the seventh day of the Creation. Resting on the Sabbath is at the core of weekly life for God's chosen, a top ten commandment, set in place and with dire and deadly consequences for those who do not rest. In the Old Testament, God's insistence to Moses to rest on the Sabbath is asserted in a number of places, but in Exodus 31:14, God makes it clear what the consequences are for breaking this rule:

> Ye shall keep the sabbath therefore; for it is holy unto you: every one that defileth it shall surely be put to death: for whosoever doeth any work therein, that soul shall be cut off from among his people.

God repeats the injunction in the next verse.

> Six days may work be done; but in the seventh is the sabbath of rest, holy to the LORD: whosoever doeth any work in the sabbath day, he shall surely be put to death.

The death order is repeated in Exodus 35:2. When the Bible is taken on the whole, the day of rest rule is the source of great drama when Jesus, liberating himself from his own tradition, questions the fairness of this rule.

> The sabbath was made for man, and not man for the sabbath. (Mark 2:27)

This tricky, polemical inversion of key words sidesteps God's Old Testament intentions. One sees a source for yet another exhaustive priestly debate over the Sabbath, where a Hebrew compromise is reached only after all agree to no compromise at all.

Once when we were covering the book of Joshua and reading the description of the battle of Jericho, Ms. Yamada, who always does her homework and who writes copious notes during class, strikes a pose and raises her hand.

"The walls of Jericho fall down on the seventh day?" she asks, then pauses. Other members of the class join her, staring at the text and focusing on the numbers. Numbers are important in Japan, and numbers are important in the

Bible. Something is numerically amiss, a possible error, and a concentrated pause is a cultural mandate. The sun stands still. We are stuck in the Bible of Earth. I am under pressure to figure out what stopped Ms. Yamada before she embarrasses me by pointing out something I missed. But then I see it, the number 7.

"The Chosen," I say, "are on the march for seven days outside Jericho, working, during one of those seven days, on the Sabbath."

"God does not follow his rule," Ms. Yamada points out in slow and deliberate English.

I fight back irritation at the irrelevance of the question. Then I fight back more irritation over the fact that I am irritated by a question that, in fact, is relevant, and then fight back more irritation at the fact that the answer that comes to my mind should have been something I had already considered. The God who commands Joshua is not the God of the Garden, the one who lets the snake wreak havoc. Joshua's God is the God of Sky. He can suspend his own commandment if he chooses. But, I dispute with myself, was this Sky God at the helm during the time of Isaac and his two sons, Esau and Jacob? That God could not overturn Isaac's accidental blessing of Jacob, who was in disguise as his brother, Esau, even when this was a clear case of fraud. How is it that the very principle of divine power insisted upon by the Bible becomes impotent at times?

This feeling of irritation over legitimate questions mark and track the Bible of Earth. You find yourself in a Jacobean wrestling match with the memory of the Sunday school teacher of yore, wanting to rejoin her by defaulting back to her Bible of Sky. But in Japan, you cannot teach from within the Christian milleaux, from inside the large Western camp of the enlisted. Tokyo. Its name in kanji means "eastern capital." This is the East, the precise East. Training students to avoid the idiosyncrasies of an inconsistent textbook, attempting to shield them from the Bible of Earth so that they might begin to imagine the high-flying Bible of Sky, would be dereliction of duty. We must always forge our way upriver with the River God, due East toward forbidden Eden, toward the Bible of Earth.

The Education of God

And he shall judge among the nations, and shall rebuke many people: and they shall beat their swords into plowshares, and their spears into pruninghooks: nation shall not lift up sword against nation, neither shall they learn war any more. —Isaiah 2:4

Moments of irritation and befuddlement flare old pains. But these moments bring discovery. After the creation stories, in the Bible of Earth, chaos arrives. And a class on the Bible has its own chaos. I do not know why God's rules change. Just hope we do not wake one morning to see Joshua on the horizon.

The cosmos is under control through the first Creation, and until the second, when the Garden of Eden is fouled. What follows are successive images of abject human failure and swift, sublime punishment. Adam and Eve enjoy immortality for a short while, then take the death sentence for a culinary misdemeanor. Cain, undone because God prefers meat to vegetables, invents Class A felony by killing his brother. Violence instead of fruit eating becomes the core human flaw, which makes more sense. We have not passed Genesis 4.

God is overwrought by human failure, a failure that cannot be parsed from flaw in his creation. He opens the windows of heaven. Water from above the firmament voids his first try. He regrets this act. He admits flaw with apology: the blessing of a rainbow. He will never do such a thing again, he promises. But we are told time and again that he will.

God learns remorse. He decrees capital punishment for shedding the blood or killing another man in Genesis 9:6, a decree he does not follow. This verse is met with vexed faces in class. We witness the approved violent slaughter of non-Chosen and even Chosen people in later books. God changes his rules; there is a management problem.

"A snake?" a student blurts out.

"Let's move on."

In the Old Testament the idea that God is infallible is not strong. This startles me. I have been shazamed into thinking that one risks damnation by seeing God and God's word as anything but infallible. The God of the Old Testament is the creator and the most powerful god. He has foreknowledge, and flaws are blamed on humans, not the Creator. But, after the flood, God struggles along with his flawed people in the attempts by both God and people to set things right. He changes his approach in idiosyncratic, experimental patterns. Flawed patterns, when reviewed by my students. The punishments for Adam, Eve, the original people on dry land before the flood, Ham, Moses, the sons of Aaron (Nadab and Abihu), Solomon, Job, and others, are excessive. God goes lighter on Cain (the murderer), Jacob (the extortionist and liar), the brothers of Joseph (guilty of attempted fratricide), Aaron (the maker of the golden calf), and David (the adulterer).

The God of the Old Testament emerges as a learner, one who experiments, if not with his mistakes, the mistakes of the flawed people he created. Trying to get it to run right, camped under the hood looking for the causes of engine failure. The God of the mountain of Moses is different in character than the God who surfaces in latter books of the Bible. This fact has not gone unnoticed by biblical scholars. But this is not a class on how pre-Christian Hebrew writers gradually absorbed Hellenic or Zorastrian influences. Cross-referencing Hebrew textual history with Hebrew history may be the most inexact science in the history of Western historical empiricism. And dangerous: It would find a man mad or leave him so.

In the world of my class, by the time we get to David and beyond, to the period of the captivity, the character of God in the perception of biblical writers morphs from warrior to the more familiar God. He is stern, still ready to punish, but he evolves into the God of tender mercies praised in Psalms, before the New Testament and the coming of the Messiah. The writers of the historical books, including both Samuels, both Kings, and both Chronicles, along with pounding their readers over the head with the idea that good kings follow God and bad kings do not, show that the God of the Hebrews creates new strategies, revisions of prior strategies that did not work.

God seems satisfied with Kings who get things partly right, a far cry from the God who attacked and punished Moses for unclear reasons. This is the same God who destroyed Nadab and Abihu, in the early days of the temple, for making a clerical error during a ritual sacrifice. Along the way, God tires of rewards and punishments and sends in the prophets Elijah and Elisha with their pre-Christ-like miracles offset by their magical weapons of mass destruction.

After the Exodus, God's chosen people witnessed what should have been enough miracles to get the point. They still turn away. God forges rules to follow, an effort that fails from the start. God uses stern punishments. He denies the Promised Land to the original exiles and to Moses himself. In later chapters, though, God is more mild and negotiable, particularly with David, who is the first human God seems to truly love, who is God's tutor in learning how to love. David does bad things. David is punished. But David lives his life throughout in God's care. He, not Moses, was the apple of God's eye.

God is taught how to forgive by his flawed people. The first full act of forgiveness that I can find is in Genesis 33, when Esau forgives Jacob for stealing his birthright in a beautiful passage. The brothers embrace and weep together. Joseph, after some understandable hazing, forgives his brothers. Moses asks God for forgiveness several times in Exodus and, finally, in Leviticus, after these demonstrations of forgiveness from God's flawed people, God allows that he will forgive his people if they carry out their sacrifices appropriately.

The God of Moses liked sacrifices and offerings. We learn, in detail, how offerings should be presented in Exodus, Leviticus, and Numbers. This God is not a vegetarian—Cain learned this much. God likes blood and burnt offerings. In Exodus 20:24, God commands to:

> Make an altar of earth for me and sacrifice on it your

burnt offerings and fellowship offerings, your sheep and goats and your cattle. Wherever I cause my name to be honored, I will come to you and bless you.

God changes this idea, even becomes squeamish about blood sacrifice. The disgusted God of Isaiah's vision says, through Isaiah, about offerings:

> To what purpose is the multitude of your sacrifices unto me? (1:11) . . . I am weary to bear them. And when ye spread forth your hands, I will hide mine eyes from you: yea, when ye make many prayers, I will not hear: your hands are full of blood. (1:14-15)

Speaking through the vision of Amos, a disgusted God says, "Though ye offer me burnt offerings and your meat offerings, I will not accept them: neither will I regard the peace offerings of your fat beasts" (5:22). By the time we reach the back end of the Old Testament, God is ready to lower his meat intake. He has learned that there is a flaw inherent to the sacrifice system, that blood sacrifices, though they signify loyalty, fail to keep people loyal. This is the God as Creator, and also the created God.

The God of Moses lays down the law in detail, emphasizing what we call the Ten Commandments. He goes into greater detail while describing the many laws and statutes for priests and leaders to adjudicate and for the Chosen to live by. But the God of Ezekiel's vision states, "Wherefore I gave them also statutes that were not good, and judgments whereby they should not live" (20:25). Through the reports of accepted visionaries, God revises his legal framework, seeking revision after failure. God will punish throughout, but a more mature, learned God than the God of Moses emerges through the Old Testament. Confounding the effort to teach the Bible is the knowledge that the writers of these books could not have seen how these independent (albeit inter-textual) books would be arranged hundreds of years later.

The editors of my classroom text and many others have pointed out that the *post facto* arrangement of these books suggests an evolution towards Christianity. Forward-looking

Daniel is placed with the prophets instead of with the traditional Hebrew Writings. This placement with other prophets—Isaiah, Jeremiah, Ezekiel—all of whom produce similar foresights indicates that as we approach the end of the Old Testament, we are in a time when all major (and minor) visionaries are looking toward the coming of the Messiah and the final days. Historic scholarship, though, has placed the actual authorship of Daniel far away in time from those books it shares a place with in the Bible.

Given that the Christian arrangement of the Old Testament canon of books came far later, even given that this arrangement in the Constantine period was also carried out by divinely inspired men, there is still something amiss here. The councilor authorities of the early church, those who insisted on the infallibility of the biblical texts they assembled and who insisted of course on the infallibility of God, inadvertently, by virtue of the order of the cannon, gave us a changing, a mutable, a fallible God.

It is a God who recreates himself and not in his own image. In the beginning, one image of God is that he is personal and very involved with his creations. He is content with two perfect humans and unready for the plot that was about to unfold. But he is of two characters: at diverse times, both close to the action and also distant. He is distant when he strands the Chosen in Egypt for 430 years. But when he finally engages with Moses, he has clearly laid out a hands-on plan to take his flock into the Promised Land, and he stays close by. As the Bible progresses, after the kingdoms split, he is more distant, delivering various messages through others instead of communicating directly with his lost and defeated people, or with me in my tiny apartment, staring at the wall.

What stands out when teaching the Bible to people who are not Christian are the frustrations of God, the teacher/learner becoming absolutely undone over a grand plan that is wrecked by wrong human action: the worship of the wrong gods, and even his own failures, the failure to gain loyalty through demonstrations of power, the issuing of laws that his people do not obey, the attempt to forge ritual practices that his people fail to follow.

God, in turn, tries new ideas, redrafts policy, has temper tantrums, commits mass slaughter, and, time and again, fails. If we read the individual books in the order they have been given to us, God's forgiveness begins to supplant God's anger and destructive qualities. The Chosen will be punished, destroyed by their enemies, but love and mercy are on the rise. There is the hope of a New Jerusalem. But this only comes by the recognition of the imperfections of man and God and the will, always and forever, to try and make things right.

The Bible of Earth shows us an imperfect divine methodology, but one in which the ideal of perfection is stronger than any modern or historic dogma about God's infallibility. The God of the Bible of Earth does not stay the course—he revises. Dis-harmonizing, dis-unifying, disengaging from prior failed efforts and policies in order to rework the system that, in the long haul, is the only way to make the world better. The most amazing feature about the God in the Old Testament is that, given his early temperament, he never gives up on the project altogether. Take away the violence and mass destruction, give him a better sense of humor, and you have a God you can work with.

The God as learner theme continues into the New Testament, with the less than systematic revisions of God's law in the reported teachings of Jesus, whose views make him the second major dis-unifying figure in biblical history. Early in the Gospels we find, if not a completely new set of laws, a new approach that is much more open minded and ecumenical. From Matthew, the disturbing notion to more than one of my students is the outlandish notion of loving your neighbors as yourself and, more outlandish, loving your enemies (5:44).

The opening up of the religion to outsiders is a wildly irreverent assertion that had roots in Old Testament prophecy, but that was clearly out of the bounds of earlier Hebrew perspectives. Without this adjustment modern Christianity would not have been possible, and it flies in the face of strict policy laid out in the Old Testament, which, after the Exodus, divided the world into Chosen and non-chosen along racial lines.

The idea of including other races and people in the new religion, along with the new non-rule that these new converts do not have to be circumcised, is a radical break from the earlier thinking of the God of Moses. Scholars of the Bible commonly make this point, but it is not so common in Cookout Christian congregations. The unifiers, the harmonizers, the people who push the Bible of Sky, want a perfect, infallible, and unchanging God we can all agree on, and they have the distribution network and the power of media.

But these folks, from their own beginnings, have been in disagreement with each other. They have biblical justification, if they turn to Joel 3:10:

> Beat your plowshares into swords and your pruning hooks into spears. Let the weakling say, "I am strong!"

They do not have to be inspired by Isaiah's vision of peace, the very reversal of this quotation. So they have biblical justification for both peace and conflict, for beating their swords into plowshares and the converse to see which side God will fight for.

Breach and dis-unification seem the fruits of the labor of those who want to pretend that the Bible is a harmonized, unified whole with a perfect, unchanging God. Given their cultural power, both in media and in many evangelical and even mainstream churches, these Bible-is-the-perfect-word-of-God followers have positioned the others, the dis-unifiers, the non-holy, the egghead Bible of Earth liberal humanists, to be the rowdy outsiders. But the source of the historical violence erupting from various competing religious practices is rooted in the disunity spawned by dogmatic attempts to round things off, to unify against hard literal evidence, as these powerful groups seek more power to shazam unto others as they have shazamed themselves.

In Japan we do not, we cannot, read the Bible under the stern binary gaze of unification theologies as they continue to demand harmonized interpretations of the Bible. There is no perfect, single God here, or the idea of the perfect God and perfect book that perpetuates such dark chaos through denying chaos. Japan can be strict, stern, close-minded at times. But when studying the Christian Bible, the humiliating words "I don't know," the acceptance of chaos as a standard for learning the Bible, creates an open-air forum here, at least in terms of learning the Bible. It is the free space without the firmament, where Bible learning, uncomfortable as it often is, can take place. Only in such an environment can the God of Creation and the Created God be brought to terms.

Here is the menacingly chaotic but lighter world of the happy River God searchers. Students learn from text and teacher and teacher learns from students and text, drawing as the great example the catastrophic experiential learning indigenous to the Bible. Learning is catastrophe, calamity. There will be more catastrophes to come. At all times you are the vulnerable, Messiah-less teacher/learner, working beyond the fragile firmaments constructed by the unifying and harmonizing cults of the shazamed.

The Double-Edged Sword

Get wisdom, get understanding: forget it not: neither decline from the word of my mouth. Forsake her not, and she shall preserve thee: love her, and she shall keep thee. —Proverbs 4: 5-6

For in much wisdom is much grief: and he that increaseth knowledge increaseth sorrow. —Ecclesiastes 1: 18

God becomes more peaceful. But the God of peace swings the sword. Like the sword of Ehud and the sword of Jesus, God's sword is double-edged. One edge is the thrust of the brutal and swift judgment of his people. The other edge protects his fold from threats. But there is also the double-edged sword of meaning that cuts both ways. Wisdom protects; wisdom brings sorrow.

The God of the teachings works the sword of meaning in sundry ways: It is difficult to confine the sharp sword of meaning to only two sides. I was put on an email list that sends out a proverb from the Bible routinely to list members. As the emails came, it became apparent that Biblical proverbs swing the multi-edge sword of meaning in haphazard directions.

Some proverbs give good advice. Proverbs 21:9 says that it is "better to dwell in a corner of the housetop, than with a brawling woman in a wide house." This is true. It is also Proverbs 25:24, almost verbatim. The idea of steering clear of a brawling woman needed repeating.

Some proverbs seem to be good advice, but are curious, such as Proverbs 13:3, which holds that "he that keepeth his mouth keepeth his life: but he that openeth wide his lips shall have destruction." This one cuts too deeply:

destruction for talking too much. But it could be true. Of the deeply cutting proverbs that ring true is Proverbs 23:27:

> For a whore is a deep ditch; and a strange woman is a narrow pit.

The exact meaning of this proverb is enigmatical to my students, and to me, but it is memorable. (I don't remember seeing this one on my email list.)

Certain proverbial bits of wisdom are not as good as we are supposed to think they are, as in Proverbs 10:4, the one that says lazy people become poor and hard working people become rich:

> He becometh poor that dealeth with a slack hand: but the hand of the diligent maketh rich.

This is not true. Hard work does not always pay off.

Certain proverbs promote ideas that we do not wish to follow:

> Withhold not correction from the child: for if thou beatest him with the rod, he shall not die. Thou shalt beat him with the rod, and shalt deliver his soul from hell. (Proverbs 23:13-14)

In the view of many of my students, the double-edged sword of the teachings of the Bible cuts the wrong way just as it is cutting the right way: good teaching doubles as bad teaching. Meaning cuts here and there. The goodly creator of Genesis 1 is not so good when he destroys his creation early on. The great God of the Garden does not have complete dominion. The all-knowing God of Abraham does not seem to know the extent of Abraham's loyalty.

These two-edged meanings persist. Psalm 10 has a beautiful ending phrased in a classic evocation:

> LORD, thou hast heard the desire of the humble: thou wilt prepare their heart, thou wilt cause thine ear to hear:

> To judge the fatherless and the oppressed, that the man of the earth may no more oppress.

The humble and oppressed deserve special care in God's world. It is the mandate of the Jubilee to free slaves and forgive debts, and it is the charge of the synoptic gospels to give over worldly belongings and adopt the humble and holy life of the poor.

But the verses before this prayer for the oppressed are angry charges delivered to a distant god to punish the wicked for iniquity. The speaker asks God to:

> Break thou the arm of the wicked and the evil man: seek out his wickedness till thou find none. The LORD is King for ever and ever: the heathen are perished out of his land.

"Dear God, please break the arms of people we don't like, Amen."

Beyond the teachings, the large, murky, books of the prophets are dark and impossible to my students. They were not talking to Japanese college students, or to us, and we do not have adequate points of reference to know exactly, precisely what they are saying. Thus in latter times they have allowed for the swinging sword of out-of-context interpretation to fly unabated.

Beating swords into plowshares: This image from Isaiah 2 is memorable and beautiful. It states God's will to bring peace to the Israelites and also among diverse nations, so that men may stop fighting and resume the divine charge to cultivate the God-given soil. This passage also looks forward to the coming of the Messiah and is echoed later in Micah and Joel. It is hopeful in spirit but is brutally offset by prophetic visions that predict and are in favor of violent conflict.

The following verses from Jeremiah 51 stand as an ugly image of how God will use Israel to treat the Babylonians and other enemy nations. Referring to the Israelites, the speaker says of Israel:

> Thou art my battle axe and weapons of war: for with thee will I break in pieces the nations, and with thee will I destroy kingdoms; And with thee will I break in pieces the horse and his rider; and with thee will I break in pieces the chariot and his rider; With thee also will I break in pieces man and woman; and with thee will I break in pieces old and young; and with thee will I break in pieces the young man and the maid; will also break in pieces with thee the shepherd and his flock; and with thee will I break in pieces the husbandman and his yoke of oxen; and with thee will I break in pieces captains and rulers.

So much for a cease-fire in the Middle East. So much for peace on earth. It is unlikely a Japanese student, or the average Christian, will wander into the relatively obscure 51st chapter of Jeremiah. It is also doubtful that a religious educator in his or her right mind would bring out this verse during service to reflect the sentiments of a loving God. This passage from Jeremiah counters Isaiah's plowshare, as Isaiah does, too. The sharp sword of visionary meaning cutting one way, then another.

There is no happy River God in Jeremiah's vision. He has been called the weeping prophet, but his deprecating tone does not signify tears during his deeply cutting rants. In Jeremiah is the auditory template for a latter day style of preaching that also cuts deeply, a semi-mad, browbeating voice that was promoted, in English, by the sharp metrics of Jeremiah and his comrades in the King James Version. The King James translators produced one of the sources for the hellfire and brimstone style so common to sermons in certain English-speaking Christian congregations, a sharp, injurious style that drives many away from Christian practice, a style that is alien to Japanese ears.

In the book of Daniel, after the hallucinogenic writing on the wall appears in Chapter 5, after King Belshazzar is killed and Darius takes over, it becomes apparent to Daniel's high-level political rivals that Daniel, the Judaic foreigner, had gained too much favor in the Persian kingdom. This story is well-known: In order to put Daniel in double jeopardy, Daniel's rivals ask King Darius to decree that anyone who prays to any god or man other than King Darius for the following thirty days will be thrown to the lions. Open to the flattery of this proposal, Darius agrees, and makes the decree, unaware of the full implications of what he is doing. Being as perfect as any Israelite, or any human being, can get, Daniel does not stop praying to his god three times a day with his window open toward Jerusalem.

Daniel's violation of the new decree is soon discovered. King Darius is distressed but being bound by his own rule of law, he has to sentence ingenuous Daniel to spend the night with the royal lions. Darius is harried with concern for his beloved subject throughout the evening and night and is first to check on Daniel in the morning. In one of the happier moments in the Old Testament, the Kings calls to Daniel in the den. Unharmed due to his faith in God, ever loyal Daniel answers, "May the king live forever." He is lifted out of the den by order of the overjoyed Darius.

The deeply cutting meaning here echoes a similar scene earlier in Daniel, during which his colleagues survive being thrown into a fiery furnace, and both scenes, however untenable their breaches of natural and physical reality, are vivid biblical reminders of how complete God's protection is for the faithful and loyal. God is just, loving, and loyal.

After Daniel is lifted from the lion's den, those who attempted to have him killed by decree are punished. This retribution against those who tried to harm Daniel seems just in the eyes of my students, but the nature and the extent of this punishment throw the story out of kilter for them. Daniel 6:24 states that, at Darius's command, "the men who had falsely accused Daniel were brought in and thrown into the lions' den, along with their wives and children."

"Wives and children?" Ms. Watarai asks. The next sentence tells us that, "before they reached the floor of the den, the lions overpowered them and crushed all their bones." The swinging sword is not wife friendly, or child friendly, or Japanese student friendly. God protects but God, through his quasi-convert Darius, destroys and destroys thoroughly. God is the God of peace who gives succor to his own and the God of annihilation, a destructive force beyond our sense of justice, beyond God's own sense of justice.

Why is the happiness of plowing through another day of work, the happiness of late night revelry after work, the happiness of a home team victory, at such a premium in this world without the River God? This multiple personality God, this revisionist God with his many-edged, and deeply cutting swords of meaning, carries over into the New Testament, when, once again, in a dark time, God begins to see.

Section Four: On The Offensive

Most holy bastard
Of the bleeding mouth:
Nigger Christ
On the cross of the South

—Langston Hughes, from "Christ in Alabama"

Gods and Christians

Life is . . . God —from a T-Shirt.

Recently while wandering through the tightly-packed streets of Shibuya, Tokyo, while darting through darting shoppers, while dodging the hawking hawkers, while ducking through a sea of bodies through blasting neon into a store to buy printer ink, I found myself thinking, once again, about the book of Job. I remembered something that one of my own college professors said about the story of God destroying the life of his best man on a whim.

Before the professor began the lecture, he paused and scratched his head, saying to the class that, in his view, somewhere between the Old and the New Testament, God became a Christian. Most of us were amused, but there were a couple of students who visibly took offense, judging from the stone cold facial expressions they held while others chuckled. I guess the offended students felt that the character of the God never changes at all and that it is bad business to suggest otherwise.

If you wanted to question the ethics of the God(s) of the Bible, you could begin at any number of places, but the first chapter of Job is the best place to start. The Tony Soprano-esque personality of this deity is nothing like what we in the Christian world see as the God of the New Testament. Early in Matthew (3:16) and later in the other gospels we are given the pre-hippy image of the joyful spirit of God as a dove lighting on his beloved son who will, in turn, bless us, whether we deserve this blessing (as Job did) or not.

College classes in the humanities—classes in literature, history, philosophy or any branch of the area some of us in the biz fondly refer to as fuzzy studies—are fertile ground for stock student characters. There are the perplexed, silent, stoic types who never speak out in class but who make the highest grades. There are the outspoken brown noses, those who restate the professor's own views and ask the appropriate questions. They make higher grades than they deserve.

Several types come to mind, but a prominent stock character is the offense taker, the student who is pre-equipped to be victimized by open discussions about politics or religion. We are all offense takers at times—I took offense not long ago when my laptop was stolen from a hotel room in Barcelona—but true offense takers operate continually on a highly sensitive offense generating software. And they have an apocalyptic disregard for grades.

My offense-taking classmates, I think, had grown up in various small and constricted religious cultures overrun by Highway Jesusites and Hooverites. Their hometown church people may have briefed them before college to watch out for professors and other students who would try to steer them away from their God. Maybe they were taught the following injunction from Paul in Romans 16:17:

> Now I beseech you, brethren, mark them which cause divisions and offences contrary to the doctrine which ye have learned; and avoid them.

If so, by coming to a liberal arts college, they were not avoiding people who thought outside of their doctrine box. One wonders how these folks ended up in a fuzzy studies class to begin with. Maybe they were thinking of conquering the infidels from within. In the years since I went to college, they have succeeded to a degree.

There are self-righteous offense takers on the other side of the ideological fence, populating the same type of classroom and often less reserved than the conservative Christian offense takers. They sit in conspicuous places, ready to jump in and snare offense from any comment that can be remotely regarded as conservative or illiberal. (You couldn't describe someone this righteous as a godless liberal if righteousness comes from God.) Offense takers on all fronts set up a force field of avoidance that seals the rest of us off from open expression. I do not know why people with such delicate sensibilities have so much power in open societies, but they do. And to be so delicate, they are adept at seizing power.

I am bound to run roughshod over some Christian sensibilities with my thoughts on teaching the New Testament in Japan, even if my Japanese students have prompted these thoughts. Those who are offended will more likely be religious conservatives than leftist junior politicos. But offense is unavoidable as we enter into Christianity proper.

I am not in a place where I can see the face of religious offense, so I don't know when to shut up. In Japan, I do not have true-blue conservative Christians who have traveled into my class with warnings about me from pastors and church people, the type of Christians who might think that they need to help keep me, and the class, in line.

There is no such standard here. Japanese people have a number of sensitive areas where they may take offense, but Christianity is not one of them. I have distance and license, maybe too much, so thinking about my old humanities class with its Christian offending Christian professor came to mind in the middle of crowded, confused Shibuya, I guess, because I have often gotten lost in Tokyo, and maybe I was free associating that lost feeling with the feeling of being lost somewhere between the Bible and that brand of Christianity that quickly takes offense.

I was schooled in a Christian environment, Furman University in Greenville, SC. I knew the terrain well. The bubbly pressure points of Christian offense were generally understood. The class I mentioned above was born of Christian thinking with a Christian professor in a college founded by Christians filled with Christian students. When I think about Christian offense takers from my current perch in not Christian Japan, I am offended by how quickly Christians offend each other.

I do not even know if the mention of being lost offends someone. I was deprived of full indoctrination as a child, and my old fuzzy studies classes in college stretched the coordinates of my provincial view of the world, and the coordinates kept stretching from that point onward. In the beginning I thought it would be a good idea to major in Business, a practical specialty I could boast about to Uncle Billy when I returned home on vacations. But I found that it was too much fun to sit in a classroom listening to god-like professors while they charted large terrains outside my little province, often with fire in their eyes. When one of them once referred to Little Orphan Annie as, "that little bitch," I wasn't offended: I was hooked, converted. No business major for me.

As powerful as these classroom experiences were, they now seem quaint when I look back: a Christian humanist professor taking on the Bible, calmly promoting the Old Testament to the important but more distant canon of historic literature while obliquely demoting its status as absolute truth. He was examining bubbles, not bursting them. Back in the now lost humanist environs of my college days, we could play around with marvelously open ideas without having to go hotfoot it out on the desert plains with Cane. We could open our minds without being cursed and exiled from the pleasant humanistic God of Comfort. And we were a comfortable distance from the careless God of Job, and what my students see as the stern, destructive, and downright mean mountain God of Moses.

Still, in this comfortable environment, people were offended. At that time their strict views seemed marginal, but over time these same strict views became more status quo as their numbers grew and as their views were adopted by many mainstream Cookout Christians. And as the strict Christians became more powerful, as they annexed the turf of my professor's comfortable brand of Christian humanism, I became even more oppositional than I already was, pushed further away from Christianity by Christians who push against humanism with sensitivities that humanism created. I went further off to wander the grumpy secular wilderness with the bubble bursters, the guys who have a problem with Little Orphan Annie.

The offense takers are right on one point: Once a mind is opened, it is hard to get it closed again, and who knows what dangerous back roads the open mind leads you to. You might find yourself teaching the Bible in Bible-deprived Japan, wandering with your students and the River God through the foreign Bible and finding that the great source of offense is the Bible itself. And the bubble bursting does not stop when we get to the New Testament, even after God becomes a Christian.

Now the professor, I have to explain the meaning of this change in the religious beliefs of God that is so apparent in the Bible. And I have to rebel against my old professor by taking a confrontational stance against his school of humanism. I have to burst the bubbles of his school by cultural necessity, because in Japan his God of Comfort is not bundled in with the actual Bible, Old Testament or New. I am uncomfortably aligned with the stricter offense-taking Christians in this regard.

As we walk through what is to my students the gauntlet of the bi-polar and ranting prophets on the rear end of the Old Testament to the more readable good news sections that begin the New, I am not sure what the Bible as book is saying about the character of God, but I find little comfort there. When covering the New Testament, you read through Christian but not yet Christianized church texts that were, long after their writing, consolidated in their selection and arrangement and their interpretation. I have to go in wielding a heavy anti-interpretation machete that my students do not even see while I prepare for class, hacking through the verdant jungle of Bible interpretation handed down and out by so many types of Christians with their various strict and comfortable gods.

Before we get to Jesus, I have to say a few words over the Apocrypha, important in many ways because of its absence during Bible roll calls. Not many people in the Christian world these days are interested in the Apocrypha, so we skip over these books inserted between the Old and New Testaments in the King James Version, and this leap confuses my students.

I do not feel comfortable with this omission either, but the stories or images from these books do not show themselves often in religious or popular discourse. The Book of Enoch gives us the idea of fallen angels, but we need not go back any further than *Paradise Lost* to absorb the memorable image of the fallen angels in their "dungeon horrible" with "no light, but rather darkness visible." That these books are placed in the King James Version means that someone important found these books to be important. But I cannot find a quick and clear way to explain why the apocryphal books became the apocryphal books. Why, in some print traditions, they continue to be included in Bibles and, in other print traditions, they have been abandoned.

It is beyond me to teach the cryptic and strange politics of the church history that formed all of the Bibles of modern times. I am not sure what single soul would be qualified to do this. Along the way, it was decided that the story of a woman drilling a tent peg through the head of a passed out drunk king was part of the true word of God. But the story about a woman who cuts off the head of a passed out drunk king and then smuggles the head out of the king's camp in her lunch basket (Judith 13) did not make the cut. I like the second story better, but I was not around when the decision was made to put it on the Bible's second string of books.

Offense takers would not be offended by my skipping over a major portion of the Bible, just so long as I did it silently and with no mention of church politics and the changing nature of God. My experience in Japan in no way mirrors the delicate Christian-esque environment my college professor was in, or that I was once in. I am homesick for this God of comfort, and oddly I also miss the strict God of the offense takers. Both of these gods helped me to chart my own turf and to create and maintain the satisfying illusion that I was disillusioned.

The New Testament is truly new and unfamiliar foreign terrain now as we move steadily and precariously upstream, on the river of Colonel Sanders and the River God, through a more complex Bible and a less multi-Christianized God, away from the Jesus who is not there and toward the Jesus who is.

The New Testament vs. Christianity

What makes the phrase "biblical Christianity" incoherent is its meaninglessness. —Robert Carroll, from *Wolf in the Sheepfold*

The late Robert Carroll is also the co-editor of the King James Version that I use for my classes. The Jesus my students see is a distant figure from their cultural standpoint, a distant figure and a fantasy figure. The text of the King James Version does little to bring this character closer or to make him less fantastical. From Matthew through John we read a mixture of reports about what Jesus did and said, second-hand reports that often relate, from an exacting Japanese perspective, excessively exaggerated events within different types of narratives with different styles. The opening books of the New Testament win the biblical contest of fantastical storytelling.

Of course we get stuck on whether or not modern day Christians believe that Jesus could feed 5,000 men (not counting women and children) with five loaves of bread and two fish. Japanese have a well-documented record of making a fish go a long way, so the math of slicing two fish into well more than 5,000 pieces puts some of my students on edge. "*Muri,*" one of them mumbled once, meaning impossible. Maybe some of them wonder how those people hauled two whales up a mountain. And the students who get nervous about whether or not I will try to make them believe in the creation stories get nervous all over again when we reach the early Christian era. I think some of them worry that they have to believe in miracles in order to pass the class.

They have answered a question I have had for a long time: Why does the New Testament make Christians nervous?

The answer is that the New Testament makes everyone, Christian or not, nervous. When we get to the Christian writings of the New Testament, it becomes more difficult to fudge or gloss over or joke away or retire from the curiosity my students have about what Christians actually believe in our day and time. We are in the New Testament now and with the Jesus of all Christians, so it is more difficult to attribute these accounts to pre-Christian thinking. A student wants to know if modern Christians really believe that Jesus walked on water. "Yes, many do."

In one particular class, something rare happened. We had a real born-again Christian in the room. We all knew she was a born-again Christian because she announced it in class early on. Instead of trying to tiptoe over the walking on water question, I directed it to her—a preemptive strike.

"Ms. Yamada, do you believe that Jesus walked on water?"

She said, "yes," and smiled.

I continued, "Do you believe that the earth was created in six days?"

"I don't know how the earth was created, but God created it," she answered.

Good, I thought privately. Maybe I should recruit at least one, self-defined, born-again Christian to sit in on future classes to answer questions about what it is exactly, precisely, that they believe from the Bible in our times. The problem is that my born-again Christian did not say exactly, precisely what she believed about the Genesis story. She made it sound like she was giving a firm answer when actually she wasn't, which, in my experience, is something that self-described born-again Christians often do.

On trips home I find it better to stay silent about the Bible and truth when flipping burgers with the saved, because the "Do you believe in walking on water?" question is appropriately inappropriate outside of church or certain appointed times and venues. Cookout Christians—the types of Christians who do not feel the constant need to announce that they are Christians—these Christians will invite you to more cookouts, may even offer you a cold beer, if you keep your mouth shut about the truth value of the Bible in the wrong place and time. They feel free to say that they follow the Bible in the abstract, but who wants to announce that he believes anyone walked on water, or that this same person can transport your inner demons to a bunch of pigs nearby and then send the pigs over a cliff. Even with plenty of cold beer, this is nervous talk at a Cookout Christian cookout.

My students, the 999 in 1,000 of them who would never, ever, announce that they believe Jesus or anyone walked on water, are still drawn in by gospel tales and want to know more about what we in the Christian world make of these fabulous stories, we who hold them so near and dear, even those of us who are not self-described born-again or mainstream Cookout Christians, and who do not really believe that someone named Jesus actually walked on water. They find these stories engaging, but they find it foolish to insist that everything in these stories is true. I think this idea lessens their respect for Christianity and for people who belong to Christianity. The Japanese communities my students grew up in neglected to give them the buy-in-or-be-burned challenge played out so often in the Christian world. But they do understand that great stories are great because they pull us over-the-top and draw us into another world. Who wants reality from hero stories?

My neighbor's wall reminds me that everyone has their delusions, or they suffer from the delusions of others. For years I believed that you would get cramps and drown if you went swimming right after eating lunch. That's what people believed in the countryside. They also believed that drinking copious amounts of milk was good for Aunt May's stomach ulcer. All of us have had delusions and have fallen short of reality. But I think that the correct word is not delusion, but misguided. I never get lost in Tokyo, just misguided.

It is easy to get misguided in the Bible, particularly in the Gospels, those of us from the Christian side, because we are drawn down the non-biblical paths of so many traditions and customs and habits of belief that make us feel comfortable with Christianity. The biblical image of Lazarus as a mummy makes us nervous because it does not fit with our Christian sensibilities. For so many of us these writings were and still are supposed to be the final authority, but in my classes they are no authority at all without the non-biblical authoritative voices that give the Bible authority. Many people in the Christian world, me included, have been misled to believe that exactly three wise men visited the Christ child. The number three comes from another authority, another source of thought. There are not exactly three wise men presented in Matthew and only in Matthew. Nor does the book of Matthew use the term, *magi*, in the King James Version. My students are free to picture as many wise men as they choose.

Onward to what the Bible says, instead of what it does not say. What my unshazamed students have forced me to see word for word makes it *muri*, impossible, to stay in retirement from bubble bursting. How can I not speak out against misguided attempts to argue for the absolute truth about ancient reports of a superhero feeding thousands with two fish, reports of the same superhero bringing dead people back to life, a scene that badly undercuts the idea of Jesus' own resurrection. And what to make of the reports of walking on water? *If he's God, why not part the water instead of walk on it?*, one of my more alert students may be thinking.

The life of Jesus is interesting to them, too, but sketchy in gospel accounts. Too much is left out to consider the life of Jesus in the Bible as an authoritative biography. What they get of the life of Jesus they get unfiltered, un-refinished by the truth-mongers from the Christian world. In this setting the stories can produce meanings well beyond the focus of the narrow cults of absolute belief.

Sometimes when I am wall gazing, I think that maybe if you stop trying to make people believe the unbelievable, a reliable, a less nervous form of understanding, even enlightenment, would take root. Allow these stories their grand fictional sway, and you may have something. Superman and Spiderman do exist, as do Achilles and Hamlet. They have been created and no amount of scientific discovery can un-create them. The writers of the Gospels, like their Old Testament forebears, knew the creative staying power of outlandish storytelling. They understood that God's power over water represents his superior command over the primal and most powerful element of the great void. God is great, and God is good. What more would a believer need to believe?

My students want to know where I stand, of course. I point them to Carroll and Prickett's notes in our King James Bible edition, where the editors assert that, "apart from shaky guesswork, we do not know who wrote the gospels, nor when, where, why, for whom, or how" (404). After spending far too much of my private time looking in to this void of textual history, all that I have found is that we can say that these gospel reports were written years after the events that they are recounting and do not exactly agree with one another.

I cannot keep my mouth shut in the classroom, as I try to do at Cookout Christian cookouts on trips home, because so many of my students want more explanation from a real instead of an imagined text. They do not care about biblical truth and only want me to make it plain before their faces what they need to study for the final exam. I tell the curious among my students that even if these gospel reports were written from first hand accounts—something impossible to verify—then we should know more about the reliability of the people reporting the unbelievable. Well, we don't. But this lack of verification should not detract from the force of the events in stories that for many represent basic truths about religious life.

Some Christians remain hungry for physical evidence and proof of the gospel truth; other Christians just want to know what it is they have to do to pass the big final exam. From the evidence that the editors of the Bible we use cite copiously throughout their notes, we can conclude that the gospel stories themselves were produced in writing from already standing Christian groups. The New Testament did not create Christianity; early Christianity produced the writings that became the New Testament. The earliest of the early Christians did not need the New Testament to be Christians.

Now Mr. Matsuda is starting to nod off again. But I continue. Members of what became a central church later selected and interpreted Christian writings for the New Testament in accordance with the needs of Christianity, or the branch of Christianity that became dominant. The writings of the New Testament, and the Old, have always been de-centered, an addendum to Christian initiatives that were and are set in place independently from what we now call the Bible. The efforts in Christian preaching to verify, to harmonize, to forge the cult of absolute belief, from, say, a modern pulpit in Tennessee, interferes profoundly with the profoundly engaging ambiguities and, yes, truths sketched by these same narratives in a modern Bible class in Japan. In my classroom in Japan there is no built-in ministerial mandate to believe that which we can never fully know. This nervous mandate often prompts a human, all too human, revulsion that we feel when we from Bible-land remember the vociferous insistence, from childhood and beyond, that we must believe the unbelievable or be damned.

I am out of the classroom, now, and back in my apartment staring at my wall. A weed has made the journey from my neighbor's yard under the wall and is giving it a go on my side. It has reached the proportion of a small tree, and it is beginning to block my view of my neighbor's wall. I should go outside and whack it down, but I am too busy thinking about religion to confront the reality that my small terrace is about to be taken over by a giant weed. Religion reflects the human search for peace and reconciliation with the unpredictable in a fearful world. Much of the New Testament charts this search among our forebears, inconsistent or inaccurate or contradictory though its books may be at times.

My students expect to encounter a religion that promotes a general understanding and thus tolerance of human frailty. But when they see the insistence for belief, even in the New Testament texts they are reading, those who have managed to stay awake put on their perplexed face, a face that, when questioned, confirms that they are thinking that the whole bit is a disingenuous sales pitch. These students, at times, have been offended by their reading.

Many of us have been told that we have to believe because someone wants us to, and this someone is not God. But it would be hard to explain to them that, beyond the Bible, their teacher believes religiously in a human gene that craves power, a need among some to make others do things they do not want to do in order to show their loyalty, their submission. In my class we see this need reflected by a God who tells Abraham to sacrifice his first-born son. There are plenty of Christian spokespeople around who think it is godly to force people to do things, sometimes outrageous things, to demonstrate belief.

We often hear the word *raw* placed in front of the word *power*. This means, I guess, that there is a raw type of power that seeks power for its own sake. But religious power does not seem so raw on the surface because religious power is so often cloaked in the corresponding images of benevolence. Evangelicals, in particular, smile and say, "aw shucks" a lot. Look once, and you see benevolent, nice folk. Look more closely and you see a need for power, but only a power that can justify itself by the idea that it is, in essence, benevolent—the type of power that summons itself in the name of all that power is not, the type of power that on the surface seems fragile and easily offended.

I am not sure if this reverse-action power could be called raw, but it certainly is powerful, loaded and triggered by the idea that it is wholly benevolent, that it is not what it is. Hamlet says that he must be cruel to his mother in order to be kind. Certain powerful forms of Christianity seem to reverse this notion. You have to be kind, at least appear to be kind, in order to be cruel, to force nervousness on a population by making them invest in believing the unbelievable with the promise of great returns in the afterlife if they believe, with the threat of pain and destruction if they do not. Maybe Ms. Yamada, my one born again Christian, is not as kind as she appeared to be.

I am still in my apartment thinking about the Bible when I should be outside cutting down a giant weed. You do not need a Bible in the end. All you need are church authorities who repeat, over and over, their version of what the God of the Bible wants. In 2004, John Kerry, then the democratic nominee for president, tried to attack the policies of the Bush administration by saying, "Mr. President, saying so doesn't make it so." This schoolmarm-ish jab at Bush was the lamest in the history of lame political comebacks. What the Kerry camp failed to understand, what Bush's chief political advisor, Karl Rove, knew from instinct, what anyone knows from a basic study of human psychology and marketing, is that saying so, time and again, does make it so.

As the writers of the Bible fully understood: Spaced repetition of ideas sells ideas, whether they are true or not. Of course saying so makes it so. You wonder why no one in the Kerry camp cracked open their old copies of Orwell's *1984*. You wonder why no one in the Kerry camp looked into why products that claim to cure hair loss in men, products that do not work, are still on the shelves, are still purchased furiously. Jesus walked on water. Saying so makes it so if you say so over and over, through the centuries, if you chant it over and over to each new generation.

I am grumbling about the Bible again because I don't want to spend a significant part of my afternoon cutting down a large, tree-sized weed that in fact belongs to my neighbor. My view of the perplexed faces of the Japanese deep, the mandate to believe, to verify the unverifiable Bible, does not point to good religion. This demand to verify, to believe, points to the weaknesses instead of the strengths of religious being. In this case the standard to believe does not even point to faith, which, theologians often remind us, is something different from belief. This mandate, this demand, this standard for absolute belief even eclipses the better side of religious faith: The hope of finding peace and reconciliation with our strange, fearful, and unknown universe.

Though this enormous effort to verify the historic truth of the Gospels, an effort promoted in the Gospels themselves, continues in Christian culture, though many defenders of the faith continue to entrance their flocks with supposed certainties from the Bible that are not certain at all, none of the charismatic shazams of biblical verification in the Christian world find traction in a Bible class in my new world.

The Japanese have suffered, still suffer, from their own shazams. They have concocted their own power-hungry gods from time to time. But our Christianized Bible God is not on their list, and sometimes the gods who are not there are easier to see than the gods who are. If we must have a God, why can't he be happier? Wouldn't it be nice to have a God who does not throw brimstone and fire at us from heaven, who does not demand that we believe the unbelievable, a God who does not ask you to kill your children, and, one who does not send his right-hand man down to kill your children? When you have a happy God, you do not need a power hungry God or any of his power hungry spokespeople, and a happy, River God, though not easily verified, is easily had.

This need for verification in the Christian tradition, this need to make people believe the unbelievable, brings on unhappy blowback—rebellion. It encourages folks to call bullshit on the whole Bible—just throw it all away. This is a shame because now I would be the first to insist that the grand but incomplete architecture of human consciousness presented in the Bible should never be sent to the valley of ashes. There is too much truth there once you purge the demand for belief, once you cut down the giant weed blocking your view. There is too much of us to be found in the Bible once we stop trying so hard to find ourselves in it.

While we are on the subject of misusing the Bible, and while I'm backsliding from my commitment to keep my mouth shut and not hurt feelings, there is also the idea in certain areas of the Christian world that there is one, clear specific Christian doctrine exposed in the Gospels. After covering these writings in class, sometimes line to line, this idea has now become repugnant to me in its inaccuracy. This one single, clearly laid out doctrine is just not there to be seen in the New Testament Gospels.

What does it mean, in any language, ancient or modern, that Jesus is the son of God and the son of Man and the son of David and that he also existed before Abraham? From the perspective of my students, the Jesus of the Gospels is not the Jesus of my college professor. His was an approachable Jesus, who was wise, kindly, and insightful, who was like my professor. The idea of Jesus as divine, as being a god himself, has biblical precedent, but the absolute divinity of Jesus, and precisely how this divinity is reconciled with his human form and also with the claim that he is the son of David, is not sorted out in the Gospels or in the New Testament.

The concept that Jesus is both divine and human did congeal by the 5th century, centuries after Christianity started and after a divisive conflict between various churches. Christians persecuted other Christians. People got whacked—in the pre-Mafia golden age of the early Roman church—for ending up on the wrong side of an abstract debate over the essence of Jesus. But my problem in Japan, where no one has gotten whacked during a Jesus debate—at least not yet—my problem is that I am teaching the Bible and not the complicated set of heated interpretive disputes that led to the Fourth Ecumenical Council of Chalcedon.

But I *am* teaching the King James Version, a translation that, in its very printing, was distributed for the benefit of people who had rebelled against the long established medieval or Catholic Church, a church that, not long before the King James Version, would have you burned at the stake for translating the Bible into English. William Tyndale, the first who attempted a full translation of the Bible into English from Hebrew and Greek texts, was strangled then burned for his efforts by other Christians in 1536.

At once I am and I am not teaching the history of Christianity, itself a rebellious religion, a religion that rebels through time in its rebellions against itself. This problem intensifies when whacking my way through the jungle of Christianity to the New Testament, when staring at my wall, procrastinating, while I stare at a huge weed that needs whacking. There is no way around at least a portion of the jungle when teaching the King James Version of the Bible, itself the physical product of Christian rebellions and disputes that happened long after the Bible.

You have to risk putting your students to sleep by explaining in an oversimplified manner, that with the help of a pagan philosophical idea about the essence of things the early church formed the idea that God and his son are both God. After all a Poodle, a Great Dane, and a Doberman, though different, are all dogs. Also, the church claimed that Jesus was both God and human. The Holy Ghost or Holy Spirit is another deity. The church gathered God, son, and spirit together after the fact and presented them as three in one. After the New Testament books were written, long after their insemination by early Christianity, the dominant branches of the early church officially deified a second and third God, new gods of different characters than the original God of the Old Testament, and still held that there is only one God. This idea confuses my students. How does 1 equal 3? "Don't worry, you don't have to understand the Doctrine of the Trinity for a final exam on the Bible."

Five minutes for the Trinity, the non-biblical Christian history of God. My students, like the powerful Christian, Marcion, in the second century, do not buy the one consistent God idea. They have already seen a changing God in their Old Testament studies and the New Testament God seems a radical revision of the Old Testament God. Despite the biblical evidence that God changes within the Old Testament and changes again from Old Testament to New Testament, despite a history of Christian efforts to add even more Gods and saints of varying character into the heavenly mix, many still believe that the nature of a one single God remains unchanged in Christian worship.

So do you teach the writing in the Gospels, the New Testament, the Bible on the whole—this group of books related by being bound together by now obscure mandates, books that are in conflict with each other? Or do you teach the various schools and the weed-like outgrowths of Christianity? I have to do some of both, of course, a problem I try to work out during extended wall gazing sessions. The problem is that church doctrines relied and still rely heavily on ideas brought on and defended, sometimes brutally, by dominant leaders within the Church. And the Church, when it wants to, trumps the Bible.

If we faced a death sentence for not believing in the human and divine nature of Jesus, then it would be best to steer clear of the study of the New Testament. We should quietly sign off on the documents pushed in our face, in history, by the men in funny hats and benevolent robes. We should nod our heads in agreement—before someone chops our heads off. I need to go chop down that weed.

But in this type of religious world we should also be careful not to read the Bible too closely because, on the whole, the Bible, with it multiple authors and multiple views, puts the doctrine itself at risk. That is why the Church killed a translator. Thankfully, these days we do not get killed by a State Church for having an understanding of the Bible that is different from the State's official position. At least I don't think so, although we will never know everything that has gone on at Gitmo.

A World Without Stained Glass

In the beginning was the Word, and the Word was with God, and the Word was God. —John 1: 1-3

For most of the history of the Bible, the Word has been absent. The books were not available to the masses, and even if they had been available they were written in languages that most people, a vast majority of people, could not read. Instead of using religious texts, Christianity has historically used religious imagery, powerful imagery, to encourage Christian conversion, to teach Christianity in its various forms, to help converts keep the faith, to help new generations to remember the religion's primary figures, stories, and themes.

Even after the Reformation in the 16th century, when printed translations of the Bible became easier to acquire, when literacy rates started going up, the historic Christian church and the newer churches and denominations used and still use religious imagery to forge popular church doctrine. It is a long way from understanding, or attempting to understand, the actual words in the Bible to understanding the vast number of Christian images presented in, say, Notre-Dame de Reims cathedral. It is a long way from the words of the prophets and apostles in the Bible to the images of the prophets and the apostles represented in the rose window of the same cathedral.

The question is how much of this imagery is actually pertinent in a Bible class? From stained glass rose windows to nativity scenes, to medieval demons, to mysterious images of the Virgin Mother, we have to avoid embarking on a pilgrimage that would lead us a long way from the Bible. A class on Christian imagery would be interesting, but a class on Christian imagery would not be a class on the Bible.

Am I sounding like a Protestant here? The imagery of the non- or pre-literate church period, the period before the printing and mass distribution of the Bible, has never gotten much competition from any Protestant close reading movement, even with higher literacy rates, even with Protestant pastors insisting, now for hundreds of years, that we study one of the abundant number of Bibles available to almost any biped. Nowadays, on our globe, it might be easier to find a free Bible than a free hot meal. One thing we can count on from the movement toward so-called biblical Christianity is that biblical texts will always take a back seat to the imagery, now often the television imagery we are afforded by fellows with their absolutely accurate haircuts. In so many quarters, being clean-cut projects the image of salvation while Jesus is portrayed with long, unkempt hair.

In my unscientific study of church imagery, my unscientific conclusions drawn from conversations with select individuals over a beer or a cup of coffee, my unscientific observations of my neighbor's wall and my large, yet uncut weed, Christians seem to be generally divided on how they respond to imagery. Although blurred, the line seems drawn along the border between the Catholic Church and Protestant denominations. If you are brought up Protestant, when entering a traditional Catholic church or cathedral, you are probably stunned by the prevalent and graphic, often bloody, images of the crucified Jesus on the cross and with the many images of the Virgin Mother.

If you are brought up in the Catholic tradition, you may be, if not shocked, curious about the absence of these images in a standard Protestant church, where the cross, sans Jesus, is often on display. Mary is hard to find. The imagery in the Catholic tradition, though, is there to be a stunning, if not a shocking, reminder of the physical man and his mother, the mother of God. On the Protestant side, the cross is a more abstract reminder of the spirit of God. In the Protestant tradition, this is an imagery of the absence of imagery. The plain steeple church in a quiet meadow is still an image, a reminder of an ever-present God with whom Everyman might have a special relationship.

I do not think Protestant denominations, though sparked by a mission to be more biblically or textually based and less driven by physical imagery, could ever return to the Bible, because Christianity, though it made the Bible what it is today, never came from the Bible. Christianity, in all of its forms, gained—gains—converts through preaching, not comprehensive reading, through oral and visual renderings of the good news, not through passing a final exam on the Bible, as my students have to do.

What is the central message of the biblical book of Habakkuk? Maybe you do not know a thing about the prophet Habakkuk, and maybe you do not know much about much of the Bible. Does this lack of knowledge about the Bible make you any less of a Christian? Christianity is based, not on holy texts, but on the potential salvation of any living being. Of course one cannot hold this salvation principle to be true and then say that only those who are literate enough to read and study the Bible can enter the everlasting kingdom.

Christianity comes from sight and sound more so than words. Christianity is maintained by imagery, even in the Protestant tradition, where the Bible as bound book is the core image. There is plenty of stained glass in the Protestant tradition, and, when you consider the endurance in the Protestant tradition of such non-biblical doctrines as the doctrine of the Trinity, you realize that the Protestant Reformation—this movement against the established church in Rome that made the Texas Baptists all that they are today—the Reformation was about reforming imagery and redefining church hierarchy and not a re-creation of Christianity as a Bible-based religion.

There are a plethora of images, or physical reminders, in Protestantism, of its religious mission, despite the fidelity most Protestant denominations claim to hold for the written Bible. No branch of Christianity, or any religion for that matter, can hold up without its own imagery. Both my old Protestant professor and the Protestant offense takers in my old college class had given fealty to Christian religious imagery rather than biblical texts—anti-imagery, imagery that arises when you glue together bits and pieces of textual support from the Bible, an imagery less direct than the bloody Jesus, but an imagery that, though amorphous, is still strongly present and heartfelt.

When distant biblical texts compete with close and heartfelt hometown religious imagery, the imagery wins out. God the father is an abstraction in most forms of Christianity, but Jesus is not an abstraction. In the Christian world, Jesus is the physical representation of God—the Jesus who lived and who still lives—but the problem is that we have many images of Jesus to choose from. There are the many Jesuses, bleeding on the many crosses. None of these Jesuses come from the Bible.

The largely Protestant offense takers in my college class had their Jesus, the less intellectual cousin of the more abstract divinity school Jesus of our humanities professor. The Protestant Jesus was and is often the white God Jesus that we see in various venues, an image of Jesus that Langston Hughes vandalized in the lines included at the beginning of this section. Carrying the tint of the stern mountain God in his eyes, the WASP God Jesus is a blue-eyed American guy of northern European descent, Charlton Heston's first cousin, looking a little distant and a little stoned in his robe with his beard and hippy hair. With his hands held out, he fills the framed picture you see in so many church fellowship halls.

My unshazaamed Japanese students do not know about the conflicts between the martyred Jesus of the Catholic tradition and the white fellowship hall Protestant Jesus. They do not know how these physical Jesuses conflict with the comfy Galilean Jesus of my professor, the finely finished and reformed barefoot rabbi who reminds us that life is more about gaining a profound understanding of God and self than about acquiring big houses and nice cars. This intellectual image of Jesus, though, is not very physical. It is too abstract, which explains why this non-image image has failed to win the hearts and minds of big room, hometown religious folk in either the Catholic or Protestant traditions.

My Japanese students have not been bombarded by Christian Jesus images before we get to Matthew's Jesus. They might know something about these images, but they have not been shazamed into receiving these images with awe or wonder: the many Jesus images, some obliquely draw from biblical texts, some just simply made up—the Romanesque Jesuses tortured on the cross, small and large, the Grecian statue of Jesus with disciples, appearing as if they have taken over the School of Athens, the squared-off concrete Christ of Rio, the obscure black baby of the black Virgin of Montserrat, and so many other statues, large and small. The praying Jesus in stained glass profile, the many baby Jesuses in the many mangers, Jesus as movie star, superstar, Jesus as athlete, Jesus as CEO, Jesus for president, or the more humble porcelain Jesus standing on the table by Aunt May's telephone. They did not grow up with the images and pictures that are tattooed on memory, often from childhood in Christian cultures, so they do not carry these images into an exploration of the New Testament.

I cannot make the joke about God becoming a Christian in the New Testament because Mr. Yoshida and most of his classmates do not know very much about who The Christ is, in any of his physical forms. They do not know Christ, not because they have not read the Bible but because they do not have the imagery of a physical Jesus embedded in their minds as they are growing up in their culture. If I tell the joke about God becoming a Christian, about God changing into the image of Christ, no one in my Japanese class would likely get it nor would they likely take offense because the joke itself would not evoke the competition in the Christian world between hometown and gown projections of the living God.

My university department requires students to take a class on Christianity offered by a Christian minister, but it is not considered a pre-requisite for my class, nor is my class a pre-requisite for his, and in fact our classes are not connected. My class is just another elective on a general menu of classes in the humanities. I used to think that the disconnection between Christianity and the Bible was a flaw in our curriculum, but now I am not so sure. A course in Christianity for Japanese students, even for those who decide to convert to Christianity, could not really shape the images forged in the minds of those who grow up Christian in one of many Christian cultures. And still, the Bible, with its many images that are often counterposed to the religion that created it, has many questions, and we do not have the answers.

My students do not understand that the book we are studying did not shape Christianity; Christianity, in its many forms, shaped the book. It is troublesome to explain major New Testament doctrines, sometimes doctrines that disagree with each other. It is troublesome that I have to attempt to do this, as it were, without the formal images of Christianity pre-installed, either in the mind of the students in my class or in the minds of the writers of the biblical writings we cover. It hurts me to do these things because I know how much this type of close reading would disappoint, would harrow the hearts of so many of my cousins from the Christian world, folks I know and respect—folks whom I love. Their beloved Christianity, in its whole form and with its Jesus, is not there to be found, with these students in this culture and in these texts. It is not there.

But it is a blessing that I do not have to plough through layers and layers of imagery with offended and argumentative students who want to defend myriad bundles of pre-installed stained glass with the attendant spiritual reckonings. I do not have to ramble on about the vision of Bernadette of Lourdes, or about any of the many visions of the Virgin Mother. I don't have to explain the Apostles Creed, the Doxology, John Wesley, or the Rapture, before we read the Gospels.

The Jesus There

> *"How can I help it?" he blubbered. "How can I help seeing what is in front of my eyes? Two and two are four."*
> *"Sometimes, Winston. Sometimes they are five. Sometimes they are three. Sometimes they are all of them at once. You must try harder. It is not easy to become sane."* —George Orwell, from *1984*

My students, by cultural disposition, see Jesus first in the King James Version of the Bible, the Jesus in reverse. They read about the baby in an animal food trough, un-reinforced by the many pastoral but not-precisely-biblical Christmas manger scenes. They read outlandish reports about the feats of a Jewish man who spoke harshly against Jewish religious authorities, without the image in mind of the fair and long haired savior with a halo over his head or of the deceased, languid Son of God in the arms of the grieving mother of God in Michelangelo's *Pieta*. They read second-hand reports of the life events, the deeds, and sayings of this person in words, instead of being taught about Jesus first through the many Jesus images that are distributed and embraced in Christian cultures.

We on the Christian side of the world interpret biblical writing and particularly New Testament writing with what is called intentionality in the interpretation business. If your Jesus is a white church fellowship hall Jesus, you will intentionally, on some level, carry that image with you into any reading of the Jesus stories in the Gospels. But, in Japan, we are reading the Gospels without pre-delivered and embedded images of a person who is not physically described in the Bible. All my students can gather about the image of Jesus is that he was Jewish and from what we now call the Middle East, which does not suggest that he looked like an inspired pothead from Utah. What they see first in the New Testament are uncomfortably inexact ideas about the Son of God and the son of David. We find a fundamental inconsistency that shapes the New Testament, one that, in my new view, neither the Christian architects of the Bible nor later theologians or theoreticians interpreting the Bible as book ever reconciled or will ever reconcile. In the Jesus stories, two plus two never equals four, even from the beginning.

There is the Jesus as Jew forwarded in the first three gospels, who opposed the status quo, yet defended beliefs and practices of the religion he was born into. But also there is the Jesus of the fourth gospel of John, the writings of Paul and other New Testament writing who is culturally separated from the Jews. This inconsistency carries other inconsistencies—the conflict between Jesus' human nature and his divine nature, his gentle nature and not-so-gentle nature—that make the Jesus character in the Bible difficult for Japanese students to understand, difficult for me to understand.

In the first three gospels Jesus is not presented clearly as a God, but we do see him as:

(1) a direct Jewish descendant of the warrior leaders and kings of Israel,

(2) a cultural protégé, of the Hebrew priests and prophets of yore (a category that includes teacher), and

(3) a man who has a DNA problem.

These three depictions come from a collection of authors, about whom we know too little, transcriptions and translations of their texts, with many textual variants in extant copies, and, when it was decided to collect them together, closed meetings with no exacting minutes, during which certain narratives were selected and ordered for reasons that are eternally obscure.

The people who eventually compiled the Gospels and the rest of the biblical books in the order that we have them now, according to Carroll and Prickett, "had to approach the past not as a sequence of time but as a problem with a meaning that had to be explained" (xix). Certain themes, primarily the gradual extraction of Jesus and his teachings from the Hebrew tradition, are forwarded by the ordering of books non-chronologically.

The ordering of the books was based, not on when they were written, but how their arrangement shows us the coming and going of Christ, the beginnings of Christianity and the Christian church, and the prospect of the return of the Risen Christ. But the first three gospels of the New Testament present us with a non-traditional Christian view of Jesus in any current Christian denomination.

(1) Jesus as Jewish King. At the onset of the New Testament, Jesus is identified as the direct descendant of the leaders of the chosen Israelites, a fact that is not promoted in evangelical or mainstream Christian churches. In the first verse of the first book of Matthew the author proclaims that Jesus is "the son of David and the son of Abraham" (1:1). In Luke, the lineage of Jesus, though much different from Matthew's genealogy, is traced, through David and Abraham, back to Adam who, like Jesus, was the son of God (3:38).

We Christianized folk do not think of Adam as a Jew or of God as a Jew. The un-Jewish and un-kingly image of Jesus as an itinerate but inspired teacher and miracle worker and as the self-proclaimed Son of God is strong in all of the Gospels, and these images have won out in modern Christian cultures. But throughout the first three gospels, my students see a Jesus who is repeatedly referred to as the son of David, who my students remember as the great albeit flawed warrior king of ancient Israelite glory. Not only is Jesus Jewish by these accounts, he descends from the highest line of the fathers of the Israelites, and he is given a first family, first son, regal birthright.

Though his people, his race, had lost power, Jesus has, by these Gospel accounts and by Old Testament judicial precedent, the strongest legal claim to the kingship should his people regain power, should he wish to lead them in this effort. In Matthew, but in Matthew only, King Herod's paranoia even about the rumor of such a person provokes him into ordering the mass slaughter of children. It was Herod who would have been by order of the Roman Senate the "King of the Jews." Herod's horrible response is used as verification, again in Matthew, of the strength of Jesus' claim to this same kingship from birth.

Also in Matthew the wise men ask for the child who was born King of the Jews (2:2). In all four of the Gospels, the issue of Jesus' illegal claim to kingship under the Roman government is the legal means by which Pilate seeks a criminal conviction. Jesus reportedly does not answer to the charge that he believes himself to be the King of the Jews, which complicates matters at his trial. But the writing that was placed with or over Jesus on the cross, though the exact words are recorded differently in different Gospels, appears in each Gospel, leaving the reader with the bitingly sardonic image of Jesus, a crucified Jesus, as King of the Jews.

In modern democracies, we have abstracted the idea of kingship to an honorary status. The dual roles of Jesus as a Jewish King and Jesus as son of God do not press us into thinking just how different these roles are. Both indicate Jesus' extreme importance, and this status is enough for modern Christianity. But in Japanese culture the period of the King or Emperor, a person who is both leader and God, has only recently passed. Many of my students have grandparents or great-grandparents who remember Imperial Japan.

Even as recently as 2000, Yoshiro Mori, then prime minister of Japan, stated that Japan was a "divine nation" with "the emperor at its center." The statement whipped up a strong reaction from a large number of Japanese who would like to keep such thinking in the past, and in my experience it mostly is in the past. But the universal acceptance of the divine role of King or Emperor is still a living memory in Japan. One question that has not come up, but that I am sure will come up is, "did the ancient Israelites view their human kings as divine?" The answer is: absolutely not. King David is close to God, but he is not God. Jesus makes this point.

In modern democracies, presidents and prime ministers call us to wars, not kings; generals, not kings, execute these wars. But a strong king, in the Bible and throughout most of Christian church history, if not divine, is an able warrior who is backed by God (when he wins). Joshua and David are excellent biblical examples of Israelite warrior kings backed by God. Jesus follows in this line. Many of us in the Christian world have been led to see Jesus as peace loving. But my students read his recorded outburst in Matthew 10:34 and see a different fellow:

> Think not that I am come to send peace on earth: I came not to send peace, but a sword.

This sentiment, repeated in Luke 12:51, would not surprise a reader who understands the relationship between kings and swords. And it does not surprise a typical Japanese student entering into Bible study without the shazams of Christian church imagery and doctrine. Students do notice that this statement contradicts the peace-loving Jesus, who reportedly said, "Blessed are the peacemakers; for they shall be called the children of God" (Matthew 5:9).

This classic verse, found only in Matthew from what we now call the Sermon on the Mount, along with injunction to turn the other cheek and to love one's enemies, found in Matthew as well as other Gospel sources, give us rich source material for the peace loving Jesus that has made its way into modern Christian thinking. As Jesus repeatedly refers to himself as a child of God, as the Son of God (not the son of David), he must rank himself among the peacemakers.

The benevolent Jesus has a large presence in the Gospels. On balance, the Jesus of the Gospels—when he is not ransacking the Temple and running out the merchants with a whip, when he is not harshly denouncing the priests and the rules of the established religion in extended verbal outbursts, when he is not insisting that we gouge out our eyes or cut off our hands when either cause us to sin, when he is not offering to weld a sword and suggesting that people should make enemies within their own households—comes across as a peace loving fellow, akin to the nicer images of Jesus we have throughout the Christian world. In a Japanese Bible class, though, the modern Christian imagination has no filter for the other Jesus who is presented strongly in the Gospels. This other kingly, sword-bearing, hard line Jesus is far harsher in the Gospels than in many standard Christian church traditions, but this often-agitated warrior king without his kingdom is manifest in the eyes of my students.

There is no intentionality, no pre-recorded Jesus in the minds of my students. You would have to cross many roads before you found a Jesus on a cross in Tokyo, cross even more crossings before finding a church fellowship hall Jesus. My students are freer than I am, than we are from Christian cultures, to conjure their own images of the Jesus of the Bible. But consolidating an image of Jesus simply as peacemaker is difficult to do in our Bible class because of the great variation in the things he is reported to have said and done in the Gospels.

(2) Jesus as Prophet. The Gospels report this double-edged Jesus, the Jesus of the sword and the Jesus of peace, combined with the Jesus who has a double-edged sword protruding from his mouth in Revelation 2:12-16, and insert him among the prophets with their double-edged world view. This is the second distinct idea about Jesus that comes out in a Japanese classroom. The prophetic writings are stacked on the rear of the Old Testament and, if you skip over the Apocrypha, the book of Matthew follows hard upon. Jesus descends from Israelite kings. His blood ties set, he is then given a spiritual link with the great prophets of Jewish tradition, first with the observation in Matthew 1:22-23 that he is Emmanuel (or Immanuel), the fulfillment of the prophecy of Isaiah (7:14) and second by showing that, after his baptism and temptation, he is naturally drawn to teaching and preaching and working miracles and, importantly, seeing the future:

> Repent: for the kingdom of heaven is at hand. (4:17)

Jesus is the prophetic fulfillment of prophecy. He is the prophet himself and among the highest order of priests of what was, even in this time, the ancient Levite tribe (maybe this is the reason for the long hair). In Hebrew biblical tradition, high marks are given to birthright and further to those who have the magical gift of interpretive insight, which includes the gift of seeing into the future. Here is the priestly, prophet king, the fulfillment of prophecy itself.

Early in the New Testament, Jesus condemns the powers of the existing religious order with what my students see as a condescending rant. This section begins in Matthew 23:13 with:

> But woe unto you, scribes and Pharisees, hypocrites! for ye shut up the kingdom of heaven against men.

Many woe-unto-you salutations follow. This passage brings to mind a style of verbal condemnation forged by the Old Testament prophets, particularly in the book of Jeremiah, and specifically when Jeremiah is angry:

> Woe unto the pastors that destroy and scatter the sheep of my pasture! Saith the Lord. (23:1)

In Matthew 5:17, Jesus makes it very clear that he is in line with the earlier prophets when he says, "Think not that I am come to destroy the law, or the prophets: I am not come to destroy, but to fulfil."

The writers of the New Testament read sections of the Old Testament closely. Old Testament prophets, particularly Isaiah, project peace on earth, but prophets also rant about the eminent destruction of those who do not follow God's law. Prophets do not hold back when they see problems with the existing order. They often show their tempers. Jesus, too, has a temper. Jesus is drawn to the synagogue, a place that comes off in the New Testament as a verbal fight bar.

But my students live in a culture where temper tantrums are considered excessive, a sign of emotional failure. And in the woe-unto-you passage they see a speaker calling too much attention to himself. But Jesus is squarely in line with the old prophets, who gave lengthy public condemnations of powerful religious leaders and even kings and who are often just plain irritating. This characteristic also positions Jesus with a type of person, in the standard Japanese way of thinking, whose argument is ineffective because he cannot calm down and negotiate, even if he is completely in the right.

By the time we reach the New Testament my students know the Bible well enough to know that the Hebrew world of the Bible was less patient with contrarians than modern day Japan or any modern-day democracy. These contrary traits place Jesus, and more immediately, John the Baptist, on the short list for extreme punishment and even untimely death by assassination or execution. Prophets get angry, and prophets also anger people.

Prophets distance themselves from the people. They have special gifts, but you do not want to go drinking with, go to a baseball game with, a prophet. Jesus' prophetic qualities make him even more of a distant, even disengaging figure in the minds of Japanese students. In the view of my students, Jesus is one of them, not the nice, comfy fellow who helps us find strength when we go on a diet or quit smoking or forgive Aunt May for all those bad things she said about us while talking to her friends over the phone. To make this point more understandable to us, the shazamites, how often does someone, after reading the book of Jeremiah, begin to feel that he or she is developing a personal relationship with Jeremiah? He has no wailing mother, no *Pieta*.

The Gospel writers want Jesus to be distant. He is a man, but he is also a king and a prophet. He is not like the rest of us. Jesus operates on another level. The words "personal" and "relationship" do not appear with each other anywhere in the King James Version.

Developing a personal relationship with Jesus or God is not a biblical concept. In the Bible, Moses, Abraham, and Adam have personal relationships with God. But those heroes would be the first to tell you that having a personal relationship with God can be rough going. As we move into the New Testament, we are implored by the writers to develop more empathy with the life of Jesus than we are with the life of Jeremiah. And this life is brought closer to us by the repetition of scenes in the first three Gospels—Matthew, Mark, and Luke—and with John's independent but highly inspired rendering of the Jesus story. Still to my students the imploring voices and repetition of the same story in the New Testament comes from distant voices, distant figures, not from the living people who form modern church societies.

There is an emphasis put on "knowing" Jesus in the New Testament. It is made clear that he is a superman. He feeds the hungry, he heals horrible diseases, he runs out demons that enter your body and mind, and he can bring the dead back to life. You would want to be on his side and not the side of his enemies. There is nothing mysteriously personal here. In the Gospels Jesus is not buttered over again and again by the history of Christian mysticism and, more recently, the various cults of religious qua self-help currics that are stirred up throughout the Christian world.

The biblical Jesus is demanding, very demanding. If he calls on you to follow him, it would be best for you follow the example of his first disciples, Simon Peter, Andrew, James, and John, and to drop everything you are doing and immediately walk away from your livelihood (Matthew 4:18-22). He famously suggested to a rich man in Matthew and elsewhere that he sell off of his possessions (19: 21). He calls on his flock to turn against the members of their own family if necessary, saying that "he that loveth father or mother more than me is not worthy of me" (10: 37). When polled, my students find these positions too demanding, even from the Son of God. Jesus speaks as the powerful prophet king: He is not in a cheerful mood or ready to be your best buddy.

These demands come from a charismatic man who is dispossessed of his birthright and is not happy about it. He is what those from my country crossroads call a tough customer. Not only will he challenge the members and wannabe members of his flock with difficult demands, he is ready to challenge priestly leaders even though he and his followers know that these leaders are ready to punish, even kill. And these are priestly leaders who are of the same race and religion that the Old Testament writers side with. What my students do not see is the warm and fuzzy hug buddy/genie out of the bottle/teddy bear that so many hold this Jesus to be in many modern Christian denominations.

But in the accounts of the life of Jesus there is an image of a person who is more interesting to my students than Jeremiah or Isaiah or even Daniel, who has the most alluring personal narrative of any of the Old Testament prophets. There are brilliant and memorable Jesus moments in the Gospels, moments that we do not have in the stories of the other prophets or kings of yore. There is a wonderful and revealing humanity involved in feeding the masses, in turning water into wine, in proclaiming that only someone who has not sinned should throw the first stone. These are the happy reports of a miracle worker who understands basic human needs and flaws, who delivers the fine message that life can be hard but that we all should relish those times when we can enjoy eating and drinking and not stoning people to death. Instead of participating in a bloody public execution this afternoon, let's have a cold beer and enjoy a cookout.

More so than the Bible's insistence on the resurrection of Jesus, which my Japanese students see as more contrived Old Testament exaggeration, another fish story although more morbid, my students are affected by the grand finale of the life of Jesus, the images of crucifixion described in various ways in the Gospels. This ending, the way in which it is variously detailed in the Gospels, the foresight of the prophet Jesus, the betrayal, the arrest, the trial, the torture, the final scene on Golgotha, sets the Jesus story apart from the stories of prior kings and prophets.

But in the first three gospels, my students see a Jesus who is yet another persecuted Jew, albeit a contentious Jew, but one in a long line of contentious spokespeople for the God of the Israelites. The Christian church tradition tends to portray Jesus as a mistreated non-Jew, the son of a new and curiously gentile, Christianized God. We from Christian backgrounds are prompted to have more sympathy for a religion that, as we move farther into the New Testament, draws more spokesmen who accept Gentiles, the uncircumcised, into the faith. Of course we are inclined to identify more with the gentle Jesus figure than we would be with *them*, the Old Testament kings and prophets who also undergo extreme trials and punishments. In a Japanese classroom, Jew or

Gentile or Jesus or Old Testament prophet, none of them are us.

Jesus is portrayed as a non-Jew in Christian cultures because he seems closer to Christians as a non-Jew or, more accurately, as a non-primitive Hebrew prophet. In Japan, though, the suffering of Jesus, though memorably and repeatedly depicted, is more in line with the general theme of Israelite suffering presented in the old prophetic world of the Old Testament. In the Bible, all the big guys suffer, even God.

Once, when we were beginning the New Testament, I overheard a student quip in Japanese, "These Christian things are scary, too." The Christian elements that surface in the New Testament, the idea of forgiving and being forgiven, the prospect of finally being able to return to God, of God returning to man, these Christian elements should represent the harmonized hopes of more tolerant and less fearful communities of earnest do-gooders. In this student's naïve view of things, Christianity should not be positioned so closely with the ancient and often harsh Hebrew traditions of the Old Testament. In the mind of this not Christian young man, something about Christianity led him to believe that it is a harmonious and peaceful religion, not scary like before. The New Testament surprises you with its own scary things.

When you read the New Testament without another Jesus pre-installed, he is seen by my students on one level as yet another distant prophetic figure from a highly intolerant Hebrew or Jewish tribal culture, a superman who can be a tough and scary figure himself at times, and who has a really tough time in a tough, and scary world that will soon come to an end in one big, scary, shock and awe campaign.

(3) Whose Son? The third distinct idea about Jesus is the most troubling for my students, with their unbending insistence that two plus two equals four. Jesus is called the son of David and the Son of God. I have tried to skip over the family line problems Jesus has in the New Testament in the same way that mainstream Christian teaching has skipped over it for time eternal. But there is often a diligent student in class who will not let me pass over this problem in silence. So I have had to do an excruciating amount of research into

the Jesus genealogy problem, excruciating not only because it involves exacting details, but because this area is populated with people and their books and websites who were already nuts before they looked into this problem or have driven themselves nuts by trying to deal with problems like this.

In order to explain the problem of Jesus' father, I also have to go headfirst into the deep, dark void of "More Than Anyone Ever Wanted to Know." Unless you are talking about your own family, genealogy is boring. The Archbishop of Canterbury's description of Henry V's genealogical claims to French lands, though thematically important, is one of the most boring speeches in Shakespeare. I would wager that most readers of the New Testament, when they start at Matthew, skip over the opening verses on Jesus' family line.

Two different genealogies are presented for Jesus in the Gospels. The first is in Matthew 1:1-16, which links Jesus to the line of David. Jesus cannot be the Messiah without this link because, according to tradition, the forthcoming Messiah has to descend from the old kings of Israel, from the Chosen. He must spring from the line of Abraham and David.

Matthew's genealogy starts with Abraham and ends with Joseph, who is vaguely described as "the husband of Mary, of whom Jesus was born" (1:16). The author does not state that Jesus was the son of Joseph, no doubt because he will soon claim that there are higher powers behind the conception of Jesus, a claim my students see as strange in Matthew 1:18:

> Now the birth of Jesus Christ was on this wise: When as his mother Mary was espoused to Joseph, before they came together, she was found with child of the Holy Ghost.

The next point, one that has often popped up in class, one that is missed by shazamed Trinitarians like me, is spooky when you think about it. In both Matthew and Luke, the fatherhood of Jesus is given to or claimed by the Holy Ghost. The Holy Ghost or Holy Spirit is seen by Christians to be the spirit of God. This Spirit is at one time the same as God but separate from God.

But in the book of Matthew, where the Holy Ghost first appears in the King James Version, and in later references to the Holy Ghost, it is not made clear exactly who or what the Holy Ghost is, at least not in the view of my students. The Holy Ghost is presented as a paranormal spirit that can expand itself communally into a group of people (Acts 4:31) and, after this bodily entrance of the Holy Ghost, an individual can see the future and speak in languages the individual did not know before (Acts 19:6). So we have modern cults of people babbling incoherently in their churches. But the Holy Ghost is also a separate entity in the Bible. Jesus, in Matthew 28:19, calls to his flock to "teach all nations, baptizing them in the name of the Father, and of the Son, and of the Holy Ghost."

It is easy enough to presume that the Holy Ghost is felt to be the spirit of God by the writers of the New Testament, the same spirit of God that "moved along the face of the waters" in their reading of Genesis 1:2. This view of the Holy Ghost as an extension of God's own being, even physical being, works well thematically throughout the Bible.

The world starts in Genesis with the interaction between the Spirit of God and the waters, before God separates the waters. Moses parts the Red Sea or Reed Sea. The Jordan is parted more than once, and this same Jordan water is used later for baptism, again a parting of the waters. The Jordan waters are parted for the baptism of Jesus. Through parted water, and walked-on water, the Holy Spirit or Spirit of God is manifested in New Testament salvation. The Holy Spirit impregnates Mary. By doing this, the Holy Spirit again interacts with water, this time the water of the womb, which is separated by the child growing inside. This explanation, after I gave it a go, stunned my students. This was the first and last time I used this idea in class.

Too over the top—but over the top is where explanations of the over the top New Testament often lead you. My students do not get the idea that the Holy Spirit is separate and, at one and the same time, God, and also in Man, in people. Later, when Jesus, son of the Holy Spirit, also claims to be the son of God, my students are not sure what this means. Enter a third father.

The Jewish tradition requires the Messiah to be in David's line. Jesus is the son of David. The Jesus story told in Matthew and elsewhere also states that Jesus is the Son of God and also the Holy Ghost. My students wonder, *How can you have it all these ways?*

Some biblical commentators argue that Jesus is only the adoptive son of Joseph, and adoption, according to the laws in those times, gave you legal birthright. I cannot imagine a punishment harsh enough for Christian apologists who slough off all contradictions in the Bible by making vague claims to what was the case "in those times." Those times? What times—epochs covering hundreds of years and massive political and social changes?

The first-born male, the male clearly born in the blood of the father has the strongest possible claim for legal birthright throughout the Bible, and my students know this from the story of Jacob and Esau. Also Jesus' reported status as being the son of David gives him credibility among the people to whom he ministers. Joseph has to be the blood father of Jesus. My students view the adoption argument for Jesus' dual parentage as weak. Some of them suspect foul play in this story about virgin birth.

Another possible explanation for the duel lineage of Jesus is based on the genealogy presented in Luke 3:23-38, which is far different from Matthew's genealogy and which traces Jesus back to Adam. This explanation argues that Adam is the Son of God. So Jesus is the Son of God through his direct link to Adam. This argument only holds if we disregard what is said about the Holy Ghost being the real father and accept the idea that Joseph is Jesus' natural father, which would be a contradiction of what Matthew actually says.

Another explanation for Jesus' duel descent from God and David is that Mary, mother of Jesus, provides the blood link to King David. Mary's background is not given in the text. But using Luke's genealogy, some have suggested that Mary was the daughter of Heli, also descended from King David, so Jesus follows in Mary's line, and because of this is the Son of David and the Son of God (or the Holy Ghost). This explanation also seems stretched to my students because the linkage between Mary and David is not made clear in the text itself.

The largest contradiction to the above arguments comes from what Jesus reportedly says. First, he does not seem to be impressed with his earthly parentage. At one point, while he is speaking to a crowd, Jesus is told that his mother and brothers are outside and have asked to speak to him. Jesus asks, "Who is my mother? and who are my brethren!" then gestures to his disciples and says that his disciples and in fact anyone who will "do the will of his Father which is in heaven" are his family. This event is recorded in Matthew 12:46-50, Mark 3:31-35, and also Luke 8:19-31.

This pronouncement is crowd pleasing, but it is also made at the expense of his direct family members, and it indicates that Jesus was not concerned about tying himself to his blood relatives or, for that matter, with King David. The modern Christian "family values" qua Jesus movement seems out of touch with these reports of the biblical Jesus. Jesus reportedly says in Matthew 9:29:

> And every one that hath forsaken houses, or brethren, or sisters, or father, or mother, or wife, or children, or lands, for my name's sake, shall receive an hundredfold, and shall inherit everlasting life.

This bent against family values is repeated in Mark 10:29-30 and even more sternly in Luke 14:26. Jesus' admirers, the blind men, the Canaanite woman, the crowds who come to hear him, refer to him as the son of David, but Jesus never refers to himself as the son of David, at least I cannot find where he does. When talking to a group of Pharisees, he asks them whose son is Christ. They answer "the Son of David," to which Jesus replies with an interpretation of Psalm 110 that David saw the Messiah as his "Lord" so how could David's Lord be his son also. In Matthew 22:45, Jesus says:

> If David then call him Lord, how is he his son?

This statement is repeated with different wording in Mark

12:37 and in Luke 20:44. Theologically complex, particularly with Jesus' own interpretation of his own lineage, the debate with the Pharisees indicates, on the whole, that Jesus did not see himself as the son of David. This idea also seems to undercut the importance of the two lengthy genealogies in the Gospels. What does Mr. Yamauchi think? He thinks very plainly that what is said about Jesus and what is reported that Jesus said contradict each other.

That is if Mr. Yamauchi can stay awake through all of this genealogy. Mr. Matsuda, of course, is in a coma by this time. This whole complex matter is made more complex when you come across one of Paul's rhetorical flourishes, the one in the opening of Romans that proclaims in Romans 1:3 that Jesus Christ is the son of God and also "made of the seed of David according to the flesh." Paul sees Jesus as the son of David. But in the second book of Timothy, ascribed to Paul, in 1:9, there is a praise to the God who "hath saved us, and called us with an holy calling, not according to our works, but according to his own purpose and grace, which was given us in Christ Jesus before the world began" (2 Timothy 1:9). The statement that the grace of Jesus was given "before the world began" indicates that Jesus existed even before mankind. There is no King David in this flourish. John 8:58 reports that "Jesus said unto them, Verily, verily, I say unto you, Before Abraham was, I am."

The onus is not on me to explain how all of these views can be molded together to form one unified understanding of where Jesus came from, of who, in sum, Jesus is. My students would not buy it, but then, they have not been Christianized. I doubt that the attempt to collapse all of these views into a single understanding of Jesus' origins would work out very well even at a local Sunday school. When you explain Jesus to a Japanese class, you get the sense that much of the Bible seems to be made up as the writers go along. A good example of this type of thinking out loud is in Proverbs 6:16-18 which says:

> These six things doth the LORD hate: yea, seven are an abomination unto him: A proud look, a lying tongue, and hands that shed innocent blood, An heart that

eviseth wicked imaginations, feet that be swift in running to mischief, A false witness that speaketh lies, and he that soweth discord among brethren.

There are two questions, no, one question I would like to ask the writer of this passage: Why is it that he didn't know how many abominations there were before he started writing?

This revisionism, placed as it is in the writing itself, does not come off as writing that is inspired by God, but a rough draft that might be changed later. Unclear thinking occurs in the Bible, and my students get it. In their view, much of the New Testament's depiction of Jesus is a work in progress. These inconsistencies are nowhere more pronounced that in the New Testaments' flip-flop on whether you need to follow the law and do good works or simply have faith. We will get into this thicket later.

But first, let's explore some scary Christian things.

Scary Christian Things I: Eating Jesus

Yea, brother, let me have joy of thee in the Lord: refresh my bowels in the Lord —Philemon 1:20

There is a story floating around my hometown about a man, a good Christian guy, who married his long time wife on the Saturday of Easter weekend. Each year for the next 24 years of their marriage, he gave his wife an anniversary card on the Saturday of Easter weekend. On the 25th year, on Easter weekend, his wife, a mild woman, mildly called him on it: "Honey, think about it."

Yea, brother, Easter is a tough one. Most Christians know that Easter Sunday jumps around from year to year, but most are not exactly sure why or how Easter is figured. I say this because, having been brought up with Easter Sunday, having done the Easter services along with the people my family went to church with, I knew little about how Easter was set up before I began looking into it, finally, as middle-aged Bible teacher who lives in a tiny apartment in a not Christian land.

A recent *Newsweek* poll concluded that 78% of Americans believe that Jesus rose from the dead. The trouble is that no one knows exactly when that happened or can even set a firm annual date to observe that happening. One wonders what the poll results would be if the same believers were asked how Easter, the religious day in which Christians observe the most important event in Christianity, is determined each year.

When I first started teaching the Bible, I naïvely felt that it would be good to include some explanations about traditional Christian holidays and observances as part of the class. I ran into problems (a) because I found—Easter being the best example of this, and Christmas not far behind—that I did not know nearly enough about traditional church holidays and observances to teach them, and (b) because a number of Christian holidays and observances, including Easter and Christmas, do not appear in the Bible.

They had not become traditions yet. By looking into Easter, or Christmas, I was going off-syllabus. There is one arcane reference to Easter in the King James Version, in Acts 12:4, but this probably points to the Passover, which is far different, of course, from the Easter of Christian tradition.

In Exodus, the Passover, the event itself, is described in bloody detail. More than enough time passes in the Old Testament for the Passover to become a traditional observance by the time we get to the Gospels. The Passover is not Easter. There is no Christmas in the Bible, no framework for the observance of the birth of Jesus. There is the birth, the announcement by the heavenly hosts to the shepherds and the wise men—but "O Holy Night" had not been written yet, and it is hard to imagine Christmas trees, particularly North American Douglas-firs, in fig land.

Christian spokespeople point to how strange it is to have pagan symbols such as Santa and the Easter Bunny and, I guess, Douglas-firs, too, hanging around or to hang things on during their religious holidays. In the Christian imagination, the Christians were there first, and now their world is being encroached upon by outside, un-Christian, unholy forces. No one knows exactly how Christian holidays that are not in the Bible shoved their way into pagan holidays, but there was a clearly a trade off.

Concerning Easter, maybe it was this scenario: Around the Year of our Lord 593 an Irish Christian missionary moves in with a Northern European tribe of boar hunters who have never heard of Christianity. He comes bearing trinkets, so they let him stay for a while, long enough for him to learn the 17 words of their language. He manages to set up a meeting with the spear-welding elders of the tribe. They eye him suspiciously when he explains that he can show them how they can live forever.

First they have to recognize the resurrection of Jesus, a story that even the pre-scientific elders voice suspicions about. The missionary does not have a bible. Hand copied bibles are too expensive and too heavy to carry around, and the elders would not be able to read a bible in Latin anyway. Instead, the missionary shows them a picture book, a dark age Manga, with colorful drawings of Jesus nailed to a cross. After grunting at each other, after sloshing down another round of rotgut mead, the elders are at first delighted by the primal cruelty of nailing someone you do not like to a piece of wood. Why hadn't they thought of that? The elders admit that the eternal life idea sounds attractive. But they wonder if they can still do the fun pagan things they like to do in the spring, when it finally warms up to just below freezing and people start feeling frisky. They ask the missionary if they can still drink and have sex like rabbits and eat sweet bark on the first full moon after the spring equinox in celebration of *Eostre*, their goddess of fertility.

The missionary understands that his welcome might run out any minute and that these gentlemen, when they are not killing boar, are out killing people from neighboring tribes, just for the fun of it. So the missionary goes for a compromise. He speaks directly to Thurthwat, the lead elder, while the others elders listen carefully, saying that, yes, the original spring celebration can stay intact—just as long as sex is not had with another man's woman.

The elders pause and look at each other silently. In unison they grunt and nod in agreement. They already had the rule that you cannot have sex with another man's woman, but they do not tell the missionary because this is now a negotiation. The missionary continues. He tells Thurthwat and company that they will have to phase out Eostre, the fertility goddess, and also *Zanock,* the Boar God. These gods are no good anymore. Thowg, another elder, asks if it is okay to keep the Zanock design on their new kilts that their women have just sewn.

"Yes," comes the answer, "but you can't worship him." Everyone grunts. Done deal.

After the missionary goes off to his early bedtime, the

tribal elders, over another round of rotgut, all grunt in drunken agreement that they made out pretty well. They have given up a couple of gods they didn't care that much about, and picked up the new live-forever God who they can use, come to think of it, to weld more power over their own people and other people they will overrun in the future.

And they still get to have their new spring festival, which is like their old spring festival. They even keep calling it Eostre or Easter, in remembrance of their old Goddess of fertility, who is not a goddess anymore, but whose name still carries for them much more than the nuance of sexual ecstasy. Generations later, after the now Christian tribal people have all but forgotten about their pagan roots, after they now kill boar and people in neighboring tribes in the name of God instead of just for the fun of it, after they have forgotten that the very name of their festival is pagan and not Christian, certain Christians among them get pissy.

"What do the sweet things and those Easter bunnies have to do with the resurrection of Christ? And why are those boys over there drinking so much? And why are people still running around having sex like rabbits on holy Easter Sunday?"

Easter is an after-the-fact assimilation of old, and presumably fun, pagan rites and new Christian, and not so fun, evangelism. And so it goes, also, with the appropriation of fun pagan winter festivals. Now we call the winter festival Christmas, and now there is something wrong with shopping in certain Christian circles because shopping is too much fun—too pagan, even though these festivals came from the pagans.

There is an Easter framework in the Bible, though no Easter. The framework adopted for Easter is in several short sections of writing, but it is important to the overall theme of the Bible as a Christian institution. It is the period of time traditionally celebrated between what has been named the Last Supper or Lord's Supper through to the resurrection of Jesus.

In my Bible class, you cannot start with Easter as a modern religious holiday and quote snippets from the Bible as you do in Christian cultures. You have to start with the Bible, then show how a church observance called Easter has been pieced together partially from the text. The Last Supper (Holy Thursday? Maybe, maybe not) in most Christian denominations is the source for a separate ceremony now called the Holy Communion or the Eucharist, and it is not a supper. It is usually just a thimble of wine with a dry wafer. As unappetizing as this sounds to my students, I explain that many people like the ceremony—in fact they welcome it—because at least communion breaks up a deadly boring and not-fun church service.

I don't really say this. But I do explain that this ceremony, in its various forms, can occur, depending on the church, at various times of the year, frequently or infrequently. It is not part of the Good Friday to Easter Sunday cycle. Any church service in Christian culture is an observance of the resurrection of Jesus.

We spend some time with these sections, as they are recorded in the Gospels and in the book of Acts, but I have not yet found a way to cover the story of the end of the life of Jesus without confusing myself and without confusing and also disturbing my students. At first I was confounded by the completely non-biblical images of Easter that were embedded in my own memories, pleasant memories, the memory of a service held in the spring, when it was sunny and the flowers were in bloom. Plenty of pollen in the air, so the trees, at least, are having sex.

I remember the woman and girls of the church showing off new, brightly patterned dresses, the Easter Egg hunts, chocolate bunnies, of course, and a Sunday morning service when even the sober preacher seemed happier than normal because the weather was warming up. No last supper, but all was capped off by a big Sunday buffet lunch with good roast beef and mashed potatoes and gravy, followed by a long nap. It was all wholesome and pleasant, if not a substitute for eating boar and drinking gallons of rotgut mead and having sex like rabbits.

Our way was better for the general welfare of our tribe. Roast beef tastes better than boar and without the mead and sex, you can skip the disorienting headache, and the terrifying revelation, when you wake up the next morning, that you are not with Helga the Handmaiden but one of Thurthwat's 17 wives. Why do the dancing women insist on covering their faces? Time to beat it to the woods before Thurthwat, open to new improvements in the field of ritual torture, nails you to a piece of wood.

Pre-bike biker gangs aside, in the Bible the images from what has become the Easter cycle are far different than a wild old pagan or a tame modern Easter observance. Throughout the Easter weekend in the Bible, there are funeral shawls instead of pretty dresses, no Easter egg hunts or chocolate, for sure, but betrayal, slaughter, and execution through bloody crucifixion. These things with the morbid images of graves splitting open to release the dead into the holy city, of an abused and mutilated man coming back to life and leaving his tomb to walk again among the quick.

Were you to focus on the precise wording of the Bible, none of these topics would be fit subjects during or after church, not fit for hometown chitchat over roast beef and mashed potatoes at the Sunday buffet, not fodder for Cookout Christian cookouts. But they are sound topics during Bible study because these images belong to the Bible. The Easter weekend of the Bible is confusing to me, but not to my students, who have not been confused into thinking that Easter and the Bible have something in common. Each Gospel has a different way getting through the Easter timeframe, different narratives relating different details, which are difficult to sort out when your not under the impression that each gospel tells the exact same story.

The imagery of each Gospel is scary, even more scary to my students because they will have to master what they think Christians have mastered: a summary explanation of the differences between each Gospel and how each one independently and variously throws in outtakes after the stunning image of the death of Jesus on the cross. Students imagine test questions like this:

> (1) According to the book of Matthew, how many women initially approached the sepulcher of Joseph of Arimathaea in which Jesus had been laid?

(2) According to the book of Mark, how many women initially approached this same sepulcher of Jesus?

(3) In which gospel was there a "great earthquake" as the women approached the sepulcher?

(4) In which gospel is there the story of a "doubting Thomas"?

My students naturally assume that Bible readers in Christian cultures would know that the answers.

But Easter is about a church service with pretty dresses, a sprinkling of some old pagan rituals, and a big Sunday buffet—all pleasant reminders that we should not let the Bible or early Christianity kill off the fun of a good spring holiday.

The answers to the questions above, respectively, are,
(1) 2
(2) 3
(3) Matthew (only)
(4) John (only)

The content of the Easter timeframe in the Bible makes a number of my students queasy. A good preacher knows not to go too deeply or thoroughly into this content during Easter Sunday service or any service because the content makes nice, good Christians queasy. Beginning with the Last Supper or Lord's Supper, the disciples are asked to make preparations for the Passover, scary enough on its own, which Jesus wants to observe. From Matthew 26: 17-19:

> Now the first day of the feast of unleavened bread the disciples came to Jesus, saying unto him, Where wilt thou that we prepare for thee to eat the passover? And he said, Go into the city to such a man, and say unto him, The Master saith, My time is at hand; I will keep the passover at thy house with my disciples. Say ye to the goodman of the house, The Master saith, Where is the guestchamber, where I shall eat the passover with my

disciples? And the disciples did as Jesus had appointed them; and they made ready the passover.

This Passover supper is also mandated in Mark 14:14 and Luke 22:8.

The Passover observance itself, its remembrance of the Exodus of the Hebrew people from Egypt after a mass slaughter of lambs and people, comes to the minds of my students from their studies earlier in the year. We are nowhere close to my pleasant memories of roast beef and mashed potatoes.

Jesus is observing the Passover, an event that includes the follow description from Exodus 12:29:

> And it came to pass, that at midnight the LORD smote all the firstborn in the land of Egypt, from the firstborn of Pharaoh that sat on his throne unto the firstborn of the captive that was in the dungeon.

Now that we have the image of Passover bloodshed and the slaughter of first born livestock and people, including children—a number that will soon include Jesus, first born of Mary and also, if we put him in front of Adam, first born of God—now that we have the image of the mass slaughter of firstborns reintroduced, let's eat some meat. Not human meat, of course, but animal meat—no—maybe human meat, too. My students are puzzled, sometimes noticeably shocked, by the association between the slaughter of lambs and cattle and the slaughter of people, particularly in relationship with a special supper. From Matthew 26: 26-28:

> And as they were eating, Jesus took bread, and blessed it, and brake it, and gave it to the disciples, and said, Take, eat; this is my body. And he took the cup, and gave thanks, and gave it to them, saying, Drink ye all of it; For this is my blood of the new testament, which is shed for many for the remission of sins.

The image of eating the body and drinking the blood of

Jesus is difficult for my students to swallow. When I cover this section of Matthew (this request appears again in Mark 14 and Luke 22) the class falls silent. I know what they are thinking:

Do modern Christians really have ceremonies to eat the body of Jesus and drink his blood?

But the thematic importance of the Last Supper is its brilliant reversal of symbolism and imagery. In the Old Testament, God tells his people to sacrifice first-born animals to him. The Last Supper combined with the sacrifice of Jesus on the cross is backwards—the Passover in reverse. God is giving his first born to be consumed by his people.

This is a perfect inversion of the will of the Old Testament God. Later, Paul says, "the truth of Christ is in me." This statement comes in one of his letters to the Corinthians in reference to a Lord's Supper ritual that seems to be already in place. Paul is not speaking purely from an abstract position: The consumption of Christ is a physical reality. Eating the flesh of Jesus and drinking his blood has been, since the earliest days of Christianity, the way to bring Jesus inside of you. But my students, when asked, do not see a Holy Communion; they see ritualized human sacrifice and cannibalism in a scene that would even make pagan Thurthwat blanch. That this ritual exists into modern times is disturbing and scary to many of them, especially to Mr. Matsuda, who is now wide awake, staring at his text, and biting his fingernails.

The image of cannibalism presented in the Last Supper is quickly followed by the betrayal of Jesus, his trial, the deliberate Pilate, the scornful priests and multitudes mocking Jesus, the torture, his death, and the removal of his body from the cross. All of this is scary. All make for a lively class on the Bible.

Students wonder why all four stories are not the same. I explain that there are many Christian preachers and speakers who will argue that all four stories of Jesus are perfectly harmonized. Saying so makes it so.

But problems arise:

(a) During Easter timeframe episode, there are two

earthquakes in Matthew. "Why are these earthquakes not reported in the other stories?" Japanese students, of course, are sensitive to any stirring of the Great Catfish.

(b) What does it mean when Jesus "gave up or yielded up the ghost" on the cross? Only in Matthew do people actually rise from their graves at the renting of the temple curtain at the death of Jesus. From Matthew 27: 52-53:

> And the graves were opened; and many bodies of the saints which slept arose, And came out of the graves after his resurrection, and went into the holy city, and appeared unto many.

Students have problems reconciling this image of the departed ghost or spirit of Jesus with the image of the physical bodies of the saints arising and wandering around the holy city. They also want to know why such a memorable albeit God-awful event was not reported in the other stories.

(c) Later we run across the problem with Jesus being missing from the tomb and the idea that he becomes another dead person wandering around, appearing incognito and/or in the flesh and saying various things to his disciples before telling them to go spread the good news. After absorbing the shock of these morbid scenes, students typically do not understand how these various reports, each offering very different descriptions of events, can be collated into one single Jesus story.

After pondering these and other thought points brought to the fore by students, I am ready to quit and go home, or maybe head to a local bar for a round of mead. With their Bibles-sans-Christian tradition, they miss the miracle of the resurrection and instead get stuck on the morbid and confusing and scary details of the empty tomb. They get stuck on the different ways the stories are told when each writer insists that his story is the absolute truth. But most of all they have trouble reconciling the physical details with the spiritual elements of the stories. So do I.

"Did the ghost return to Jesus' body after he died?" one student wanted to know. "Wouldn't his body look really bad after the ghost returned?" another queries. "Do Christians believe that your whole body comes back to life after death?"

The thought of a dead body coming back to life is scary for folks on this side of the not Christian world. There are a lot of answers for these questions out there in the Christian world. In Acts 2:31, Peter, according to Acts a witness to the resurrection event, says of Jesus that that, "his soul was not left in hell, neither his flesh did see corruption." The flesh wasn't corrupted but it had puncture wounds that are shown off and other wounds if we are to believe the torture stories.

There is no one set answer in the New Testament to what exactly happens when you are resurrected from the dead. To say abstractly that you will be with God in Heaven just is not enough for my students. "Who is God? Where is heaven exactly?" It is best to stay fuzzy about the origins of Easter. This way we can keep our pleasant Cookout Christian Easter, the closest thing Christianity has to a River God celebration. It is best to keep Easter, with its pretty dresses and chocolate, a safe distance from the Bible, with its human sacrifices and empty tombs and zombies.

Scary Christian Things II: Going to Hell

To Hell with Georgia.
—A bumper sticker seen on the campus of Georgia Tech, the University of Georgia's in-state football rival.

How we from the English speaking Christian world adopted a noun from an Old English verb that meant "to cover" or "to conceal" and over time transformed it into a ghoulish signifier to scare the hell out of people, particularly children, would be a subject of great curiosity to my students. I do not go into hell much as a Bible teacher because the idea of hell, the district of the damned—Dante's circuitous *Inferno*, Hamlet's speculative "undiscovered country," Milton's cavern of darkness visible—has been the vast domain of Church tradition and folklore (and some fine poetry) but not the Bible.

The word *hell* is used in a scattered manner in the King James Version. The word is prevalent in Matthew, but the place it signifies is never described in detail. There are four old words in Hebrew and Greek source texts used to point to an underworld or a place where people, bad people or sometimes all people, go after they die: *Sheol, Gehenna, Hades, Tartarus*. They are not the same place. Sheol is a Hebrew or Old Testament underworld—often a bleak place but not necessarily. Fiery Gehenna is the preferred bad place of the Gospels. This word finds its root meaning from what was a large garbage dump outside of Jerusalem. In Gehenna both "soul and body" are destroyed. I cannot find where one burns in eternal flames in Gehenna, but it is a good add on idea, if your intent is to scare the hell out of people.

Hades is the underworld, imported from the Greeks, and Hades is familiar to those of us who had to read the Odyssey in high school. It was a ghoulish place in a cool piece of ancient adventure literature, but not a place we believed in or were asked to believe in. Hades is also the preferred underworld term for the writer of the book of Revelation. And there is Tartarus, not very well know, probably because it is mentioned only once, and you will come across it only if, unlike me, you are able to read an ancient Greek version of the New Testament. Tartarus is a bad place below, and even worse than, bleak Hades. It is important because it is where angels who sinned were placed in "chains of darkness," and more than likely one of the sparse biblical sources for Milton's grand epic view of the fall of angels in *Paradise Lost*.

The King James Version, in what I think is a purposefully sloppy manner brought forward from prior translations of the Bible into English, paints over all four words with the one word, *hell*. By the time of the King James Version, hell proper was already a church institution, an idea that probably rose from a merger with a similar pagan word for a Norse underworld.

By the early 17th century in England, hell had long had its coming of age, and had become the established giant subterranean burning landfill where the Church could dump anyone who did not agree with the Church. The images of circular walkways, vast dark caverns, fires, demons, and whatnot change depending on which Church is in power (or what poet is having a vision).

In the Bible, though, Gehenna, the source term for the image of hell most embraced by the Christian tradition, is a physical area on earth and not deep below earth. The source image for Gehenna is a huge valley, with its ugly burning trash dump, one that no doubt included the stench of animal remains, maybe the remains of human, including child, sacrifices practiced by competing religions the writers of the Bible abhor—for the right reasons. It was this ghastly place that the writers of the Gospels would assume people knew about in legend if not from experience. It does not come with the vivid descriptions, the detailed and brilliant poetic architecture, of Dante's *Inferno* or Milton's Hell.

It is not even the unimaginatively imagined hell that certain church people near my hometown had in mind when they erected a billboard that says, "Love Jesus or Burn in Hell." The writers of the Bible stayed away from graphic descriptions of hell, and, for that matter, heaven.

Hell is a word that the powers of the medieval church, packed with devotees of creative and not-Christian folklore, adopted as a quick way to plant in the minds of their flock stories of potbellied, horned demons and fires and pitchforks and any other horrible dead teenager flick image you can conjure to herd common folk to church. The great literary names of demons were developed through oral and written tradition, names that came to carry horrific nuances, names sometimes obliquely drawn from the Bible, sometimes just made up and used strategically: Lucifer is a proper name drawn from a good Latin word combination that means light bearer, a reference to Venus or the morning star that brings first light. Good Christian translators found a way to plug the word *Lucifer* into the Bible, referencing the King of Babylon and other things. Eventually the word was merged with the Satan or Devil of Christian tradition, but not necessarily a biblical Satan.

There is Beelzebub, the famous Lord of the Flies, origin obscure, but maybe a Philistine God. There's the devil, Mephistopheles, whose origin is medieval, not biblical, and whose fame was promoted by Christopher Marlowe in his version of the Faustus legend:

Faustus: Where are you damned?
Mephistopheles: In hell.
Faustus: How comes it then that thou art out of hell?
Mephistopheles: Why, this is hell, nor am I out of it.

Here, hell is any place where you are separated from God. This is another church tradition reinforced in Marlowe's *Faustus* through the perspective of a demon. Good for dramatic effect, and the pain felt from being separate from God is an idea that is strong in the Bible. All of these devils make for an interesting consideration that charts the course of human imagination, human consciousness, all too human fears, but this after-the-fact pagan folklore has no business in a Bible class.

My mates from the hellish utilitarian world sometimes see me as an overpaid academic whose classroom efforts are of questionable value. I would like to think that my single most redeeming purpose in life has been in the struggle to preserve the brilliant thoughts of those who went before us, yet there are those dark times when I begin to think that the horrible thoughts from past times are the most enduring, while the best thoughts die too quickly. I wonder if I am not a small part of an engine that preserves the wrong type of culture. Maybe it is time to go out and find a real job, to join the ranks of those who would be satisfied to let the memory of the past die a complete death each generation.

If I had a choice, I would like to be rid of forces that attempt to block us from forming our own mythology by drawing inspiration from the cannons of the ephemerally brilliant rather than the enduring insipid. I do not know what type of mythology this would be. Maybe one in which a round earth is saved in the end, instead of a flat earth being broken apart and destroyed with so many good souls being thrown into a lake of fire. We could opt for a mythology that is more positive and less fearful.

I grew up without the threat of the barbarian hordes marching through my hometown, sacrificing and eating our children, raping and maiming our woman folk, chopping us up or chaining us to a cart to be led off to slavery or burned or nailed to a piece of wood. I grew up without the fears of the northern tribes storming through with their horned helmets, those pot-bellied pagans from beyond who might terrorize any given sunrise with their silhouettes spanning the hills of our horizon, those killers sent by their angry Gods who keep us terrified of the certain death of our entire tribe every desperate minute of our short lives, should our own God not protect us.

We of the soft modern middle class have our own terrors. In Japan, at any moment the earth may shake and the sea may surge. But we should be able to create our own gods and demons without being dominated by the imagination of people who thought the earth is flat. The threat of hell may not work so well these days to herd people to church, but in these more democratic times, it is still too easy to gain ownership of hell, to superimpose some vigilante justice on the afterlife for those people you do not like.

God's love, unrequited, will be punished with eternal torture. This idea is not clearly laid out in the Bible that my students read. And thank God. Eternal torture for unrequited love? This heaven must be run by a consortium of horribly petty and bitter and down right mean folks whose mommas didn't love them.

Scary Christian Things III: Members and Persecution

But I see another law in my members, warring against the law of my mind, and bringing me into captivity to the law of sin which is in my members. —Paul, Romans 7:23

"Before Abraham was, I am", says Jesus in the book of John. But before Jesus was, Paul is. Paul, who scholars think was writing before some of the Gospel accounts of Jesus were written. It may be that Paul took over the narrative of the Risen Christ before others were writing about the life of Jesus. And he has a tricky understanding about how we should view the Risen Christ.

Paul is more the inspired rhetorician, the pre-Emersonian engineer of quotable quotes, than he is a concise theocrat, but the ambiguities in Paul's work are at the source of the Christian theological world that gave him the status of theocrat and saint. Paul's flourishes, though compelling in almost any language, I suppose, are heavy on feeling but light on concise explanation.

His most famous work, the book of Romans, is unreadable in the context of my class. From the beginning of Romans 5:

> Therefore being justified by faith, we have peace with God through our Lord Jesus Christ: By whom also we have access by faith into this grace wherein we stand, and rejoice in hope of the glory of God. And not only so, but we glory in tribulations also: knowing that tribulation worketh patience: And patience, experience:

and experience, hope: And hope maketh not ashamed: because the love of God is shed abroad in our hearts by the Holy Ghost which is given unto us.

This is strong writing and beautiful in its translation. It has the powerful cadence of profound inspiration. But how do you explain the meaning to those who cannot feel the meaning?

I would be able to explain part of this passage to my students by echoing Nietzsche's pithy remark that what doesn't kill you will make you stronger. Add the ideas of justification, faith, and grace and then you are at the heart of why an irritated, enraged, Nietzsche said that Paul had, "a mind full of superstition and cunning." My students are not predisposed to be irritated or enraged with Paul. But the lofty words are at the heart of what drives my better students into fixated trances while they stare at their electronic dictionaries in earnest attempts to understand Paul. Among evangelicals and large segments of the Catholic church, Paul's Christianity rules, so we have finally reached a place, at the back end of the Bible, where direct connections can be made between the Bible and modern Christianity. If only we could understand the vocabulary.

I feel Nietzsche's pain when I cull words and phrases from Paul and throw them out to fly, like the Methodist minister's Bible, over the heads of my congregation. The abstractions of Paul's Christianity are hopelessly convoluted when you attempt to explain them. We need faith, and we need, through tribulation, to build hope. This need to build hope suggests to my students that faith is lacking, maybe unattainable.

If we have faith, why do we need hope, too? Here may be the nerve center for what makes modern Christians, including Cookout Christians, nervous, at least when they start thinking about the meanings of faith and hope. In English these are two feel good words, but it makes me nervous, too, to think about how to teach faith and hope, how to transmit the meanings of these words when placed beside each other in the abstract. These words make my students nervous, too, but for different reasons. They are horrified by what type of hopelessly unanswerable test questions will lurk behind this type of diction. And they have no faith that the answer will be sent to them from on high.

What is the problem with Paul's members? And how does his problem with his members expand to us? From 1 Corinthians 6:15:

> Know ye not that your bodies are the members of Christ? shall I then take the members of Christ, and make them the members of an harlot? God forbid.

We should avoid harlots. My students get this. But what is this about our bodies being members of Christ? What exact meaning do we assign to the word *member*? Later in 1 Corinthians 7, Paul states that it is best to live, like he does, without sex. But for those who cannot control their sexual impulses, he begrudgingly allows that they should take a wife, uttering the famous phrase, from Corinthians 7:9, that is "better to marry than to burn."

When you throw this body-forbidding notion out to polite Japanese students, it appears as if the first officer of the Starship Christianity sees the body as necessarily in conflict with the godly. The idea that God-is-alive-in-you is more scary than it is cunning. God is alive forever—and in you, and this being so, God is ready to make us alive forever, too, before and after our bodies die. God does not need sex. Being Godly ourselves, why should we? This idea, because it is so frequent and forceful in Paul, presents itself on the whole as fretful and compulsive and weird in Paul's writings. In Ephesians 3: 20-21, he insists again that God will make us immortal:

> Now unto him that is able to do exceeding abundantly above all that we ask or think, according to the power that worketh in us. Unto him be glory in the church by Christ Jesus throughout all ages, world without end. Amen.

God's power is our power, the power that works in us, but my students do not understand this need to be god-like.

"Christians think they are God?" says a perplexed young Japanese man. World without end. Eternal life. These ideas sound attractive on the surface, but is there not more to being God than simple existence? If we have choice in life, will we have choice in the afterlife?

There is more to Paul than can be covered in an eternity. At the core of the problem with understanding Paul, of making vain attempts to teach Paul's thinking, is that most of us don't feel *his* pain. This pain is rooted in the confessions of an inspired, if not completely obsessed man who persecuted Christians himself—we are told—before he saw the blinding light that made him see that he was persecuting his own people, himself, his own God, the God in him.

This everlasting life God is a God of comfort at first, but the punishment, the pain continues. This God of comfort is not so comfortable. Paul repeatedly and continually reprimands himself in his writing for his persecution of others. He wrestles with self-loathing, not only of body but also of mind. The source of his struggle is simply put in 1 Corinthians 15:9:

> For I am least of the apostles, that am not meet to be called an apostle, because I persecuted the church of God.

He turns persecution inward, from the persecution of others to the persecution of self. Paul sends a strong message to all he speaks to: He does not deserve the love of God.

Neither do we, those of us who have never persecuted people. In Paul's writings, God loves us, God loves Paul, but Paul has trouble loving himself, and none of us deserve the love of God. The love we receive from God is God's grace. This idea does not float in a room full of people who do not believe that they were born in sin, who believe that they were born okay the first time. Here you start to see why early Christians were persecuted, beaten, as people cried out, "speak for yourselves and leave us be."

Moving through Paul's writing, this undeserved divine love is a strange, foreign love to him, even as it springs from indigenous Hebrew sources. He is not able to reconcile the ancient, time-held laws of God from his Pharisee heritage (Acts 26:5) with the a new view of the law produced by a renegade Jewish sect he first despised but later became a self-proclaimed leader of.

Paul was intimately acquainted with the old idea that faith means faithfulness to God's law. Ezekiel (18:9) expresses the idea that he who follows God's "decrees faithfully keeps [God's] laws. That man is righteous; he will surely live." But in Romans 3:28, Paul says:

> Therefore we conclude that a man is justified by faith without the deeds of the law.

But what of the idea that having faith *actually is* being faithful to the law? Three verses later, in Romans 3:31, he says:

> Do we then make void the law through faith? God forbid: yea, we establish the law.

But what law is being established when you take away the necessity for following the law? Following the law also carries the charge of doing good works. As many good Christians have pointed out, there is a nervousness when you remove faith from the idea of following the law and make faith into something else, something that needs hope, not fidelity or loyalty to God's law, to maintain.

What to do with the rules of Paul's Pharisee legacy, the old rules of the all-powerful and vengeful and brutally loving God who gave his revered laws to Moses. The God of the fathers, the great leader in his people's bloody struggles from oppression to glory to oppression again. Paul's people: the sons of Abraham, Isaac, Jacob, Joseph, Moses and David, these men, the great monuments, the adoptive brothers of God, who are flawed but loyal, enduring, and, in David's case, the seat and origin of God's own love.

This great God, this divine lover, creator, and destroyer. How unjustified the rules of this God, the God who understood faith itself as the ability to follow the law, how unjustified this God seems with the God who has become the father of the Christ, the great rule-making commander now turned laid back folksinger but who still has not forgotten how to damn us all, this loving perfect God, this God who does not require human betterment in following the law, this new God made perfect in Christianity, this new God, who understands his own imperfection as the savior of the flawed human race.

So goes the thinking of a religious radical, who succeeds in hot wiring and driving forward what became a powerful new religious order. New rules have to be made on the fly. As with the idea that sex is the new forbidden fruit, these rules seem to be more Paul's rules than God's rules—that is, the old Old Testament God who, with his rule against adultery, is more interested in pre-empting property disputes and social disarray than urging us to despise our own members.

God's people are supposed to be fruitful and multiply. If Paul's unhappy member thoughts had to do with same-sex desires, as has been speculated, then there would be a problem breaking with one of the clearly stated laws of Moses. But Paul is first in line after Jesus when it comes to rethinking Hebrew practice and law. He falls in with Leviticus on homosexuality, but breaks with other, arguably more important laws.

His most radical affront to the laws, in what is a blasphemous and reckless challenge to a foundational principle, is his repeated amendment that no one has to cut the end of his member off to go with God. In Romans 3:30, he states most clearly that the circumcised and uncircumcised can equally be justified with God. This is radical. Abraham, God's servant of unbending loyalty, had to be circumcised, according to tradition, at the age of 99.

Are we to include member-less women in any of Paul's thinking? In 1 Corinthian 14:34 Paul says:

> let your women keep silence in the churches: for it is not permitted unto them to speak; but they are commanded to be under obedience as also saith the law.

Most of my students are women, and my female students of the new Japan find Paul's injunction regressive and unsavory.

I am sure that there are scholars and theologians and preachers and lay people in Christianity who feel that they can discern exactly what Paul is saying. I am not one of them, and the final failure of each class I teach on the Bible is the failure to make the thinking of Paul clear before the faces of my students. Faith, which once was the following of laws and rules, faith, which has now become something larger than even being faithful, faith now supercedes law and rule. But we have to follow laws and rules still, although we are not clear exactly, precisely, what these rules are.

While explaining these ideas to a class of, say, 42 Japanese students, 10 will look at you and nod slowly, as if to say—*I hear you but what are you saying?* 10 will stare into their electronic dictionaries. 10 will stare at their texts, and there will be 12 heads bobbing, fighting off sleep.

Paul's ambiguities, those markers in his writing that put my students into suspended animation, makes one wonder how firmly set his own belief is. And these ambiguities make him one the most believable characters in the Bible. He sounds real, he sounds like many modern-day Christians, and I think this is why many of us from the Christian world, me included, give him latitude. My students do not, at least those who have questioned Paul's position on religion. If we take the Paul accounts in the book of Acts as either truth or fiction, we find either way the story of a man who puts himself in danger and who seeks and finds persecution. In this religion of love, there seems at its root the #1 scary Christian thing: persecution. Paul's writings and the reported life of Paul give us a fit finale for the Bible, from Genesis until the end. Throughout the Bible, I am reminded repeatedly of the Prince's statement at the end of *Romeo and Juliet*: "All are punished."

Aside from trying to explain such words as *faith* and *grace*, the problem with teaching Paul in Japan is that my soft middle-class students do not carry Paul's guilt, his feelings of unworthiness, and his self-seeking self-loathing. There are times that we all feel that we have fallen short of the mark—I'm thinking in particular of certain days when I blow off going to the gym and have a couple of beers instead—but you must travel downward through far deeper levels of guilt before you reach Paul.

Paul says, "O wretched man that I am! Who shall deliver me from the body of this death?" Paul is carting about unhappy thoughts and feelings at a most profound level. My students get this part. The part they do not get is when Paul projects this self-loathing onto everyone else. I was surprised at first by the response by some of my students to the famous statement in Romans 3:23:

> For all have sinned, and come short of the glory of God.

I like this equalizing idea from the Bible, and I see it as important to understanding Christian thinking and human nature.

"*All* are bad?" Ms. Yoshikuni says, with an emphasis on the word *all*. "How would he know?"

I pause, thinking, *Paul never made it to Japan. How can you say such a thing if you have not met everyone in the world?* The word *all* in my classroom is not an abstraction: It is an exact number.

So being people who have never had Paul's words seared into their minds, the general consensus is that Paul should speak for himself and leave the rest of us alone, those of us who Paul never met, those of us who have not found the time to persecute Christians or do other things to make us despise our own members. Paul identifies a branch of Christianity that is recognizable to me. It is one that is rooted in people who have willfully hurt others and want to make things right again through a convoluted formula that begs for persecution and self-persecution through self-loathing. These breast-beating confessions are used as a means to balance the ledger that these same folks insist can never be balanced without God's intervention.

Paul tells us that he did terrible things to Christians. After he saw the light and became a Christian himself, he felt that, in order to redeem himself, he had to do extra work for God, even though work, he reminds us, does not win God's grace. This is a perfect formula for self-persecution. Paul traveled according to biblical accounts to what was then most of his world, to tell people about Jesus and also helped to set up Christian churches. This in the effort to redeem himself, but after his efforts, he still does not feel that his work is enough to even the ledger with God, to become *at one* (at-one, atone) with God, to be justified with God.

My students are confused. "Paul did bad things to people," one said, "so he should start his redeem [still having trouble with word usage] with people he hurt or their families, not with God."

"Why not with God," I asked.

"Because it's just his idea," the student said. I did not pursue this, but I think she was following the idea that if God is in you, then all you have to do to redeem yourself is to make things right with your self. Paul wanted to atone, to be at one with God, a version of self that in my student's view is neglectful of others.

I explain to my students that Paul felt that he had been a bad person, but that Jesus came to him for a special reason. It is revealed to him that the bad things he had done were part of the badness of all human beings. We cannot be with God because we are all bad, but Jesus takes away our badness so that we can be with God.

"Why are we all bad?" one student asks.

"Because of Adam, I think."

But Adam wasn't Japanese. Wrong passport.

I continue by saying that Paul believed that God sent Jesus to help us go to heaven after we die. Jesus suffered, and he did that suffering for us. Now I am getting blank stares. I explain that it is like when you throw a baseball through a window of someone's house, accidentally or not, and a nice guy comes and pays the owner of the house for the window, so you do not have to pay. The nice man redeems the owner, and he is also your redeemer. This is what Jesus does. He's the nice man.

"But if you don't throw the ball through the house, then you don't need the nice man," says a student.

"No, in our case, we are born having already thrown the ball through the window, born in debt." Students stare at me. I know what they're thinking: "In *our* case?"

Next class: Paul believes that all of us can be at one with Jesus. This is atonement and through atoning, we receive the pure spirit of Jesus, the Holy Spirit. Then we are justified, we are good, pure, and then we can go be with God after we die.

"But what about the people Paul hurt?" comes the question.

Epilogue: Shinjuku

"Holy cow," he said.
"Where?" she asked.

I am thinking about Ecclesiastes, the book written, in some traditions, by "The Teacher." The Teacher begins his book with the famous quotation, "vanity of vanities; all is vanity" (1:2). Many times I wished that I had not been so arrogant to take on teaching the Bible, so vain to have thought that I could manage it with ease. And now it is too late. Once you enter the Bible, you are in for good. The Bible has no back doors.

It is hot and a little mean spirited at 19:33, rush hour in Shibuya station. There is some pushing, but it's not personal. You cannot move without displacing air, and there are more people than air on the platform. Still a couple of apologies escape over the screeching of brakes and the guy announcing the arrival of the train.

He is energized—the trains on the Yamanote Line come every two minutes, but he is determined to present each one like it is the Orient Express barreling in from Istanbul. The doors open—the train exhales its payload—mass humanity surges out, mass humanity lunges forward refilling space in its destiny to force every body, every limb, every microscopic gene of its recombinant DNA onto Car 5, Yamanote—the circle line. The train jerks forward, the human cargo is held up by itself.

Hell bent for Shinjuku, 3 stops away, 7 long, hot minutes. The train stops between stations, the lights flicker. This isn't usual, but it happens. Everyone is quiet, stoic. There is an implicit understanding among the Japanese that sometimes the train stops—the train is like life that way. But one foreign guy wrapped in the human luggage has a burst of individualism.

"Jesus Christ," he says, "what tha hell's going on?" From the sound of his accent he might be a Brit or an Australian.

There is an announcement in Japanese, a rapid, crackling sputtering series of utterances over a PA. The car falls silent again.

"Wot's wrong?" the guy says.

"It's an accident," a female voice answers timidly with a Japanese English accent.

"Right—well why didn't you say anything the first time?" he says.

"I didn't understand," she says under her breath.

I wanted to turn, if I could turn, to tell the guy in good redneck fashion, to shut the hell up. *Shut the hell up.* We are all miserable, all 17 thousand of us baking on the stopped train, so why does he think he's so special? A bead of sweat drops from my nose.

The girlfriend didn't respond to her boyfriend the first time because she didn't understand him. I hear the non-conversation again in my head: "*Jesus Christ, what the hell is going on?*" A few years before, I would not have thought twice about this sentence. This was before I started teaching the Bible in a place that does not have much of Jesus Christ, either as a religious figure or an angry figure of speech, in a place that does not have a Christian Hell or a way of understanding what the hell "what the hell" means.

The train starts again after some long minutes, the cargo sways backward in sync against forward movement. Recently a Japan Rail spokesman proudly announced that they can clean up a *jinshin jiko,* a human body accident, in 15 to 16 minutes, unless, he said, the body gets tangled in the train. So today we are lucky, no entanglement. But I keep thinking about diction, word usage, relieved to have something to keep my mind off the compression and heat.

I am The Teacher—I am paid to think, and now I am thinking about the country crossroads where I grew up, a place with a name, but not big enough to rank a post office, a place with a thick accent, a place that had roughly one-tenth of a human every 10 square miles. I muse about my situation now, finding a place on earth where being crushed against people was a daily rite of passage, where a human body accident is little news. The heat was the same, both in this energetic new crowded world and in the old hot world with no people.

Even in the county seat only twelve miles away they laughed at my accent when I was a boy. Gradually I made adjustments, adjustments that Mr. Outback, somewhere in the train car, had not made yet. Still, I understand his English. His young lady friend understands most of his English, too. No, there wasn't a problem with English. That boy is from the other side of the world from me, far from the swamp English spoken where I grew up. But I understood him when his girlfriend couldn't. *Jesus Christ*, I thought, *the girlfriend couldn't understand him, not because of his English, but because she can't speak Christianity.* I wanted to teach him this, show him the error of his ways in good biblical fashion.

I am nearly carried off of my feet by the crowd dashing for the door at Shinjuku station. I surge from the netherworld of the Yamanote line and cross the platform to board the next train, the gentler, happier yellow train that will take me home. Not so crowded here. I even find a seat, which is special. I reach in my backpack for the large book. I open it to a section that I was rereading, the story of Daniel. I am at the part where the hero's buddies survive being thrown into the fiery furnace.

I can't keep my mind on the story. I am still angry with a rude guy I have never met, who I want to set straight in his ways, who assumed that the term Jesus Christ, in all of its non-meanings, is known to all, who reminded me, in an offhanded way, of a religion that is hell bent on becoming everyone's religion, who reminded me of my own religious arrogance. And I am angry about being detained for roughly 15 to 16 minutes.

A Japanese guy probably just hurled himself into oblivion, and all I can think about is me. All is vanity. This anger segues into another form of anger, the anger that I have been trying to edit out of a book that has turned into another failed mission to unhinge the Bible from theology. Wrong from the start.

Much of what I have put forward in this book is evidence enough that I do not fall in line with standard Christian denominations. I would like to say that I am an atheist and be done with it, but I cannot. Atheism is another branch of Christianity, named by Christianity just like Adam named the animals. My un-Christian anger might point to the fact that I am not Christian enough to be an atheist.

Why would a self-proclaimed atheist be vexed about the Bible on the Tokyo train system? Why do I, a vain older man, have to project my vanity toward a vain young man who is oblivious to the fact that he is in a culture where the term Jesus Christ as a curse makes no sense? No Japanese person I've ever encountered would ever say, "Buddha, what the hell is going on?"

I am in a constant fight with the arrogance and the vanity of Christianity, when it claims ownership of the Bible, when it feels that all should understand curses that erupt from Christian tradition. As The Teacher I find this fight also within me. Why am I thinking over and over about these topics to purge my own arrogance and vanity for thinking I was qualified to teach the Bible? There is too much arrogance, vanity, and anger in my soul these days to say that I am not a Christian.

I think the answer might be found back at that crossroads of the old Scots Presbyterian Southern home. I'm still a rebel. There is no way to detach rebellion from Christianity, so my rebelliousness is itself a sign of my Christianity. But there would be so many Christians who would read this book say that, no, this rebellious boy can be no Christian.

So the answer is no, I'm not a Christian. I'm a Presbyterian.

I am an old-school Presbyterian, a branch of religion that will soon go the way of the dinosaurs if it has not already. Explaining the religion I grew up with would require another book, one in which I would attempt to describe the curious religious attitudes of a country crossroads where I grew up and how this religion differed from itself even twelve miles away in the county seat, how this religion differed categorically from what we saw as the wild new forms of Christianity bleeding through our borders. No one ever took to dancing in the aisles during services where one served God by sitting still. It would be a book that has already been written by Senator Jim Webb and other books written by other fine authors on this subject.

Mine was a conservative but thoughtful branch of Presbyterianism inherited from the old Scottish kirk, a religion that had Jesus, of course, but that had no use for any outsider, son of God or not, who would advocate that you reject your family on his behalf. Those would be fighting words. It was a religion of the crossroads home, but also a religion of county seat Sunday school teachers, city folk, trying to insert a more refined God in the heads of young country boys, trying to educate them in the strange, uncomfortable ways of their God of Comfort, the God of juice and cookies, the God we must turn to, the God of Judgment. Their religion was more suburban, one that was unwittingly being assailed by mutant forms of Christianity that claimed to be older.

But my country religion was old, old time, dating back to the God of the still swamp and surging river. It was the religion that produced young boys who knew, a priori, given in their DNA, that the effort to educate them on God should be met with the hard questions incumbent to vigorous democratic discussion. You could not buy out our countrified questions with juice and cookies.

God may be holy, but in that childhood world, the holy of holies was resistance, keeping a hard eye on this new foreign God who judges us when we were already damn sure we knew a God who had stood beside us all along the way. And he was not a God of judgment, of turning, of conversion. The site of religious education by some unknown, primal genetic charge, we took to be, like members of Thurthwat's clan, the site of negotiation, not rote learning and certainly not indoctrination. But we lost our battle in a religion that fought against itself while new gods were slowly killing off the old God of the fathers.

We did not turn to this new God. We did not convert. Not often, because we had been eternally packed in with our original God from birth in the same way that I am packed in with my colleagues on the Yamanote line daily. When you are packed in with the God you know, it is difficult to turn to a foreign God. Our Scots Presbyterian DNA was resistant to turning. That would be mutiny. *All* is vanity, and what is more vain than turning, than converting? This stiffneckness is what made me categorically reject the evangelical Methodism of my mother's father at the age of ten. It is what still gives me the heebie-jeebies when I hear the chimes from the Methodist hymnal at my university. He was a preacher, a bright man. But he was loyal to the harsh God of judgment, the God of turning, rather than our tough but accepting and communal God of the kirk.

Our God. No, we weren't Christians. We were Presbyterians. We did not look kindly on people who tried to convert us, whether they were mild Cookout Christians or I am a Christian Christians or Hooverites or the Dinosaur Lovers of Kentucky. Along the way there were always those, even some among us, who pressed for conversion—all along the way and still. Sometimes I think of them when pressed in a crowded train. They were and they are met with silence, mostly. To each his own.

But press our stubborn souls hard enough, and you might get a peek at the anger, the country temper that flares on a hot day when someone needs to be set straight, to be taught a thing or two, about the assumption that his new God is better than the one we had always had. We had the exquisite privilege of being blessed and saved from birth by our God and could never garner the absurd notion that we would ever be among the dammed. We were old Presbyterians. And plenty flawed—too arrogant, often vain—but that was between our own God and us. Try to force a foreign God on us and you might see us at our worst. We carried a pugnacious distain for things novel and suspiciously disingenuous. Show some respect for us and for our old God, and you might see us at our best. We were energetic, open to debate, we could love and trust, we were gentile and full of grace.

This Presbyterianism, for the most part, has now given in to the new citified, suburban God, the God of conversion, of turning—the God of judgment. Our old country God, the crusty old tough but kind soldier, the grand good old boy who blasts you at birth with rowdy but divine DNA, is in retreat. He was a good, loyal god, and I miss him.

My reflections in this book, too, are rear guard. Trying to give readers a glance of Japanese incredulity while learning the Bible, trying desperately at times, to bring light to often bitterly dark religious thinking that so badly needs light. Trying vainly to be The Teacher, but knowing that my resistance to so many flawed ideas about the Bible can only stand as a small, arrogant and vain skirmish against the Herculean institutions marching forward to keep these ideas in place.

It is a shame that church tradition paired a fine name, Lucifer, the bearer of light, with the diabolical. There is nothing diabolical about bringing light. Ask God. We teachers are the vain ones who want to set things straight. Even for those of us who have been made cynical along the way, our greatest hope is that we can be the bringers of light. So often we fail. In *Look Homeward Angel*, Thomas Wolfe gives tribute through the perspective of the character, Eugene Gant, of an old grade-school teacher who was dying of tuberculosis, but who still found the energy to teach, who "remained" after Gant's idols, his "gods and captains," had fallen away:

> She remained, who first had touched his blinded eyes with light, who nested his hooded houseless soul. She remained.

There is the divine, the eternal, in teaching, in learning. Maybe we can reach the summit if we can look through the mirror darkly and learn to purge ourselves of arrogance and vanity—a distinctly Christian pursuit.

Writing in a cabin in the mountainous Blue Ridge of North Carolina, Wolfe closes the tribute to Gant's beloved teacher with the following evocation:

> O death in life that turns our men to stone, O change that levels down our gods, if only one lives yet above the cinders of the consuming years, shall not this dust awaken, shall not dead faith revive, shall we not see God again, as once in morning, on the mountain? Who walks with us on the hills?

This tribute to a remarkable teacher, one that presses back for a moment the prevailing mood of disillusionment in Wolfe's work, upholds the idea that we as teachers might be capable of inspiring faith in the mind of a student, that we might, through humble dedication, produce divine light. Even the glimpse of such a possibility makes our failures, when we do fail, so distressing, so unmanageable.

I did not realize at first that my teaching assignment was one of leveling down the gods. Doomed from the start. I come into a Bible class, not to create, but to destroy. Not The Teacher, not the bringer of divine light, but the destroyer. Even if my students are not aware of just what it is I am destroying, or that they participate with me in the destruction, I feel as if I am carrying out a pedagogical Passover in my Bible class, and often botching the job. What light there is to be had is the light borrowed from my Japanese students. And there is plenty more light to go around in Tokyo.

Until I sort out what it is exactly, precisely, to conclude about the Bible and its religions, you will find me still reflecting and gazing at walls, still traveling the great circle, looking ahead and homeward at the same time, maybe reading a big, scary book, wondering if I am misguided or truly lost, looking for the signs that are not there and the signs that are, reckoning that I may have arrived too early for the divine light and too late for the gods.